# Grand Finales

## The Art of The Plated Dessert

# Grand Finales

## The Art of The Plated Dessert

TISH BOYLE and TIMOTHY MORIARTY

*Editors of* Chocolatier *and* Pastry Art & Design

*Preface by*

MICHEAL SCHNEIDER

*Editor-in-Chief,* Chocolatier *and* Pastry Art & Design

Van Nostrand Reinhold

I(T)P® A Division of International Thomson Publishing Inc.

*New York • Albany • Bonn • Boston • Detroit • London • Madrid • Melbourne*
*Mexico City • Paris • San Francisco • Singapore • Tokyo • Toronto*

*Van Nostrand Reinhold Staff*

*President:* Marianne Russell

*Vice President, EDP:* Renee Guilmette

*Publisher:* Melissa A. Rosati

*Art Director:* Mike Suh

*Manufacturing Director:* Louise Kurtz

*Editorial Production Director:* Stephen McNabb

*Marketing Manager:* Mary Fitzgerald

*Marketing Associate:* Michelle Agosta

*Support Staff:* Karren Abrams, Ginsen Chang,
Elizabeth Curione, Jill Elias, Dionicia Hernandez,
Carolyn Holfelder, Jackie Martin, Laura Morelli,
Andrea Olshevsky, Amy Beth Shipper

I(T)P® an International Thomson Publishing Company
       The ITP logo is a registered trademark used herein under license

Printed in the United States of America

For more information, contact:

Van Nostrand Reinhold
115 Fifth Avenue
New York, NY 10003

Chapman & Hall GmbH
Pappelallee 3
69469 Weinheim
Germany

Chapman & Hall
2-6 Boundary Row
London
SE1 8HN
United Kingdom

International Thomson Publishing Asia
221 Henderson Road #05-10
Henderson Building
Singapore 0315

Thomas Nelson Australia
102 Dodds Street
South Melbourne, 3205
Victoria, Australia

International Thomson Publishing Japan
Hirakawacho Kyowa Building, 3F
2-2-1 Hirakawacho
Chiyoda-ku, 102 Tokyo
Japan

Nelson Canada
1120 Birchmount Road
Scarborough, Ontario
Canada M1K 5G4

International Thomson Editores
Seneca 53
Col. Polanco
11560 Mexico D.F. Mexico

1  2  3  4  5  6  7  8  9  10  RRD - WL   01  00  99  98  97  96

Library of Congress Cataloging-in-Publication Data

Grand finales: the art of the plated dessert / [compiled by] Tish Boyle and Timothy
Moriarty
      p.  cm.
    Includes bibliographical references and index.
    ISBN 0-442-02287-5
      1. Desserts.  3. Pastry.  I. Boyle, Tish  II. Moriarty, Timothy, 1951–

TX773.G683  1996                                            96–2852
641.8'6—dc20                                                CIP

http://www.vnr.com
product discounts • free email newsletters
software demos • online resources

email: info@vnr.com

A service of I(T)P®

# ACKNOWLEDGMENTS

My sincere thanks and appreciation to the following VIPs: to Michael Schneider, for dreaming up this book concept and putting up with my stubborn (but always rational) little "fits" during this entire project (and for always letting me think I had won the latest argument). To Stephanie Banyas, for making every phone call I ever asked her to make and never complaining (MUCH), and for her help and encouragement in selecting, decoding, and testing these somewhat tricky recipes. And finally, to my family, especially my parents, for their unwavering love and continued support.

TB

My thanks to Christopher Thumann, Susan S. Lee, Anne Thomas, Joanna Rend, Catherine Brophy, and, especially, Stephanie Banyas, for their invaluable help in the preparation of the manuscript. To Mark Kammerer, who kept this project rolling. To Melissa Rosati and Amy Shipper, for their support. To Mary Goodbody and Janice Wald Henderson, for their guidance. Thanks also to Michael Schneider, who first conceived the idea of dessert schools. My love and gratitude to Richard and Rita Moriarty (at last, a book you can show your friends), my wife Geri, and Ryan and Evan (you can show it to your friends too, but wash your hands first). And to Theresa and Jerry Doolan—courage is inspiration.

TM

# CONTENTS

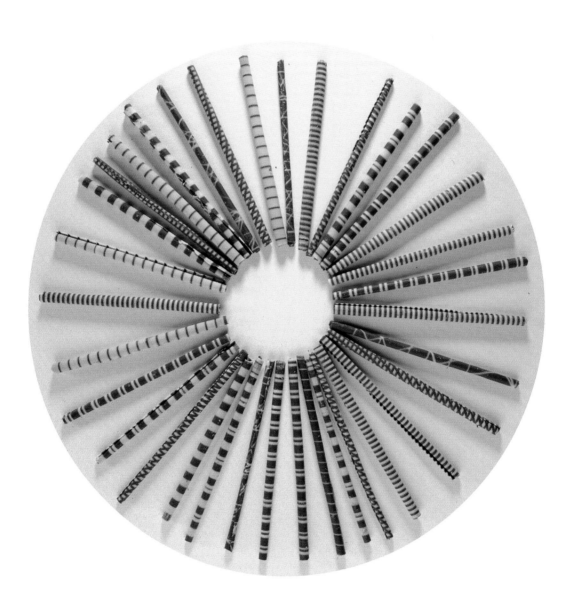

# RECIPE CONTENTS

# PREFACE

Twelve years ago I had an idea to start a magazine about desserts and more specifically chocolate desserts, figuring if we could present great recipes coupled with fabulous photos we would have a reasonable chance for success. I remember telling my staff to make sure each recipe "tastes homemade." From that philosophy *Chocolatier Magazine* was born.

As time passed, the talent level of America's pastry chefs improved greatly. As a result, the philosophy of "tastes homemade" was replaced by a newer philosophy, "complex flavors with a stylized appearance." Dessert preparation became so complex *Chocolatier Magazine* could no longer bridge the chasm between home bakers and professionals. Enter *Pastry Art & Design Magazine*, the first magazine written to pastry professionals.

Once pastry chefs were released from the bonds of slices and soufflés, there was no stopping them. Today, as never before, dessert has taken the appearance of art, with the plate as its canvas. *Grand Finales: The Art of the Plated Dessert* defines the various styles of plated desserts being presented today. I emphasize today because who knows where this journey will eventually lead us?

However, this journey could not have begun without the cooperation and efforts of many talented, hardworking people. Mark Kammerer, Stephanie Banyas, Chris Thumann, Susan Lee, Tom Singer, Melissa Rosati, Marianne Russell, Michael Suh, and the staff at VNR—you have my admiration and respect as truly gifted professionals and friends.

To the pastry chefs who contributed to *Grand Finales*, you are artists in every sense of the word. Also, my thanks to Anne Hersley and the people at the Ritz-Carlton Hotels in Palm Beach and Chicago, The Phoenician Hotel in Scottsdale, and The Culinary Institute of America at Greystone.

# I N T R O D U C T I O N A L I S M

*"Styles are not usually defined in a strictly logical way ...The characteristics of styles vary continuously and resist a systematic classification into perfectly distinct groups."*

MEYER SHAPIRO

*"I prefer what I make today, because I hate what I did yesterday."*

HANS PETER GRAF

Hubert Keller's father was a pastry chef, and Keller spent most of his boyhood in his father's pastry shop in Ribeauville, France. Keller recalls with fondness his father's baba au rhum. After the cake was baked and poached in syrup, Keller's father would set one aside for young Hubert. "He would put a scoop of ice cream inside while it was still cooling," says Keller. "It was delicious. But that was not something that the customer could experience—the warmth of the pastry just as it had been made."

Keller, a chef who also makes desserts, is pleased to be able to serve plated desserts to the customers at Fleur de Lys, his San Francisco restaurant; plated desserts are designed, in part, to capture the experience Keller enjoyed as a boy. "That's what we're able to do in a restaurant," says Keller. "Desserts are baked to order, and we are able to present them on china that we select."

This book presents masterpieces of the relatively new art of plated desserts. Fifty of the finest pastry chefs and executive chefs in the country—men and women who work in some of the finest restaurants, hotels, bakeries, wholesale operations and culinary schools—have contributed their recipes and visual designs. Their goal when presenting these desserts is the same as that of any chef who works in a refined setting with the finest possible ingredients: to offer an incomparable, exquisite taste experience coupled with intricate, visually pleasing presentation. Flavor is always the primary goal, and the recipes presented here deliver that; however, in this book, the emphasis will be on how well chefs achieve the second goal, presentation. As you will see, many of the chefs disagree on the style and flavor combinations in desserts, not to mention the degree to which presentation should be emphasized. But all would agree that presentation is important. Art may exist for its own sake, but presentation sells. "As long as people are aware of what they're doing and why, it's fine," says Ruben Foster, pastry chef at the Arizona Biltmore in Phoenix. "We're in a business. We're about selling things and about people coming back. If you stay in business, you keep your job."

The concept of plated desserts (Chris Northmore calls them "composition desserts"; his opinion matters, as we will see) is best understood if we visualize the plate as a frame and the components as the medium with which the chefs "paint." "We teach that there are four components to a plated dessert," says Meridith Ford, a food writer, pastry chef and instructor in the International Baking and Pastry Institute of Johnson & Wales University. "Ideally, there is the main item, the star of the show, whatever you would name the dessert. Other components will complement or contrast with this item. The second component is sauce or sauces. Most complicated is the third component—the garnish. This encompasses everything from scoops of sorbet to sugar work to a mint leaf. The final essential component is crunch. If the main item doesn't contain flour, you should include some crunch elsewhere. Of course the rules are stretched," she adds. "Some people use a cookie whether the main component has crunch or not. There are many objectives and concerns to consider. But that's where the fun is."

Ford admits that, under the definition she outlined, a slice of cake with a drizzle of sauce and a mint leaf qualifies as a plated dessert. But let's step outside of the dictionary definition and into the fine print: Most plated desserts include at least one component of perishable ingredients. Although beautiful presentation is integral to the concept, a plated dessert is created to be eaten, not exhibited. Some components of a plated dessert may be prepared beforehand, but the plate itself is assembled à la minute. Because plated desserts are labor-intensive and demand fresh, sometimes exotic ingredients, they can only be achieved in fine restaurants and hotels. "Every single plate you do should look like the only one you did," says Meridith Ford.

Plated desserts are a far cry from the desserts of yesterday, meaning ten years ago; the classic American desserts such as fruit pies, cream pies, chiffon pies, custards, and bread puddings. A slice, a crumble, a bowl, a sundae. In fine European-style restaurants, it was a tart or a slice of cake, served with a flourish. They were fine and delicious, they still are, our memories reside there and we can visit anytime we like, but change was inevitable. "We have evolved from a slice on a plate to more composition and depth," says Mary Cech, an instructor in the pastry program of the Culinary Institute of America at Greystone, St. Helena, California. "A combination and a composition on a plate."

Why this evolution? Certainly, economics plays a part: as the price of entrées and appetizers rose during the upscale, up-and-at-'em eighties, desserts had to keep pace; it wouldn't do to have a $24 entree and a $4 dessert on the menu. Complexity is one way to enhance a dessert's appeal and value. And it is justified: if you apply meticulous plating, distinct forms and over-the-top presentation to the savory food, it feels like a gimmick; you do the same with dessert, it feels...right.

But in the opinion of Ferdinand Metz, President of the Culinary Institute of America, the reason for the emergence of plated dessert presentations is two-fold: "Being able to control what comes before the customer, and the lack of skill of servers," says Metz.

According to Metz, there was a quiet movement in restaurants in France in the 1980s toward à la minute presentation of plated desserts. "Desserts, by and large, do not lend themselves to presentation of ten or more," Metz explains, "unless you're talking about cakes. For example, if you serve soufflés for ten or more, you spoon each portion out and plop it on a plate; it loses its eye appeal, its fluffiness. If you serve crème caramel for ten people, the moment you cut it into pieces it doesn't look so good.

"And, during the 1980s, chefs began to observe that the waitstaff, in general, had become less and less knowledgeable," Metz continues. "They are now more carriers than servers. Chefs wanted to finish a plate in the kitchen rather than relying on someone else to present it. They wanted to know what the plate would look like once it reached the customer. Of course, desserts traditionally lend themselves better to individual presentation than food does. Desserts are cold, and much intricate work can be done beforehand. That gave the trend more of a purpose."

The event which ignited interest among American pastry chefs in à la minute, artful dessert presentations was the Culinary Olympics of 1988, which was the first year that desserts were included in competition. Up until 1988, each team had prepared a soup, appetizer, and entrée. Pastry chefs had been welcome at the Olympics, but only to provide desserts and breads for the meals before and after the events. Ferdinand Metz and Tim Ryan, also of the Culinary Institute of America, were instrumental in bringing about a change. "I proposed to the Frankfurt committee that a pastry chef be included on each team," says Metz. "The idea being that a meal is not complete without dessert. But dessert for 120—their first reaction was, oh no, it can't be done." Eventually, the Olympic Committee agreed to include desserts as part of the cold competition. The pastry chef selected for the team was Chris Northmore, now of the Cherokee Town and Country Club in Atlanta.

The challenge for Northmore was the conditions set by the committee: the 100 to 120 dessert portions had to be completed in three hours and had to be made in the limited space and equipment conditions of the Culinary Olympics. "And it had to taste great and have good presentation," notes Northmore. He began to work with Stacy Radin on concepts and procedures.

"It was an attempt to highlight dessert presentations so that multiple skills could be demonstrated," says Noble Masi, Senior Chef Instructor in pastry at the Culinary Institute of America. "If you were to present a savarin by itself, it represents the skill of making the dough, the flavoring of the rum syrup and the sauce. But if you enhance it with three or four different textures, a sauce, a cookie and so on, you begin to balance the delicate characteristics with more robust characteristics. It moves it from a singular presentation to more like a dessert entrée.

"But it was more than creating desserts, it was a whole system," Masi continues. "When Chris used his skill and his speed, he demonstrated that it could be done. Until then, people thought it would take 30 minutes for each plate. He demonstrated that it could be done efficiently." The dessert that Northmore, Radin and other members of the team agreed on was originally Northmore's: "We wanted to do 'a new twist on apple pie,'" Northmore says. "We wanted to take the elements of apple pie and give it presentation. We called it The Big Apple."

The first chronicled American plated dessert was created by first piping an outline of a large apple in cinnamon-flavored white chocolate on a plate. Northmore then filled in the outline with dried cherry sauce. He placed a timbale of apple-flavored Bavarian cream set on a walnut cinnamon cookie in the center, and warm sautéed Parisian apples alongside. At the top of the apple he placed a hippen leaf and a stem made of chocolate; the stem came vertically off the plate. "It's one of my favorite desserts because it is simple and elegant," says Northmore.

But what really amazed people at the time was the volume. "It was a very dramatic presentation, and we devised a method of production so that it could be done in quantity," says Northmore. "Most piping you think of as being done free-hand. But I came up with a template for the apple shape. I cut a stencil out of hard carboard and set it on the rim of the plate. We then piped the outline. It was awkward, but once I got used to it I could just go with it."

The American team won the gold in 1988, and pictures of the Big Apple were seen in magazines such as *Art Culinaire.* "It flourished after that," says Lars Johansson, Director of the pastry curriculum at Johnson & Wales University. "Once the pastry chefs saw it through the books and magazines that were published with it, it flourished in hotels, country clubs, fine dining restaurants." By 1990, estimates Noble Masi, the trend was fully established.

"I'd love to say I invented it," Northmore says, "but that's not the case. Plated desserts were in their evolution at the time. The industry was getting away from dessert carts and more toward à la carte desserts. It was an opportunity for more creativity by moving it back into the kitchen."

Now the question becomes: Is this a fad (which will suddenly one day be gone, and the next day ridiculed), a trend (which will linger and metamorphose), or a permanent facet of dessert presentation? "I see it receding," says Noble Masi. "Maybe they have gotten a little over-creative. They are not meeting what the customers want at the end of the meal. Some of them have gotten too complex. Too much presentation, not enough flavor."

Meridith Ford says no. "This is not a fad. All fine dining establishments will have some level of plating. Once something this impactful is introduced, it's hard to dismiss. It will never disappear. Maidda Heatter said, 'Good flavor never goes out of style.'"

As with any sudden, dramatic change, there have been excesses. "You only have to taste some of the desserts that are out there to know there is too much emphasis on the visual," says Marshall Rosenthal, pastry chef at the Renaissance Harborplace Hotel in Baltimore. "I believe in being on the cutting edge, but you can fall off too."

"I have been guilty of over-complicating things. Cutting edge is very important to me," admits Mary Cech. Cech is a seasoned chef and innovator of impeccable reputation, but many of the chefs blame Those Damn Kids for the excesses that everyone concedes are rife—kids, and pesky books like the one you hold in your hands. "Less-trained or less-skilled chefs often emphasize presentation over flavor," observes David Pantone, Director of the Florida Culinary Institute. "Kids just out of school tend to be more interested in presentation. But if you don't know how to cook, it doesn't matter what it looks like."

Dan Budd, an instructor at the Culinary Institute of America in Hyde Park, New York, agrees. "Students see these presentations in the press, and they think that's what they have to do. And maybe they get a pastry chef job too soon and they feel compelled to make everything flamboyant. But it's so delicate. I value simplicity," Budd adds, "but I would never relinquish the belief that a pastry chef should be able to express him- or herself."

"I like what other chefs do with their fun presentations," says Andrew MacLauchlan, author and pastry chef at several Coyote Cafe restaurants in the Southwest. "Chocolate is formless. Once it's liquid, heck, you might as well have fun with it. We want to astound people. This is not what people will do at home. That's why they go out."

"If the customer can go home and reproduce one of our desserts, or if it reminds them of something they had at home, then we have missed our opportunity," agrees Hubert Keller.

"What's good about this is that there are different styles emerging, and nothing is right or wrong," says Emily Luchetti, pastry chef and cookbook author. "When the Architectural style emerged, it was like, this is right and everything else is wrong. But now we see that nothing is right and nothing is wrong. It's great that we can fight and argue."

If it is arguments about style, visual emphasis and flavor balance that you seek, you will find them in the pages of this book. The fifty contributing chefs represent a variety of backgrounds, training, sensibilities and venues: each one's style is a synthesis of his or her own aesthetic and the theme of the restaurant, hotel or bakery in which he or she works. They are not shy about expressing their opinions.

We have divided the desserts into nine schools, using schools and disciplines from the visual and theatrical arts as touchstones. We did this partially because we thought it would be fun—it's all about dessert, folks—but primarily because the Impressionist, Minimalist and other movements provide a useful frame of reference with which to analyze the visual presentation of these desserts. Only one, the Fusionist school, uses flavor as a standard of definition.

It was never our intention to identify a particular chef with a particular school of visual presentation. Some chefs' plates appear in more than one chapter, but many are included in only one school. The fact is, all of these chefs present a variety of visual presentations and ingredients in their individual restaurants, running the spectrum from dense flourless chocolate cakes to light sorbets and fruit. Even Dan Rundell of Aureole in New York is not, we insist, an Architectural pastry chef, even though he is closely identified with that mode; for our purposes, he is a pastry chef who presents in the Architectural school, among others.

The desserts pictured in this book will strike some as needlessly ornate, even decadent. It is important to remember that pastry kitchens are becoming major profit centers for restaurants and hotels; the customers who flock to their dining rooms order desserts at a 60 percent, 70 percent clip and higher. When all is said and done, the bald fact remains: Presentation Sells. "Recently I costed out my desserts and discovered that my sauce painting and garnishes—tuiles, berries, mints and so on—are two-thirds of the cost," says Thomas Worhach, Executive Pastry Chef at the Four Seasons Ocean Grand in Palm Beach. "But I am within my budget. That's how important presentation is. I didn't realize it myself. But my management is very happy. See, a lot of companies are coming out with pre-done mixes, mousses and sauces, but they're expensive. I make everything from scratch, and that's less expensive. It gives me money to do these extra garnishes."

We all know how it works. An exquisite dessert is placed at the next table, and we want it. So we order it, and we anticipate it, and then it is placed before us: a sophisticated chocolate ring in a shimmering pool of sauce and crowned with crème fraîche, cookies and pulled sugar. We take a moment to appreciate the colors, the forms, the artistry of the presentation—to acknowledge the work that went into its creation. That is part of it, but hardly all. "We taste with our eyes," says Alain Roby, pastry chef of the Hyatt Regency Chicago. And perhaps it is literally true: perhaps in the hot-wiring of our brains, in the secret, elusive realm we call The Mind, the wickedness we feel because we're straying from our diets and the anticipation we feel as our spoon hovers over this food sculpture are tied into our memories, which now kick into gear: we see chocolate and whipped cream and Bosco; Mom and Dad beaming down at us and Little Brother, who can't wait, never could, already a dervish with his spoon; the people at the next table are stealing glances, delight and envy flickering, tasting it with their eyes. We conjure the chocolate and cherry-on-top of yesterday, tasting this plated dessert in our minds. Our sophistication and seen-it-all urban chic fall away, and as we scramble for our spoon and Mom tucks a napkin under our chin, we are already tasting it.

# CHAPTER TWO

# NEO·CLASSICISM

*"Beauty is composed of an eternal, invariable element whose quantity is extremely difficult to determine, and a relative element which might be, either by turns or all at once, period, fashion, moral, passion."*

JEAN-LUC GODARD

*"There's nothing sexier than a poached pear with a perfect sorbet."*

LISA HERSHEY

Eric Bedoucha recalls his apprenticeship in pastry, and the man with whom he studied in France: "My teacher, chef, second father and friend was Monsieur J.P. Weiss," says Bedoucha, the pastry chef at La Grenouille in New York. "Monsieur Weiss was, and still is, a man very deeply in love with what he does. He is a purist. And he was open to anyone who wanted to learn. Secrecy had no part in his politics. My love for my craft was like a second skin to me, but still Monsieur Weiss knew how to make it grow even further."

Randy Gehman, pastry chef at the Four Seasons Resort and Club in Dallas, recollects *his* apprenticeship: "Having no experience, everything I touched I did wrong, and the pastry chef let his feelings be known. He was German, and very belligerent at times. But I have a little German blood in me too, and we can be very stubborn people. I was not about to let him drive me out of pastry, so I took the brunt of this. I made a lot of mistakes, but I never made the same mistake twice."

Chefs' experiences in pastry training invariably run the gamut from the nightmarish to the sublime and back again: the hand that gently guides one day can be raised in a roundhouse slap the next. But no matter what the state of French patisserie is at any one time — and it is in flux in the mid-1990s — the fact remains that classic French training — whether the training takes place in Switzerland, Austria, France or New Jersey — is a part of most (not all) pastry chefs' rite of passage. Why? "To work under these disciplines makes us stronger," says Eric Bedoucha. Training imparts a means of organization, a proper respect for food itself, and time-honored methods of preparation — peeling, seeding, segmenting, zesting and dicing fruits. Toasting nuts. Clarifying butter. "Many chefs are enormously talented, but haven't found the balance between craft and creativity," says Roxsand Scocos of RoxSand in Phoenix. "Classicism is good because it teaches you what works. The flavors that have an innate relationship to each other. It's important to defer to the classics, use them as a base point, then evolve from them."

*ERIC BEDOUCHA, pastry chef at La Grenouille in New York City, was born on May 24, 1958, in Constantine (French Algeria), though his family moved to France when Eric was two. After working for a while in the fashion industry —"to be around the girls," he says — he began his training in pastry as a pre-apprentice and then an apprentice under J.P. Weiss until age 18. He worked in a pastry shop before doing his time in the army, then found a position at Dalloyau in Paris, where, for 3 1/2 years he studied under Pascal Niau — "the best in the field," says Bedoucha. "He taught me organization, volume, and quality." When he came to the United States, Eric worked with Gray Kunz at the Peninsula Hotel before moving on to La Grenouille. "I learned a lot from Gray, especially flavors. It must make sense, he told me." When Bedoucha is creating a new dessert, the flavors are designed first, and then the visual approach. "But I will quickly know whether it will be round or square or at an angle, and high or low on the plate." As to his future, Bedoucha is unsure, but his goals will remain "to stay honest with myself, my customers and my peers." He would like to study Spanish, and perhaps food chemistry for research or business classes. Currently, he spends his free time in the gym. "Get motivated," he exhorts his peers.*

And no matter what the public clamors for at any one time ("Do you by any chance serve green tea cheesecake?"), the classic recipes remain. In France, classic is opera cake, genoise cake, miroirs, choux pastry, pâte sucrée, charlottes, baked custards, fruit tarts, vacherins, macaroons, meringues and petits fours. In America, pumpkin pie, the ice cream sundae, chocolate pudding, fruit pies, cobblers, and crisps are classic.

## CLASSICS  ILLUSTRATED

Classic French cuisine was codified in the writings of Auguste Escoffier, particularly in his *Guide culinaire*. Other important books include *La répertoire de la cuisine* by Gringoire and Saulnier and — for French patissiers in particular — *Traité de pâtisserie moderne* by Darenne and Duval. Didier Berlioz of La Panetière in Rye, New York, also credits Yves Thuries for "showing the way. He took the time to put everything in his book. All the recipes for the modern era are in his book." Berlioz then goes on to make a crucial distinction between the classicist and the neo-classicist: Of Thuries, he says, "His job was to make cakes, and he doesn't see the plate the same way I do."

François Payard had a similar experience. "When I was working at Lucas Carton, most of the chefs were making cakes like they would in a bakery," says Payard, now pastry chef at Restaurant Daniel in New York. "But a pastry chef there, Alain Senderens [now the owner], said to me, 'Sit down and take a look at these desserts.' He taught me to look at desserts the way a customer would."

In classic preparation, a cake or tart or pastry is made at 4 a.m. according to an established formula and placed in a display case or on a dessert cart until it disappears, slice by slice. In plated desserts, recipes are sometimes formulated in the morning based on the produce that is received; some elements are made ahead, but the plate is, by definition, assembled upon order.

Not all chefs can or should work in this way, but certainly there has been a change in patisserie. Even among the classically trained chefs in France, there is now a grudging allowance for experimentation; more vigorous flavoring, including Asian spices and ingredients; more use of chocolate, including milk and white; an emphasis on fresh fruit over glazed fruits, and the increased use of tropical fruits, with a simultaneous reduction of added sugar for sweetness; a decreased reliance on sugar, butter and cream, even when not creating a so-called "light" dessert; the ascension of ganache, mousse and buttercream; a de-emphasis of fondant.

In the 1990s, food has gone international: the culinary traditions of different cultures are overlapping, a greater variety of ingredients is available, there is an eagerness and allowance among chefs to experiment, and competition is forcing even the unwilling chef to reconsider his menus and methods.

## THREE FLAVORS

A Neo-classic plated dessert is one that features a *classic dessert as one major component,* although that component may contain a contemporary *variation;* this variation can entail a slight *alteration of the classic recipe* or it can involve a *change in the customary presentation* of the dessert. But the classic formula must be clear, vivid and at the forefront of the plate. This is the least exclusionary school of all; most plated desserts qualify to some degree.

David Blom characterizes his work in this way: "I like desserts that flow — sauces that mesh properly with each

*DIDIER BERLIOZ, pastry chef at La Panetière in Rye, New York, was born on June 24, 1963, in Nice, France. He attended the Nice Technical School of Cooking and Tourism, thus earning the right to learn pastry with the most in-demand and demanding pastry chef in Nice.* But "at the time I was more interested in tennis," says Berlioz, who had ambitions to become a professional. As a result, he failed the program. But then, so did the entire class. "The teacher took it badly," Berlioz recalls. "So, out of respect for him, I became determined to succeed." He earned his degree, worked at La Réserve de Boilean and L'Oasis outside Cannes. After a stint in the French army, he worked at Negresco with Jacques Maxima and Jacques Torres. Berlioz came to the United States in 1985, spent a year in Washington, D.C., and eventually found a job at La Reserve in New York. He has been at La Panetière for over five years. When he ponders his future, he thinks perhaps of a teaching career or ownership of a pastry shop or tea salon— "but like a Japanese restaurant, where desserts are made to order," he says.*

*FRANÇOIS PAYARD, pastry chef at Restaurant Daniel in New York City, was born on July 16, 1966, in Nice. His father being a pastry chef, Payard's path was clear. He trained at Ecole Lenôtre before taking jobs in the pastry kitchens of La Tour d'Argent and Lucas Carton. Coming to the United States, he worked under Daniel Boulud at Le Cirque, was Executive Pastry Chef at Le Bernadin in New York City, and then rejoined Boulud in his new venture. He loves the unpredictability of the restaurant life. "My father made the same Napoleons for forty years," he says. "That would make my life very, very boring." In just over two years, Payard has had more than 200 different offerings on his menu at Daniel. "We get better with age," he insists. "When I was 24, 25, I started to understand better what people want." What they want, in Payard's view, is simplicity. An over-complicated plate "is like a beautiful woman with too much makeup." Payard would like to open a pastry shop someday.*

*DAVID BLOM, pastry chef at Chef Allen's in North Miami Beach, Florida, is the third generation of a family of bakers. Born on March 20, 1968, in Philadelphia, Blom spent the first eight years of his life playing with flour and helping his father egg-wash danish in their small German bakery. When the family moved to Wilkes-Barre, Pennsylvania, Blom's father and oldest brother built a large bakery, Bakery Delite, where Blom worked until graduating from high school, and which is still in business today. "When it comes to my father and my brother, they do it once, and they do it right the first time." Blom enrolled at the Culinary Institute of America, trying to escape his destiny by learning to cook savory food, but it was at CIA that he was exposed to the more artistic side of pastry, and he was hooked. He moved to New York City and worked as an assistant pastry chef at three restaurants before meeting Drew Nieporent and becoming pastry chef at Montrachet for six years and then TriBakery, also in New York. "Every day is like an adventure," Blom says, referring to a typical day in the pastry kitchen of a fine dining establishement, "all based on the produce that comes in on any given day."*

*LISA HERSHEY, a pastry chef in New York City, was born on May 18, 1967, in Brewster, New York. As a teenager she took a job at a bakery, making cookies, but "my original interest in pastry was sparked by Albert Kumin," she says, when she studied under Kumin at the International Pastry Art Center. She went on to take jobs as a pastry cook at Glorious Foods Catering, at the River Café and Le Bernadin. At Soleil, she assumed the role of pastry chef, and then worked at the Four Seasons Hotel and at Chanterelle before signing on at Le Chantilly. She describes her goal in creating desserts as "simple but not minimal. Sophisticated but not flamboyant." As to her ambitions for the future: "I've been at a four-star restaurant," she says. "So where do I go from here? Maybe someday I'll open my own place or do some teaching."*

other, or the sauce with the dessert. Everything comes together yet all tastes are experienced individually. And I like to put a little twist on it, whether it's sugar work or painting with coulis — a slight abstraction to the dessert." The Neo-classic formula in a nutshell.

As always, the milieu of a restaurant will determine to some degree the approach the pastry chef must take. So it is not surprising that many of the chefs who offer desserts in this school can be found in classic French restaurants.

"For me the visual is important, but the taste has to be simple and there should not be too many of them," says Didier Berlioz of La Panetière. "By the time a customer of a sophisticated restaurant gets to dessert his palate is saturated. If he knows the dessert looks good, he may give it a try. But you don't want to saturate people with flavors. I would say, two or three." Other chefs agree with the three-flavors rule: "I don't like to have more than three flavors on the plate," François Payard says. "When I get an idea for something — an apple dessert, for example — all elements contribute to apple. There should be no conflict. Chefs now tend to make too many sauces of so many different flavors, and they do it for the look. We are not painters. We are artists, but not painters."

"With more than two or three flavors on the plate, then you don't know what you're eating," agrees Eric Bedoucha. "I believe in one dominant flavor. Different textures can contribute to the one flavor. It's like in advertising — they want one idea to get across."

The Neo-classic approach involves, perhaps above all, a respect for fresh produce. "I try to look at food as itself," says Lisa Hershey. "I like to come up with a plate that's clean and tastes good. I don't want too many things on the plate." "I take a very simple approach," says David Blom. "I'm partial to fruits, and depending on the condition of the fruit you might not have to do a thing with it."

This reliance on fruit also produces, in Neo-classic plates, vibrant, rich color schemes. And most of the forms seen here are classic and familiar: rings, cigarettes, spun sugar nests, fruit fans and scoops. But the visual feature that most closely ties these desserts together is the simplicity and conventionality of the plating: the major component sits squarely at the center of the plate. The eye is never confused by these plates; it is drawn to the primary component and anchored there while admiring the garnishes. These plates are carefully, meticulously composed. Contrast this approach with the (purposely) careless plating and primitive forms of Minimalist desserts.

Chestnut Cake is a classic French dessert, but François Payard alters the formula with his ginger-infused chocolate sponge. The tuile is classic, but Payard gives it a contemporary spin with the "stenciling" technique, using cocoa-infused tuile batter. And the ascending chocolate drops on the plate are an exquisite modernist touch.

David Blom's Banana Gratin is pure classic: linzer crust, caramel, chiboust; even the sauce painting is in the restrained, classic mode. But Blom adds a frozen ganache sphere in the center; when the dessert is baked, the chocolate will partially melt and then ooze forth when the customer applies a spoon.

Eric Gouteyron's Imperial Apple Chocolate Cakes are classic in form — the apricot crown mimics a miroir, the cigarettes nest snugly, the cakes sit in a pool of cinnamon sauce — but the pairing of classic green apple mousse with a chocolate biscuit and chocolate mousse is contemporary. Stanton Ho's Hawaiian Gold takes the classic joconde and runs with it, all the way to his native Hawaii; rather than use almond flour, he employs macadamia nut flour in the cake, and adds crunch elements with finely chopped macadamias and crushed cigarette cookies. While the form of the overall dessert is classic, the flavors of the crème anglaise (Kona coffee), syrup (Kahlua) and mousse (dark chocolate and Kahlua) are Ho's invention, as is his preference for Hawaiian Vintage Chocolate, which lends a distinct, fruity note. In his presentation, he adds "neo" elements such as gold flakes and a striped chocolate ribbon. Hubert Keller's Apple Crisp is pure, classic Americana, complete with crumbly topping and caramel sauce, but his presentation is distinct and contemporary.

## START MAKING SENSE

There are practical reasons to employ the restraint of the classical artist in a kitchen setting. François Payard points out one: "If you make a dessert too complicated, it cannot be replicated if you are not in the kitchen," he says. "You cannot be there all the time. The other guys must be able to do it. No one should know that you are not in the restaurant." But for the most part, the chefs who present Neo-classic desserts as part of their repertoire do so because of strong aesthetic beliefs. "The plate must make sense," maintains Eric Bedoucha. "The flavors should be clean and be in harmony with the rest of the meal. Ingredients and their combination should be tasty and fresh and sometimes amusing."

Chefs who work in the Neo-classic mode — and their cousins, those who present Minimalist desserts — can be

*ERIC GOUTEYRON, Executive Pastry Chef of the Plaza Hotel in New York, was born on April 17, 1962, in France. He served a two-year apprenticeship in pastry, then attended several technical schools and worked in a series of pastry shops; during this time he came under the tutelage of Chefs Rix and Siennat. "Mr. Rix taught me the basics of pastry making and the love for the profession," says Gouteyron. "I discovered a higher level with Gerard Siennat." Once his training was done, Gouteyron had acquired an uncanny skill in working with chocolate. In 1988, he came to the United States and found a position at the River Café in New York. In 1992, he assumed his post at The Plaza Hotel. "Create a plated dessert with harmony, beauty and care," he says. "Moreover, create it as if it was the first or even the last one you will ever make. This is my philosophy."*

*STANTON HO, Executive Pastry Chef of the Las Vegas Hilton, was born on April 20, 1952, in Honolulu, Hawaii. He attended the University of Hawaii, Kapiolani Community College, where he studied with Master Pastry Chef Walter Schiess. "He was creative, energetic and very well rounded," says Ho. "He was the first to make me aware how creative this field could be. " Ho studied at Ecole Lenôtre in Paris, then returned to Hawaii and worked in a several hotels and resorts while continuing his education through seminars and competitions. "A number of people have influenced me," says Ho, "and two of the most influential were Master Pastry Chef Wally Uhl, who shared his knowledge in sugar craft, modern techniques and technology of pastry production, and Paul Houdayer, who was responsible for bringing me to the Las Vegas Hilton." Ho joined the Hilton in 1984, and is in no hurry to move on. "The Hilton has not only been supportive of me, but has given me a lot of flexibility," he says. Someday he would like to write a production pastry book.*

*HUBERT KELLER, chef de cuisine of Fleur de Lys in San Francisco, was born on June 14, 1954, in Ribeauville, France. He trained at the École Hôtelière in Strasbourg, then served an apprentice- ship at the Auberge de L'Ill before train- ing with both Paul Bocuse at Collanges and Gaston Lenôtre in Paris. After stints with restaurants and a cruise line, he worked as a sauce chef for Roger Verge at Moulin de Mougins. Keller went on to work at the Hotel Negresco in Nice and Hotel Prieuré and to manage two restaurants for Verge in São Palo and San Francisco. In 1986, Keller became co-owner of Fleur de Lys with Maurice Rouas. "I loved San Francisco from the first day," he says. Keller also has the distinction of being the only guest chef at the White House, making a pre- sentation on low-fat cooking and preparing a meal for President Clinton and his family. "I was one of the first chefs to talk about health," he says. "The goal is to keep the customer happy and healthy, keeping that fine line between what the doctors want and what the people want."*

passionate in their denunciation of what they perceive as overkill in many plated dessert disciplines. "It's confusing," says François Payard. "People don't know what they're eat- ing anymore. And sauces too, what are they doing in the middle of the plate? We cannot forget that we are making food. I don't like it when people see something and they have to ask, 'What is that on the plate?' Most of the time, they should know what they're eating."

"Taste is first, the look is second," says Eric Bedoucha. "If you can marry them, then you win. I dislike sampler plates and busy plates. It's like a bag of surprises — the biscuit, the mousse, the sorbet, the cake. To identify so many fla- vors and forms, it's not a guessing game, it's food."

Still, these chefs are not entirely unmindful of the impor- tance of extravagant presentation in some settings. "I don't think it's gone too far or that there is an overemphasis on the visual," says John Hui of Cottage Bakery, Inc., ever the practical businessman. "I think it's great. It shows creativ- ity. As long as it matches up with profitability…it's never too much as long as a customer is willing to pay for it."

Critical as chefs can be, most understand the demands that different restaurants impose, and respect the individuality of their peers. Although restraint is the watchword of Neo- classic desserts and the focus is on flavor — an aesthetic shared by chefs who present Minimalist works — there is respect, even admiration, for the more ornate works of oth- ers. As Eric Bedoucha recalls, his tutor, J.P. Weiss, said to him many years ago: "Whatever will come out of your hand will be a reflection of you, of the artist that sleeps in you."

# CHESTNUT CAKE

. . . . . . . . . . . . . . . . . . . . . . . . . . . . . . . . . . . . . . . . . . .

FRANÇOIS PAYARD, RESTAURANT DANIEL, NEW YORK

*A chocolate cake with a hint of ginger complements the chestnut mousse and candied chestnuts*
*— a clever complexity to this pure flavor experience.*

## YIELD: 10 SERVINGS

Special Equipment:  Ten 2 1/4" x 1 1/2" (5.7 x 3.8 cm) high ring molds
1 dot-pattern stencil
15" x 1 3/4" (38 x 4.4 cm) acetate template, tapered at one end

### TUILE RIBBON BATTER
*3.5 oz/99 g unsalted butter, at room temperature*
*3 oz/85 g confectioners' sugar*
*4.2 oz/119 g egg whites*
*1 tsp/5 ml vanilla extract*
*3.7 oz/105 g all-purpose flour*
*1 Tbs/5.8 g cocoa powder, sifted*

1. In a mixer with the paddle attachment, beat butter and sugar until light and fluffy. Gradually add egg whites one at a time (the mixture will look curdled). Add the vanilla and flour and mix until smooth. Transfer one-third of the mixture to a bowl; whisk in the cocoa powder until smooth. Refrigerate dark and light tuile batter for 2 hours.

2. Place a dot-pattern stencil over a silicon baking mat. Using a spatula, spread the dark tuile batter over the stencil in a thin, even layer (see illustrations *a* and *b*, page 16). Carefully remove the stencil. Place the mat in the freezer until firm, about 1 hour.

3. Preheat oven to 350°F (175°C). Place the mat on a sheet pan and, using a spatula, spread a thin layer of the tuile batter over the dark tuile batter pattern. Bake the tuile layer for 5 minutes until partially set. Using an acetate template as a guide, cut the tuile layer into ten 15" x 1 3/4" (38 x 4.4 cm) strips, tapered to a point at one end (see illustration *c*, page 16) with a pizza cutter. Return the tuiles to the oven and bake 3–5 minutes longer, until golden around edges.  Remove the tuiles from the oven and immediately wrap each tuile strip around the outside of a 2 1/4" ring mold, allowing the tapered end of the strip to trail away from the ring mold (see illustration *d*, page 16). Allow the tuiles to cool completely; remove from ring molds and store in airtight container until serving.

*Page 8: "I like the shape of this dessert," says François Payard, "the sweep of the cookie. And almost everything here contributes to the fla-*
*vor of chestnut. Only the whipped cream on top breaks the flavor, but you need that, too."*

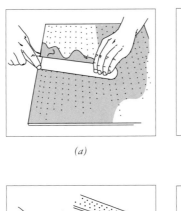
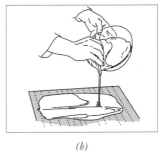

(a)

(b)

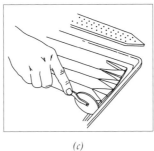
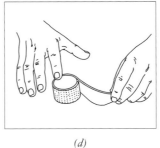

(c)

(d)

### CHOCOLATE SAUCE

*5.6 liq oz/166 ml water*
*5.25 oz/149 g granulated sugar*
*4.25 oz/120 g crème fraîche*
*1.05 oz /30 g alkalized cocoa powder*

1. In a saucepan, combine water and sugar and bring to a boil. Remove from the heat and whisk in the crème fraîche and cocoa powder.

2. Return the mixture to the heat and bring to a boil. Strain through a chinois. Cool.

### GINGER SOAKING SYRUP

*4.1 liq oz/121 ml water*
*1.75 oz/50 g granulated sugar*
*.5 tsp/2 g alkalized cocoa powder*
*4 oz/113 g fresh gingerroot, grated*

In a saucepan, combine the water, sugar and cocoa powder. Bring to a boil and add the ginger. Infuse for 15 minutes and strain into a bowl in an ice bath.

### FLOURLESS CHOCOLATE CAKE

*8 oz/227 g bittersweet chocolate, coarsely chopped*
*4 oz/113 g unsalted butter*
*3.25 oz/92 g egg yolks*
*3 oz/85 g granulated sugar, divided*
*3 oz/85 g egg whites*

1. Preheat oven to 350°F (175°C). Line a half sheet pan with parchment and butter lightly. Place chocolate and butter in a bowl over a hot water bath until melted.

2. In a mixer with whisk attachment, whip the yolks and 1 oz (28 g) of the sugar to the ribbon stage.

3. Gently fold the melted chocolate into the yolk mixture.

4. In a mixer with whisk attachment, whip the egg whites and remaining sugar to stiff peaks. Fold into the yolk/chocolate mixture and scrape into the prepared pan. Bake for 7–9 minutes. Cool completely.

5. Using a 2 1/4" (5.7 cm) biscuit cutter, cut out twenty circles from the cake. Brush each circle with the ginger soaking syrup.

6. Place the rounds on a sheet pan lined with parchment paper. Place a 2 1/4" ring mold over each circle.

### CHESTNUT MOUSSE

*1 tsp/4 g powdered gelatin, softened*
*1 liq oz/30 ml water*
*5.9 oz/167 g chestnut purée*
*2.9 oz/82 g sweetened chestnut cream*
*1.3 oz/37 g granulated sugar*
*2 oz/57 g crème fraîche*
*.48 liq oz/14 ml dark rum*
*8.12 liq oz/240 ml heavy cream, whipped to soft peaks*

1. Soften the gelatin in the water; clarify in bain-marie.

2. In a mixer with paddle attachment, cream together the chestnut purée, chestnut cream and sugar until pale. Add the crème fraîche and rum, and continue beating for 1 minute. Add the clarified gelatin and beat until combined. Gently fold in the whipped cream.

### WHIPPED CREAM GARNISH

*8.12 liq oz/240 ml heavy cream*
*8.8 oz/264 g superfine sugar*
*.5 tsp/2 ml vanilla extract*

Whip ingredients to soft peaks. Cover and chill until serving.

### ASSEMBLY

*Candied chestnuts*
*Caramel-dipped candied chestnuts*
*Chocolate cigarettes*
*Chocolate decoration*
*Mint*

1. Spoon 2 Tbs (24 g) of the chestnut mousse into each of the cake-lined ring molds. Place another cake round on top of the chestnut mousse. Press down and place 1 Tb (12 g) of mousse onto each cake round, filling the mousse to the top. Level the mousse with an offset spatula. Cover the sheet pan with plastic wrap and freeze for 3 hours.

2. Unmold the mousse rings.

3. Fill a pastry bag fitted with a medium star tip (Ateco #4) with the whipped cream.

4. Place an unmolded chestnut cake in the center of a dessert plate. Carefully slip a tuile ribbon over the chestnut cake, allowing the tapered end to trail off the plate.

5. Pipe several small rosettes of whipped cream onto the top of the chestnut cake. Garnish the whipped cream with a sprig of mint, half of a sliced candied chestnut, a chocolate cigarette, and a chocolate decoration. Spoon five graduated dots of chocolate sauce on the plate following the contour of the tuile ribbon. Garnish the plate with a caramel-dipped candied chestnut.

# HAWAIIAN GOLD

. . . . . . . . . . . . . . . . . . . . . . . . . . . . . . . . . . . . . . . . . . . . . . . .

STANTON HO, LAS VEGAS HILTON, LAS VEGAS, NEVADA

*Coffee, chocolate and macadamia blend seamlessly in this silky dessert experience. The chocolate bow and accompanying fruit add texture and tartness.*

### YIELD: 12 SERVINGS

Special Equipment: Twelve 2 1/2" x 1 1/2" (6.3 x 3.8 cm) high ring molds

#### MACADAMIA NUT CAKE
*7.8 oz/221 g egg yolks*
*8.6 oz/244 g granulated sugar, divided*
*8 oz/227 g all-purpose flour*
*4 oz/113 g almond flour*
*4 oz/113 g macadamia nut flour*
*7.3 oz/207 g egg whites*
*4 oz/113 g unsalted butter, melted*

1. Preheat oven to 375°F (190°C). Butter and flour two 9" round cake pans.

2. In a mixer with whisk attachment, beat yolks and 4.6 oz (130 g) sugar to ribbon stage.

3. Sift all-purpose flour, almond flour and macadamia flour together.

4. In a mixer with whisk attachment, whip egg whites until soft peaks form; gradually add remaining 4 oz (114 g) sugar and whip until stiff peaks form.

5. Gently fold sifted flours into egg yolk mixture.

6. Fold 1/3 of meringue into the yolk mixture. Fold in remaining meringue. Fold in melted butter.

7. Pour batter into prepared pans. Bake 20–25 minutes.

#### CHOCOLATE CRUST
*4 oz/113 g gianduja chocolate, melted*
*1.7 oz/48 g Hawaiian Vintage Chocolate, melted*
*3 oz/85 g toasted, chopped macadamia nuts*
*8 oz/227 g crushed cigarette cookies*

*Following page: "Many times chefs will try to make an impression on their bosses or their customers," says Stanton Ho. "I try to stay with the traditional but find new flavors, new blends. This works out better for everyone in the long run."*

1. Line a half sheet pan with parchment paper.

2. Combine chocolates in bowl and stir in macadamia nuts and crushed cigarette cookies. Spread mixture onto prepared pan in a 1/16"(.16cm)-thick layer. Chill.

### HAWAIIAN VINTAGE CHOCOLATE AND KAHLUA MOUSSE

*1.95 oz/55 g egg yolks*
*1.75 oz/50 g whole egg*
*2 oz/57 g granulated sugar*
*3 Tbs/44 ml Kahlua liqueur*
*1 gelatin sheet, softened*
*8 oz/227 g Hawaiian Vintage Chocolate, melted*
*16 liq oz/473 ml heavy cream*

1. In a medium bowl, whisk together yolks and egg; add granulated sugar and Kahlua liqueur. Place bowl over hot water bath. Whisk mixture to ribbon stage.

2. Add gelatin and whisk until dissolved.

3. Whisk melted chocolate into egg mixture until combined.

4. Place mixture over ice bath and stir with rubber spatula until it just begins to set. Remove from ice bath and fold in 1/3 of the whipped cream. Fold in remaining whipped cream and refrigerate.

### KAHLUA SIMPLE SYRUP

*7.5 liq oz/222 ml water*
*2 oz/57 g granulated sugar*
*1 liq oz/30 ml Kahlua liqueur*

1. In a small saucepan, combine water and sugar and bring to a boil.

2. Continue to cook until mixture becomes a light syrup. Allow to cool.

3. Stir in Kahlua liqueur.

### KONA COFFEE SAUCE ANGLAISE

*.5 qt/.5 L heavy cream*
*4 oz/113 g granulated sugar*
*1/2 vanilla bean, split and scraped*
*2.6 oz/74 g egg yolks*
*1 Tbs/15 g instant Kona coffee*
*1 Tbs/15 ml Kahlua liqueur*

1. In a saucepan combine heavy cream, granulated sugar and vanilla seeds. Cook over medium heat. When cream begins to boil, stir in instant coffee until dissolved.

2. Slowly temper hot coffee/cream with egg yolks.

3. Return mixture to pan and continue to stir with a wooden spoon over medium heat until mixture reaches custard stage.

4. Immediately strain sauce through a fine chinois into an ice bath and stir until cool.

5. Stir in Kahlua liqueur. Refrigerate.

---

2. In a food processor, purée banana and milk until smooth. Transfer mixture to saucepan.

3. In a bowl, whisk together egg yolks and 2 Tbs (24 g) sugar until smooth. Whisk in flour to make a smooth paste.

4. Over medium-high heat, bring banana/milk mixture to boil, whisking constantly. Gradually mix half of the hot banana purée into the yolk mixture. Return this mixture to the saucepan.

5. Continue cooking over medium-high heat, whisking occasionally, until the mixture comes to a boil. Whisk in the gelatin and chopped chocolate until smooth. Set aside, covered, at room temperature.

6. Line a sheet pan with parchment. Arrange eight 3" ring molds on the sheet. Remove the ganache from the freezer; form eight 3/4" balls out of the ganache and place one in the center of each ring mold. Place the sheet pan in the freezer.

7. In a saucepan, cook the remaining 3.5 oz (99 g) sugar and remaining 1.75 liq oz (52 ml) water to 240°F (117°C). Meanwhile, in a mixer with whisk attachment, beat egg whites with cream of tartar to soft peaks. While continuing to beat at medium speed, slowly add sugar syrup in a steady stream. Beat until cool.

8. Fold 1/3 of the whites into banana mixture to lighten it. Fold in the remaining whites.

9. Spoon the chiboust into the prepared ring molds, covering the ganache balls and filling the molds completely. Use an offset metal spatula to level the tops of the molds. Freeze the chiboust molds for at least 2 hours.

### LINZER CRUST

*4 oz/113 g unsalted butter, chilled*
*3.5 oz/99 g granulated sugar*
*.12 tsp/.61 g baking powder*
*.5 tsp /2 ml vanilla extract*
*.65 oz/18 g egg yolk*
*2.1 oz/60 g slivered almonds, finely ground*
*5 oz/142 g all-purpose flour*

1. Preheat oven to 350°F (175°C).

2. In a mixer with paddle attachment, mix butter, sugar, baking powder and vanilla until smooth. Add yolk and beat to combine. At low speed, add the almonds and flour and mix until crumbly. Turn the dough out and press into a 5" (12.37 cm) disk. Wrap and chill 30 minutes.

3. Roll the dough out to 1/8" (.32 cm) thickness. Using a fluted 3 1/2" (8.8 cm) round cookie cutter, cut out 8 rounds of dough and place them on ungreased sheet pan. Bake for 10–12 minutes, or until lightly browned. Cool on rack.

### CARAMEL SAUCE

*7 oz /198 g granulated sugar*
*1 liq oz/30 ml water*
*8 liq oz/237 ml heavy cream*
*.5 tsp/2 g vanilla extract*

1. Preheat oven to 375°F (190°C).

2. Pour clarified butter over shredded phyllo and toss to coat evenly.

3. Press about 1 oz (28 g) shredded phyllo into a 2 1/4" ring mold set on a baking sheet lined with parchment paper. Let excess dough lay over edge. Arrange the sautéed apples over phyllo in one layer. Fold excess dough inward.

4. Sprinkle crisp mixture on top. Bake for 20–25 minutes until crisp mixture browns and phyllo is golden.

### ALMOND TUILES

*6 oz/170 g confectioners' sugar, sifted, divided*
*2.5 oz/71 g all-purpose flour*
*2 oz/57 g unsalted butter*
*3 oz/85 g egg whites, at room temperature*
*2.25 oz/64 g blanched almonds, sliced*

1. In a bowl, combine 4 oz (113 g) confectioners' sugar and flour.

2. In a mixer with paddle attachment, beat butter until smooth. Gradually beat in flour mixture. Slowly beat in egg whites and continue to beat until smooth, about 2 minutes. Cover bowl with plastic wrap and chill for at least 2 hours.

3. Preheat oven to 400°F (205°C). Lightly butter 2 nonstick baking sheets.

4. Spread tuile batter by tablespoons into 3" (7.6 cm) circles, spacing them 1 1/2" (3.8 cm) apart. Top each circle with a few almonds and sprinkle with the remaining confectioners' sugar. Bake 4–6 minutes, until tuiles are golden brown around the edges.

5. While still warm, form the tuiles into cup shapes by pressing them over a tall, narrow glass. (If the tuiles become too cool to bend, return them to the oven for 30 seconds, just until warm enough to be flexible.) Cool completely.

### CHAMPAGNE SABAYON

*7.8 oz/221 g egg yolks*
*9 oz/255 g granulated sugar*
*24 liq oz/710 ml champagne*
*12 liq oz/355 ml heavy cream, whipped to soft peaks*

1. In a medium bowl, whisk together egg yolks and sugar. Whisk in champagne. Place bowl over a pot of simmering water and whisk 6–8 minutes, until soft peaks form and mixture has doubled in volume.

2. Place bowl over ice bath and whisk until sabayon is cold. Gently fold in whipped cream.

### CHOCOLATE CRÈME BRÛLÉE

*11 liq oz/325 ml milk*
*24 liq oz/710 ml heavy cream*
*7 oz/198 g bittersweet chocolate, coarsely chopped*
*6.5 oz/184 g egg yolks*
*6 oz/170 g granulated sugar*

1. Preheat oven to 275°F (135°C). In a saucepan, bring milk and cream to boil. Add the chocolate and stir until chocolate is melted and mixture is smooth. Cover saucepan and set aside.

2. In a bowl, whisk together egg yolks and sugar until lemon-colored and slightly thickened. Gradually whisk warm milk chocolate mixture into yolks. Strain through a fine sieve into bowl. Skim off any foam.

3. Divide mixture among twelve 4 oz ramekins and bake in water bath for about 80 minutes, or until custards are set. Cool and refrigerate up to, but no longer than, 8 hours.

### ASSEMBLY

*4 ripe bananas, peeled and thinly sliced*
*Sugar, for caramelizing tops*

Fan out 5 slices on top of each custard. Sprinkle sugar evenly over tops of custards. Broil until caramelized.

### PLATE ASSEMBLY

*Apricot sauce*
*Chocolate sauce*
*Sliced strawberries*

1. Spoon some apricot sauce onto one section of a dessert plate and pipe chocolate sauce over it in concentric circles. Drag a knife through the sauce to create a feather pattern. Place a cinnamon apple raisin crisp in the center of the sauce.

2. Place a chocolate crème brûlée on the plate. Place a tuile cup alongside it and spoon some of the champagne sabayon into the cup. Garnish with a sliced strawberry.

# CHOCOLATE BANANA TART

. . . . . . . . . . . . . . . . . . . . . . . . . . . . . . . . . . . . . . . . . . . . . . . . . . . .

LISA HERSHEY, LE CHANTILLY, NEW YORK, NEW YORK

*The appealing marriage of banana and chocolate is given a hint of rum with a smooth and oozing sabayon.*
*This hot dessert is cooled with vanilla ice cream and lent sweet crunch with a brûlée and a spun sugar halo.*

### YIELD: 4 SERVINGS

#### PUFF PASTRY BASE
*8 oz/227 g puff pastry rolled out 1/4"(.63 cm) thick*

1. Preheat oven to 400°F (205°C).

2. Cut puff pastry into 4" (10 cm) rounds and place on sheet pan.

3. Bake until golden brown, about 6–8 minutes.

4. Cool and slice in half horizontally.

#### GANACHE
*11.5 oz/326 g bittersweet chocolate, chopped*
*2.5 oz/71 g milk chocolate, chopped*
*4.5 liq oz/133 ml heavy cream*
*4.5 oz/128 g unsalted butter*

1. Melt chocolates together over double boiler.

2. In saucepan, bring cream to a boil; pour over chocolate, add butter and whisk until smooth.

3. Spread onto half sheet pan about 1/4" (.63 cm) thick; chill.

4. Cut ganache into 3" (7.6 cm) rounds.

#### SABAYON
*5.2 oz/147 g egg yolks*
*1.75 oz/50 g whole egg*
*3.5 oz/99 g granulated sugar*
*4 liq oz/121 ml Meyer's dark rum*
*6 liq oz/177 ml heavy cream, whipped to soft mounds*

*Following page: "Since my menu changes every month, I sometimes play with old favorites, like the caramelized peach torte I'd made for a while," says Lisa Hershey. "I'd also been playing with a rum sabayon, and needed something to do with it. This dessert was born."*

31

1. Whisk together yolks, egg, sugar and rum over-bain marie until pale and doubled in volume.

2. Remove from heat and chill over ice bath.

3. Fold in whipped cream.

**ASSEMBLY**

*4 large ripe bananas*
*Superfine sugar for caramelizing tarts*
*Vanilla ice cream*
*Mint*
*Spun sugar*

1. Preheat oven to 400°F (205°C).

2. Slice bananas and arrange in an overlapping circular pattern over the top layer of puff pastry. Sprinkle with sugar and caramelize with a propane torch.

3. Place 1 ganache round inside each puff pastry shell and top with the caramelized banana lid.

4. Reheat for 3–4 minutes until ganache is just melted.

5. Plate with the sabayon and vanilla ice cream and garnish with mint and spun sugar.

# CHAMPAGNE SORBET WITH CRISPY APPLES

Eric Bedoucha, La Grenouille, New York, New York

*Simplicity itself — a cool, intriguing champagne sorbet and crispy apple slices. "A dessert should be elegant and this is," says Eric Bedoucha. "After a long meal, it's perfect. This is my favorite."*

## YIELD: 8 SERVINGS

### CHAMPAGNE SORBET
*21 liq oz/621 ml water*
*11 oz/312 g granulated sugar*
*3 liq oz/89 ml orange juice*
*2 liq oz/59 ml lemon juice*
*25.4 liq oz/750 ml champagne, chilled*
*1.05 oz/30 g egg white, whisked until frothy*

1. In saucepan, combine water, sugar, orange, and lemon juice. Bring to a boil; cool and chill.

2. Add champagne and egg white to chilled mixture and process in ice cream machine.

### BEAUME DE VENISE REDUCTION
*24 liq oz/710 ml Beaume de Venise wine*
*24 liq oz/710 ml white wine*
*24 oz/680 g granulated sugar*
*4 liq oz/118 ml lemon juice*
*6 vanilla beans, split in half, lengthwise*
*1 medium Granny Smith apple, peeled, cored and diced*

1. In a heavy-bottomed saucepan, combine all ingredients. Simmer on low heat until reduced by 1/3 of the volume.

2. Strain the sauce and add the diced apple; chill until ready to serve.

### CRISPY APPLES
*4 medium Granny Smith apples*
*32 liq oz/946 ml simple syrup*
*2 liq oz/59 ml lemon juice*

*Facing page: For a short time, Eric Bedoucha worked for Pierre Cardin at Maxim's de Paris in New York. Some time later, Cardin came into Bedoucha's restaurant, and identified this dessert "as a duplicate of one of the dresses he designed," remembers Bedoucha. "He wanted to sign it for me, but instead he ate it."*

1. Preheat oven to 200°F (95°C). In a large saucepan, combine simple syrup and lemon juice and bring to boil. Remove from heat and set aside.

2. Cut each apple in half and remove core. Slice each apple very thinly into rings; place directly into hot syrup. Allow the apples to soak in the syrup for a few minutes.

3. On a silicon baking mat, arrange the apple slices in a single layer. Bake until dry and crispy, 75–90 minutes. Store in an airtight container until ready to serve.

### ASSEMBLY

*Eight 2" biscuit rounds*
*Mint leaves*

1. Place 1 round of biscuit on dessert plate. Top with a scoop of champagne sorbet. Place another scoop on top of the first. Press apple slices into the sorbet at 1/4" (.63 cm) intervals around the sorbet, trimming them if necessary.

2. Spoon some of the Beaume de Venise reduction onto the plate and garnish with a mint leaf.

# IMPERIAL APPLE CHOCOLATE CAKES

ERIC GOUTEYRON, THE PLAZA, NEW YORK, NEW YORK

*The uncanny pleasure of a chocolate and apple combination is brought to the fore through the details: a sautéed apple filling, cinnamon sauce, and chocolate and green apple mousses.*

## YIELD: 10 SERVINGS

Special Equipment: Ten 3" x 1 1/2" (7.6 x 3.8 cm) high ring molds

### CHOCOLATE COOKIE BATTER

*8.5 oz/241 g all-purpose flour*
*14 oz/397 g granulated sugar*
*3.5 oz/99 g cocoa powder*
*8 oz/227 g unsalted butter, at room temperature*
*5.8 oz/164 g honey, at room temperature*
*8.4 oz/238 g egg whites, at room temperature*

1. Line a sheet pan with a silicon baking mat.

2. Sift together flour, sugar, and cocoa powder; set aside.

3. In a mixer with whisk attachment, cream butter until smooth. Gradually beat in honey and egg whites until mixture is silky in texture. At low speed, mix in sifted dry ingredients.

4. Spread a thin layer of the cocoa batter over the silicon baking mat. Using a decorating comb, scrape the surface of the batter to create decorative patterns. Freeze until set, about 15 minutes.

### ALMOND BISCUIT

*1 lb/454 g whole eggs*
*12 oz/340 g almond flour*
*12 oz/340 g confectioners' sugar*
*3.5 oz/99 g all-purpose flour*
*3 oz/85 g unsalted butter, softened*
*11 oz/312 g egg whites*
*1.3 oz/37 g granulated sugar*

*Following page: "Pastry is an art that can be magic and beautiful," says Eric Gouteyron. "The beauty of a dessert is 50 percent visual and 50 percent flavor. If a dessert is not appealing to the eye there is little chance you will taste it."*

37

1. Preheat oven to 400°F (205°C). In a mixer with paddle attachment, beat whole eggs, almond flour and confectioners' sugar at high speed for 10 minutes. At low speed, mix in flour and butter.

2. In a clean mixer bowl with whisk attachment, beat egg whites and granulated sugar to soft peaks. Fold whipped whites into almond mixture. Scrape 1 lb 4 oz (567 g) of the almond batter onto the frozen cocoa batter and spread into an even layer. Bake 15 minutes until set; cool completely.

3. Arrange ten 3" x 1 1/2" (7.6 x 3.8 cm) high ring molds on a parchment-lined sheet pan. Cut ten 10" x 3/4" strips of biscuit; line the inside of each mold with a biscuit strip.

4. From the remaining biscuit, cut out ten 2 1/4" (5.7 cm) rounds. Place a cake round in the bottom of each lined ring mold.

### GREEN APPLE FILLING

*2 green apples*
*.5 oz/14 g unsalted butter*
*2 Tbs/24 g granulated sugar*
*2 Tbs/24 g brown sugar*
*.15 tsp/.75 g ground cinnamon*

1. Peel, core and slice each of the apples into 8 wedges. Cut each wedge into triangles 1/4" (.61 cm) thick.

2. Melt the butter in a sauté pan and sauté apple pieces for 4–6 minutes, sprinkling on the sugars and cinnamon and tossing frequently. The apples should be soft and slightly caramelized. Cool completely.

### CINNAMON SAUCE

*3.5 oz/99 g granulated sugar, divided*
*16 liq oz/473 ml heavy cream*
*1 tsp/4 g ground cinnamon*
*.15 tsp/.75 g salt*
*3.6 oz/102 g egg yolks*
*.5 tsp/2 g vanilla extract*

1. In a saucepan, combine half of the sugar with heavy cream, cinnamon and salt; bring to gentle boil.

2. In a medium bowl, whisk egg yolks with remaining sugar until blended. Gradually whisk hot cream mixture into yolk mixture to temper. Return mixture to saucepan.

3. Continue cooking over medium-low heat, stirring constantly for 3–5 minutes until slightly thickened. Strain the sauce and cool over ice bath. Stir in vanilla.

### CHOCOLATE MOUSSE LAYER

*3.2 oz/ 91 g granulated sugar, divided*
*1 liq oz/30 ml water*
*1.3 oz/37 g egg yolks*
*1.75 oz /50 g eggs*
*6 oz/170 g bittersweet chocolate, melted*
*6 liq oz/177 ml heavy cream, whipped to soft mounds*

1. In a small saucepan, combine 2 oz (57 g) of the sugar with water. Cook to 240°F (117°C).

2. Meanwhile, in an electric mixer bowl, whisk together yolks, egg and remaining sugar. Place bowl over bain-marie and whisk until just warm. Place bowl in mixer stand fitted with a whisk attachment, and beat until tripled in volume, about 5 minutes. Gradually beat in hot sugar syrup.

3. Temper yolk mixture with melted chocolate. Fold in whipped cream. Fill a pastry bag with the chocolate mousse and pipe the mousse into the lined ring molds to just below the top of the cake. Top the mousse with a small amount of the sautéed apples, spreading them into an even layer. Freeze until set.

### GREEN APPLE MOUSSE LAYER

*2 green apples, peeled, cored and chopped*
*1 liq oz/30 ml lemon juice*
*4.6 oz/130 g granulated sugar*
*1.75 tsp/5.4 g powdered gelatin*
*1 liq oz/30 ml water*
*1 liq oz/30 ml Calvados*
*12 liq oz/355 ml heavy cream, whipped to soft mounds*

1. In a non-reactive saucepan, place apples and lemon juice and bring to boil. Reduce heat to low, cover, and cook 7–9 minutes, until apples are tender. Stir in sugar and cook 2 minutes, stirring. Cool 10 minutes.

2. Soften gelatin in water and clarify over bain-marie.

3. Purée apple mixture in food processor with Calvados. Add clarified gelatin. Fold apple mixture into whipped cream. Spoon the apple mousse into the ring molds, filling them completely. Level tops with spatula. Cover molds with plastic wrap and chill 3-4 hours, until completely set.

### APPLE GARNISH

*6 liq oz/177 ml water*
*1 liq oz/30 ml lemon juice*
*1 Granny Smith apple*

1. Place water and lemon juice in bowl.

2. Slice apples on mandoline into extremely thin rounds. Place rounds in lemon water for 10 minutes.

### ASSEMBLY

*Apricot nappage*
*Poached lady apples*
*Chocolate cigarettes*
*Fresh raspberries*
*Mint*

1. Unmold desserts. Dry apple slices and place 1 slice on top of each mousse. Brush apple slice with apricot nappage.

2. Place dessert on plate and garnish with halved poached lady apple, chocolate cigarette, raspberries, mint and cinnamon sauce.

# DOBOS TORTE

. . . . . . . . . . . . . . . . . . . . . . . . . . . . . . . . . . . . . . . . . . . . . . . . . . . .

D A V I D   B L O M ,   C H E F   A L L E N ' S ,   N O R T H   M I A M I   B E A C H ,   F L Ó R I D A

*Mocha buttercream, white cake imbibed in coffee syrup, a rectangular shape and an (optional) croquant spatula*
*are some of the variations David Blom works on this classic torte.*

Y I E L D :   1   C A K E

### CAKE
*5 oz/142 g all-purpose flour*
*3 oz /85 g cornstarch*
*6.5 oz/184 g egg yolks*
*8 oz/227 g granulated sugar, divided*
*10.5 oz/298 g egg whites*

1. Preheat oven to 350° F (175°C). Grease 2 half sheet pans and line them with parchment paper.

2. Sift the flour and cornstarch together. Set aside.

3. In a mixer with whisk attachment, whip the yolks and 4 oz (113 g) of the sugar together to the ribbon stage.

4. In a clean bowl with whisk attachment, whip the whites to soft peaks and slowly add the remaining sugar.

5. Fold the yolks and whites together . Fold in the flour mixture in 4 additions.

6. Divide and spread the batter onto the prepared half sheet pans.

7. Bake for 10 minutes or until slightly browned. Cool in the pans and set on a wire rack.

### COFFEE SOAKING SYRUP
*8.3 liq oz/245 ml water*
*10.5 oz/298 g granulated sugar*
*2 Tbs/24 g coffee extract*

In a saucepan, bring the water and sugar to a boil. Let cool and stir in coffee extract.

*Following page: "This is a classic classic which I first made when the restaurant owner requested it," says David Blom. "I sometimes*
*add a croquant spatula, which coordinates well flavor-wise."*

### MOCHA BUTTERCREAM

*8.8 oz /250 g whole eggs*
*16 oz/454 g granulated sugar*
*6 liq oz/177 ml water*
*1 lb/454 g unsalted butter, softened*
*2 oz /57 g bitter chocolate, melted*
*2 Tbs/30 ml coffee extract*
*1 Tbs/15 ml vanilla extract*

1. In a mixer with whisk attachment, begin whipping the eggs.

2. In a saucepan, bring the sugar and water to the soft ball stage 240°F (117°C) and slowly add to the eggs while continuing to beat. Continue whipping on medium speed until cool.

3. Slowly beat in the butter 2 tablespoons at a time. Beat the buttercream until it is smooth.

4. At medium speed, beat in the melted chocolate and extracts.

### ASSEMBLY

1. Cut each sheet of cake widthwise into 4 even strips, making a total of 8 strips.

2. Soak 1 layer of the cake with the coffee syrup and spread a 1/4" (.63 cm) layer of buttercream on top. Top with another cake layer. Repeat layering, making seven layers and ending with a layer of cake.

3. Soak the top layer with the coffee syrup but do not spread with the buttercream.

4. Press down the cake to make an even and level top. Refrigerate for 2 hours.

### CARAMEL TOPPING

*7 oz/198 g granulated sugar*
*1 tsp/4 ml lemon juice*
*1 liq oz/30 ml light corn syrup*
*1 oz/28 g unsalted butter*

1. Combine all ingredients in a saucepan and boil to a medium dark caramel.

2. Immediately immerse the bottom of the pot in ice water and let cool for 30 seconds.

3. Pour the caramel over the assembled cake and spread quickly and evenly with a spatula. Refrigerate for 1/2 hour.

4. Remove from refrigerator and, using a hot knife, mark the caramel top of the cake into the classical cut shape of the Dobos Torte (a triangle with the "tip" cut off).

# M I N I M A L I S M

*"We ascribe beauty to that which is simple; which has no superfluous*

*parts; which exactly answers its end; which stands related to all things;*

*which is the means of many extremes."*

R ALPH  W ALDO  E MERSON

*"Why do you have to put it all on the plate just because it*

*exists on the planet?"*

E MILY  L UCHETTI

*BRUNO FELDEISEN,* pastry chef at the Four Seasons Hotel in New York City, was born on September 4, 1964, in Clermont-Ferrand, France. His love of food bloomed early and, at age 15, he began his apprenticeship in "a very old chocolate shop." Moving to Paris, Feldeisen found work at Robert Linxe's La Maison du Chocolat. Later, he became chocolatier for Alain Ducasse at L'Hotel de Paris in Monaco. In 1985, he moved to the United States. "When I moved here I didn't have much training in pastry," he says. "I thought I would make it big in chocolate, but it didn't work out that way." Once in Los Angeles, he found work with Joaquim Splichal in the pastry kitchens of Patina and Pinot Bistro. "I have had two mentors, Alain Ducasse and Joaquim Splichal," says Feldeisen. "From Alain I learned respect for product. Joaquim taught me to develop my own style. This is when I learned France was not the center of the world. Joaquim told me to go buy junk American pastry—donuts, Twinkies, cupcakes— to get a feeling for what Americans grew up with." Although he was happy at Patina, Feldeisin wondered about the rest of the country, and decided to try New York. In 1994, he became pastry chef at the Four Seasons. His plans for the future perhaps involve working on a cookbook.

Since Bruno Feldeisen became pastry chef at the Four Seasons Hotel in New York, people have often remarked to him that his plates are "limited. So," Feldeisen adds with a wry chuckle, "my mind must be limited."

Feldeisen is waxing ironic on a subject that many pastry chefs know well: it is more difficult to succeed with simplicity than with spectacle.

## FREUDIAN SWEET SATISFACTION

A Minimalist dessert is one that usually has *a single component supported by a spare garnish or no garnish.* The primary dessert *form* and the garnish are often *primitive* or "unfinished." The plates are not only spare—some of them look downright careless. But of course there is craft in casualness. Wayne Brachman, pastry chef at the Mesa Grill in New York, explains the philosophy he learned from working with executive chef Bobby Flay: "We always drop food—the savory food, the desserts, fruit, everything. It always seems to fall in the right places. You are capturing something in a moment of time, and that energy can be captured. It makes the food more natural. It doesn't look set."

Dropping food, splattering sauces. It's often been remarked that desserts—whether served at a fine restaurant or at Mom's dinner table—appeal to the child within. And no desserts in this volume have more subliminal appeal to the child in us than Minimalist desserts and Illusionist desserts (see Chapter 4). Illusionist desserts are those which bear resemblance to known objects; we take primal joy in seeing such resemblances in food (or sand or ice or Silly Putty, for that matter). But Minimalist desserts offer perhaps even more childish appeal because they look like something a child might create—mounds of food, heaps of whipped cream, squiggles of coulis—and because the simplified, streamlined flavor systems speak more clearly to us of the cherished flavors of our childhood. Other than music, what sensory input hurtles us back into the past more efficiently than flavor? "I like dessert to be fun," says Wayne Brachman. "I have no objection to fun things on the plate. I like candies. I like to appeal to nostalgia."

"Your memories of desserts come first before savory food," says Bruno Feldeisen. "Desserts are a link to the past, a form of Freudian sweet satisfaction."

## PURE, UNCOMPROMISING, MEDITATIVE

Although the term "Minimalism" was first coined in 1929, and some of its most vivid examples—the black canvases of Robert Rauschenberg—were created in 1952, the Minimalist movement really came to fruition in the 1960s and 70s. Minimalist art reduces visual content to the very simplest of shapes and forms. There is a low degree of differentiation in form and color and a minimal amount of noticeable "artwork," and therefore it is said to possess little "content" in the traditional sense. It strives to eliminate information that might express or refer to anything outside itself, including references to the artist himself. A single form or design principle often dominates, and is repeated or contrasted in some way with other elements. It is said of the Minimalist artist that he or she seeks to create a meditative or peaceful effect by stripping away all but the essence of shape or materials, until what is left is pure and uncompromising. Examples of Minimalist art include the monochromatic canvases of Yves Klein and the primary structures of Robert Morris, but the movement was quite diverse. For example, Andy Warhol's pop art is often included under the Minimalist umbrella, because his soup cans and Marilyn portraits are self-referential and have virtually no content.

The Minimalist movement in the visual arts was a reaction to the romantic, flamboyant Abstract-Expressionist works that preceded it. The Minimalists were seeking to do away with the emotional and expressive content, the complexity and attempts at individuality they found hopeless or distasteful in abstract expressionism. Minimalist works were therefore considered cold at best; boring, meaningless and fraudulent at worst.

The analogy between Minimalist works in the visual arts and Minimalist plated desserts breaks down because of the simple fact that in food, flavor is content. If pastry chefs who create simpler plates are reacting to the more lavish and intricate works of their contemporaries, they are also attempting to throw the focus back on pure flavor by reducing the number of flavor carriers on the plate and minimizing contrast in flavors—in a sense, their works are more pure.

"We're talking about cooking," says Bruno Feldeisen. "Blown sugar, flowers on the plate—it doesn't excite me."

"It's playing with food and it's kind of silly," agrees Emily Luchetti. "And if it's too arranged, with the different flavors all over the plate, it forces you to gather little bits on your spoon. You should be able to take one dig with the spoon and get good flavor."

Still, the fine arts have much to teach the willing chef. In the opinion of Wayne Brachman, "there are two great sources for learning how to do presentation—looking at other chefs' savory food and looking at art," he says. "If you look at other pastry chefs' work, you usually wind up copying. At best you'll do a poor version of what they're doing. But if you look at savory dishes, it forces you to think. It's the same with art—if you use art as inspiration, you'll come up with revolutionary ideas, totally new."

The pastry chef's role is to complement the chefs' dishes, which is not an easy thing to do, says Brachman. He is proud of the fact that his desserts do not mimic other objects or other pastry chefs' plates. "When I started I was

**WAYNE BRACHMAN**
"My mother was the worst cook ever," says Wayne Brachman. "Zero cooking. That's how I got into food. From necessity." Brachman, currently pastry chef at Mesa Grill in New York, was born on April 25, 1951, in Queens, New York. He went to the Manhattan School of Music, taught orchestra to high schoolers, was a punk rocker, "a Warhol hanger-on" and co-owner of a deli. A trip to Paris inspired him to be a chef, and on his return he took a job in a French restaurant When the position of pastry chef was available, Brachman asked to give it a try. "I looked up recipes in Julia Child and Food & Wine and just assembled a little menu. I learned from reading." Brachman worked in a series of restaurants and hotels in Massachusetts before moving back to New York. He worked at Odeon, Arizona 206, the Mesa Grill and Bolo. He is the author of Cakes & Cowpokes, and conducts master classes in the New York area. "I love doing this so much I want to keep at it," he says. "I love writing and teaching, so I will continue to do both."

**EMILY LUCHETTI**
Emily Luchetti was born in Corning, New York, on June 21, 1957. After college, she moved to New York City, and answering a want ad that caught her eye only because the job did not require typing, she found herself cooking in the kitchen of an executive dining room. "After a while, I realized how much I loved it," she says. "I was 21 years old, and a lot of my contemporaries hated their jobs. I thought that was sad. I always wanted to enjoy what I do." While working in a series of restaurants in New York, she studied with Nick Malgieri and with Gerard Pangaud outside Paris. She worked at Silver Palate and, in 1984, moved to San Francisco, where she got a job as a line cook at the newly opened Stars restaurant. Three years later, a position as pastry chef became available, and Luchetti asked Jeremiah Tower if she could give it a try. "Pastry was something I always loved to do," she says. "And half an hour into it, I knew I was home." Luchetti is the author of Stars Desserts. In 1995, she left Stars restaurant to concentrate on writing a second book. As to her future: "I definitely want to be baking."

doing little cactuses and cows, and everybody said, 'Look! How adorable!' Now when I see an elaborately decorated plate it tells me that four people have been pawing my food with their dirty fingers for twenty minutes."

## DISTRESSED

In a Minimalist dessert, conventional forms such as squares, spheres and rectangles will be seen but do not predominate, and the overall look of the finished plate will have a careless, "found" quality: piping of sauces is imprecise (or is calculated to appear childlike or casual), and the placement of fruit and other support components is not done in such a way as to suggest recognizable repeats or pleasing patterns. The colors in Minimalist desserts are often muted because there is rarely an attempt to enliven the plate with fruit sauces or sugarwork.

Contrast Minimalist plates with their closest relative, Neo-classic plates (see Chapter 2), where the vibrant colors of fresh fruit, fruit reductions and elaborate sugar garnishes dominate; where forms are precisely geometric or follow the dictates of conventional pastry molds; where the piping is precise, the plating is exact and often symmetrical.

Although there may be classic forms in Minimalist desserts, they are often camouflaged. The "monolith" of Wayne Brachman's Banana Butter-Crunch Cake looks even more primitive when crowned by the cookie shard and coated with the coarse, intermittent butter-crunch; also, the placement of the fruit leather is random and the sauce painting is haphazard. Brachman's Chocolate and Peanut Butter Ganache No-Bake Cake takes the form of...what? A mutant mushroom? The top is seared, giving it a scorched appearance that would be labeled unappetizing by traditionalists.

**MARY CECH**
Mary Cech, an instructor in baking and pastry at the Culinary Institute of America at Greystone in St. Helena, California, was born on May 30, 1956, in Dayton, Ohio. After some catering for a hotel in Chicago, she found positions at Gordon Restaurant, the Hyatt Regency Chicago, the Park Hyatt and Charlie Trotter's, working nights and continuing her education by day. Between jobs, she trained with Ewald and Susan Notter and with Albert Kumin at his International Pastry Arts Center as well as at the Culinary Institute of America in Hyde Park. After a stint at the Cypress Club in San Francisco, Cech became Corporate Pastry Chef for the forty-plus restaurants of Lettuce Entertain You Inc. in Chicago. "I saw the need to simplify and make pastry approachable not only for the pastry chef, but for a pantry worker who may not have had any pastry background," she says. She continues to make things simple for the students at the CIA's northern California campus. "I like it when they say, 'Wow, that looks difficult,' and then they learn its simplicity," she says. "As to her future, Cech cites, "more travel and a pastry book—the best book of course!"

Bruno Feldeisens's Peanut Butter and Jelly Sandwich Cake—perhaps in keeping with the childlike theme of the recipe—is a "distressed" slice of cake: there is no attempt to smooth seams between layers or between cake and frosting in this rectangle of cake; and the chocolate sauce truly forms a spill rather than an elegant pool. Feldeisen's Milk Chocolate Pumpkin Cake is an oversized square of cake with a finished, sleek appearance—but the dried apple slice, propped like a forgotten wagon wheel in the desert, the withered cinnamon sticks and the unformed pools of sauce once again de-romanticize the plate.

Emily Luchetti's Mocha Panna Cotta with Caramel Rum Sauce is a crater-dome (rather than an elegant demi-sphere) with a heap of whipped cream and shaving on top and an asymmetrical cage of caramel sauce at its feet. Luchetti's Caramel Hazelnut Tart is Minimalism defined: a simple rectangle standing alone. Even the minimal flourish of chocolate sauce and hazelnut is neatly camouflaged by the plate design, as if the artist were attempting to hide her craft; only the ornate swirls of white and dark chocolate reveal her artistry.

Mary Cech's Sweet Melon Cream is similarly Minimalist: a simple sphere is repeated many times in two sizes and combined to create a somewhat floral, though mostly uncanny, provocative form. The mood of unreality is reinforced by the color of the combined melon purée and mint syrup. The dried melon flower is a perfect Minimalist touch: it contributes melon flavor while adding an elegant though muted visual accent.

## FUNKY GRACE

Not surprisingly, several of the pastry chefs who contribute work in the Minimalist mode agree with the "three flavor" rule outlined in the Neo-classic chapter. "Two to three flavors on the plate and that's it," declares Emily Luchetti. "Otherwise there's too much going on." Bruno Feldeisen agrees. "I love cold and warm, crispy and creamy, texture and color…but too many flavors are confusing."

Feldeisen, long an admirer of Japanese art, loves its simplicity and strives for the same simplicity in his plates. Jacquy Pfeiffer, pastry chef at the Sheraton Chicago Hotel and Towers, defines a beautiful dessert as possessing "understated elegance." Emily Luchetti defines it as "simplicity and elegance. They are not opposite," she insists. "You can have both." Luchetti wonders why pastry chefs feel compelled to over-garnish plates. "Why a mint leaf, for example?" wonders Luchetti, citing that cliché garnish of the past. "If it's not going to be eaten, it doesn't have to be there. In fact, desserts don't have to have color. Everything should relate to the main object. What's wrong with brown? If it doesn't have color, it can have texture and shape." "Funky grace" is the term that Wayne Brachman uses to describe his favorite plates. "I love color and textures but I don't like too much organization."

JACQUY PFEIFFER
*Jacquy Pfeiffer, the executive pastry chef at the Sheraton Chicago Hotel and Towers, was born on February 11, 1961, in Molsheim, Alsace, France. "My father owned a bakery, baking bread in the old-fashioned style," he says, and young Jacquy spent much time in the shop, learning and lending a hand. At 15, he began an apprenticeship as a pastry cook at Jean Clauss,' pastry shop in Strasbourg, while also studying food technology, business and marketing. Pfeiffer worked at a confectionery shop in Alsace to sharpen his chocolate skill, was a pastry chef in the French Navy, then worked in various pastry shops and hotels in France, Saudi Arabia and California. He was pastry chef for the Sultan of Brunei on the island of Borneo, sometimes creating desserts for banquets of 6,000. He was pastry chef at the Hyatt Regency in Hong Kong and the Fairmont Hotel in Chicago before joining the Sheraton Hotel and Towers. A tireless participant in pastry competitions, Pfeiffer is a master at creating sugar centerpieces and sculptures. He recently transformed part of his living space into a school for chocolate and sugar. His most immediate goal is "to try to win the pastry World Cup in Lyons in 1997," he says. Eventually, he would like to move back to France.*

Still waters run deep, the saying goes, and there is calculation in how these simple plates are assembled. "I like to surprise the customers," says Bruno Feldeisen, "but not too early. That's why my plates are simple. The customers don't know what to expect. When they bite into it, if you did it right, that's when they are most delighted, not when it is presented." Wayne Brachman designs his plates "ergonomically." That is, he tries to anticipate how the customer will fork the plate, and ensures that each bite will be a little different, the components mixing in different ways. "I want the plate arranged so that no matter how the customer attacks it, he will taste several flavors."

## SIMPLICITY AS A TREND

Throughout history, the urge to create spectacle with food has been strong. Illusionist works, for example, have been popular for nearly as long as there has been pastry. But if you want to capture someone's attention, whisper; and if you want to stand out in a crowd, you must behave or dress differently. Perhaps simplicity in presentation will catch on.

Mary Cech is ready for that to happen. "In these days when we're trying to cut costs, cut labor, we should try to take the minimal and make it feasible," she says. "How can we take the fewest components possible and make a great end product? We need to take it easy on ourselves. This industry is so hard, burn-out happens really quickly.  The question is, how can we keep that appeal and not kill ourselves? We've gotten too complicated. We need to step back. We need to look to the future. So many things don't make sense together but we do it anyway because it's a trend. My message is, let's make 'simple' the next trend."

If that happens, Wayne Brachman is willing to take the message to the world. "American pastry chefs will be exported," he announces. "We are the center of food now. All the thinking is going on here. Restaurants around the world are copying American-style restaurants."

Around the world, at any given time, a dessert course is being served, and restaurant customers are reacting as Jacquy Pfeiffer hopes that they will, every time: "A smile is great," he says. "A memory is even better. But a tear of joy is the ultimate."

# BANANA-BUTTERCRUNCH CAKE

Wayne Brachman, Mesa Grill, New York, New York

*The fun flavor of banana sour cream cake is supported with banana ice cream and fruit sauces, with a dash of sarsaparilla. Fruit leather and buttercrunch coating add the chewy to the smooth.*

## YIELD: 24 SERVINGS

### BANANA CAKE

*32 oz/907 g cake flour*
*2 tsp/8 g baking soda*
*.5 tsp/2 g baking powder*
*.5 tsp/2 g salt*
*10 oz/283 g unsalted butter, at room temperature*
*14 oz/397 g granulated sugar*
*7 oz/198 g whole eggs*
*14 oz/397 g medium bananas, peeled and mashed*
*4 oz/113 g sour cream*
*2 Tbs/30 ml vanilla extract*

1. Preheat oven to 375°F (190°C). Line a sheet pan with parchment paper.

2. Sift together flour, baking soda, baking powder and salt 3 times.

3. In a mixer with the paddle attachment, cream butter and sugar on high speed.

4. Beat in eggs one at a time. Beat until light and fluffy.

5. In another bowl, stir together mashed bananas, sour cream and vanilla.

6. With the mixer on low speed, add the banana mixture to the batter alternately with the dry ingredients until combined.

7. Spread the batter into the prepared pan and bake for approximately 15 minutes or until golden brown. Cool in the pan set on a wire rack.

### BUTTERCRUNCH

*2 liq oz/59 ml water*
*2 liq oz/59 ml light corn syrup*
*14 oz/397 g granulated sugar*
*8 oz/227 g unsalted butter*

*Page 44: "I wanted a monolith on the plate with no layers," says Wayne Brachman, "and I wanted to play with sarsparilla. I added the fruit and mint as a foil for the sarsparilla, which is like dirty root beer, but good dirt, like farm dirty. Musky."*

# CHOCOLATE AND PEANUT-GRAHAM NO-BAKE CAKE WITH ROASTED MARSHMALLOW

WAYNE BRACHMAN, MESA GRILL, NEW YORK, NEW YORK

*Peanuts and graham crackers add crunch throughout this flavorful cake. Marshmallow is flavored with rum and the cake filling is a duet of chocolate and coffee.*

### YIELD: 8 SERVINGS

#### PEANUT BUTTER ICE CREAM
*12 oz/340 g creamy peanut butter*
*6 oz/170 g egg yolks*
*8.75 oz/248 g granulated sugar*
*12 liq oz/355 ml heavy cream*
*12 liq oz/355 ml milk*

1. Place the peanut butter in a medium bowl.

2. In a separate bowl, whisk the egg yolks with the sugar until smooth. In saucepan, combine the heavy cream and milk and bring to a boil. Temper the yolks with the milk mixture. Return to the saucepan and cook until thickened.

3. Strain about 1/4 of the yolk mixture into the peanut butter and whisk until combined. Strain in the remainder and whisk until smooth. Cool over an ice bath. Freeze in an ice cream machine.

#### CRUST
*2 oz/57 g unsalted butter*
*1 oz/28 g granulated sugar*
*3.75 oz/106 g graham cracker crumbs*
*2.7 oz/77 g roasted peanuts, coarsely chopped*

1. Preheat oven to 350°F (175°C).

2. Lightly grease and set eight 3" (7.6 cm) ring molds on a parchment-lined sheet pan.

3. In a small saucepan, melt the butter.

4. In a medium bowl, combine the sugar, graham cracker crumbs and peanuts. Stir in the butter, then pat the mixture out into the bottoms of the cake rings to a thickness of 1/2" (1.25 cm). Bake for 8 minutes. Set aside to cool.

*Facing page: "I look on this as a deconstructed s'more," says Wayne Brachman. "You have the graham as the crunchy bottom, peanut flavor throughout, and a cold, moist center once the marshmallow is roasted and the cake warms up."*

### CAKE FILLING

*10 oz/283 g semisweet chocolate, finely chopped*
*6.25 liq oz/185 ml brewed coffee*
*10.25 oz/291 g graham cracker crumbs*
*4 oz/113 g roasted peanuts, coarsely chopped*

1. Place the chocolate in a large bowl. Bring the coffee to a simmer; pour it over the chocolate. Whisk until smooth.

2. Mix in the graham cracker crumbs and peanuts.

3. Gently pat the mixture over the crusts in the cake rings to form a 1/2" (1.25 cm) layer. Form a slight indentation in the top of this layer to accommodate the ice cream. Let it set at room temperature for at least 1 hour.

### MARSHMALLOW

*8 liq oz/237 ml water, divided*
*11.5 liq oz/340 ml light corn syrup, divided*
*14 oz/397 g granulated sugar*
*.5 oz/14 g powdered gelatin*
*.5 liq oz/15 ml vanilla extract*
*.5 liq oz/15 ml Meyer's dark rum*
*Flour for forming the marshmallow*

1. Place half of the water, half of the corn syrup, and the sugar in a small saucepan fitted with a candy thermometer. Place over high heat and cook to 240°F (117°C).

2. While the syrup is heating, soften the gelatin in a small bowl filled with the remaining water.

3. In a mixer with the whisk attachment, combine the remaining corn syrup with the vanilla extract and rum. As the syrup nears the proper temperature, melt the gelatin over a small pot of boiling water.

4. Once it reaches 240°F (117°C), pour the hot syrup into the mixing bowl. Using the whisk attachment, mix the syrup at medium speed for 1 minute. Add the gelatin and increase the mixer speed to high. Continue mixing about 5 minutes, until the marshmallow reaches the consistency of shaving cream.

5. Fill a half sheet pan with flour to a thickness of 1/4" (.63 cm).

6. Fill a pastry bag fitted with a plain tip (Ateco #5) with the marshmallow. Pipe eight 2 oz (60 g) mounds of marshmallow onto the floured half sheet pan, and allow them to spread out and set up, about 15 minutes.

### ASSEMBLY

*Assorted fruit sauces*

1. To serve, unmold a cake and place it on a sheet pan lined with parchment. Place it in a hot oven for 1 minute to soften it. Unmold the cake and top with a scoop of the peanut butter ice cream.

2. Using a cake spatula, lift one of the marshmallow disks from the floured sheet pan and drape it over the ice cream. (Note: To handle marshmallow, always first dip your fingers in flour.) Torch the marshmallow or flash the dessert in the broiler for 12 to 15 seconds until the marshmallow browns.

3. Transfer to plate decorated with fruit sauces and serve immediately.

# BANANA MOUSSE WITH AMARANTH SEED WAFER AND VANILLA-RUM SORBET

JACQUY PFEIFFER, SHERATON HOTEL AND TOWERS, CHICAGO, ILLINOIS

*Rum is the classic accent to banana, and it can be found in the wafer and in the cooling sorbet.*

### YIELD: 20 SERVINGS

#### BANANA MOUSSE
*15 oz/425 g banana purée*
*1.5 liq oz/44 ml lemon juice*
*1.5 liq oz/44 ml rum*
*9 oz/255 g granulated sugar*
*6 liq oz/177 ml water*
*9 oz/255 g egg whites*
*2 gelatin sheets, softened in cold water*
*8 oz/227 g apricot glaze, melted*
*cocoa powder, for dusting*

1. Mix the banana purée with the lemon juice and rum.

2. In a non-reactive saucepan, make a caramel with the sugar.

3. Add water to the caramel, and boil the mixture to 248°F (120°C).

4. In a mixer with the whisk attachment, whip the boiled sugar into the egg whites to soft peaks.

5. In a large bowl, melt the gelatin over a water bath. Remove from heat and add the purée mixture; fold in the meringue.

6. Quickly spread the mixture in a parchment-lined half sheet pan to a thickness of 3/4" (1.9 cm). (The mousse won't cover the entire pan.) Freeze for 2 hours. Dust mousse with cocoa powder, and spread glaze over sheet.

7. Using a 2 1/2" (6.3 cm) oval cutter, cut the mousse into 20 oval shapes. Return shapes to freezer until plating.

*Following page: "This is actually a low-fat item," says Jacquy Pfeiffer. "The wafer is made of amaranth seed, and I mix it with caramel and marshmallows — still no fat."*

### AMARANTH SEED WAFER
*1 oz/28 g granulated sugar*
*.5 oz/14 g marshmallow*
*4 oz/113 g Amburst\**

1. In a non-reactive saucepan, caramelize the sugar.

2. Mix in the marshmallow.

3. Add the Amburst and immediately transfer the mixture to a silicon baking mat. Place another silicon mat over the mixture. By hand or with a dough sheeter, roll the mixture out to 1/8" (.32 cm) thick.

4. While mixture is still warm, cut the wafers into desired shapes. If the wafers cool down too much, place the sheet in the oven on the silicon mat to re-warm.

### DRIED BANANAS
*4 bananas, under-ripe*

1. Preheat oven to 225°F (110°C).

2. On a slicing machine, slice the bananas lengthwise to 1/8" (.32 cm) thick. Place slices on a silicon mat and dry in the oven for about 30 minutes. Form into desired shape; cool.

### VANILLA-RUM SORBET
*32 liq oz/946 ml water*
*16 oz/454 g granulated sugar*
*3.5 oz/99 g glucose*
*2 vanilla beans, split and scraped*
*.5 liq oz/15 ml dark rum*

1. Boil the water, sugar, glucose and vanilla beans.

2. Strain and stir in the rum; chill.

3. Freeze in an ice cream machine.

4. Form into 2 oz (57 g) quenelles.

### ASSEMBLY
*Whipped cream or Marshmallow*
*Dried banana slices*
*Banana purée*

Place amaranth wafer and dried banana on plate. Place banana mousse oval on the amaranth wafer and ice cream quenelle on the banana wafer. Top mousse with dollop of whipped cream or marshmallow. Decorate plate with banana purée.

* Amburst is an amaranth seed product available from Amaranth Resources Inc., Albert Lea, Minnesota: (800) 842–6689.

# LAYERED PUMPKIN AND MILK CHOCOLATE MOUSSE CAKE

BRUNO FELDEISEN, FOUR SEASONS HOTEL, NEW YORK, NEW YORK

*The flavor of pumpkin and coffee infuse this cake, perfectly complemented with smooth chocolate mousse.*

## YIELD: ONE 10" CAKE

### PUMPKIN SPONGE

*8 oz/227 g cake flour*
*1 tsp/4 g ground cinnamon*
*1 tsp/4 g baking soda*
*8.75 oz/248 g eggs*
*20 oz/567 g granulated sugar*
*15 oz/425 g pumpkin purée*

1. Preheat oven to 350°F (175°C). Grease and flour four 10" (25.4 cm) cake pans.

2. Sift together the flour, cinnamon and baking soda; set aside.

3. In a mixer with the whisk attachment, beat the eggs and sugar until light and fluffy. At low speed, mix in the pumpkin purée. Fold the dry ingredients into the batter.

4. Pour batter into the prepared cake pans. Bake for 25 minutes, or until toothpick inserted in center of cake comes out clean.

### MILK CHOCOLATE MOUSSE

*2 lbs/907 g milk chocolate, chopped*
*8 liq oz/237 ml milk*
*8 liq oz/237 ml heavy cream*
*1 Tbs/15 ml light corn syrup*
*16 liq oz/473 ml heavy cream, whipped to soft peaks*

1. Place chocolate in a bowl. Bring milk, cream and corn syrup to a boil and pour over the chocolate. Gently mix with a spatula. Allow mixture to set until it cools down to 85°F (29°C).

2. Fold in the whipped cream.

*Facing page: "I wanted to do something different with pumpkin, with cake and mousse, and it turned out delicious," says Bruno Feldeisen. "It's a very good marriage. Milk chocolate works much better here than bitter."*

### COFFEE SYRUP

*16 liq oz/473 ml water*
*14 oz/397 g granulated sugar*
*1 cinnamon stick*
*1 Tbs/12 ml coffee extract*

In saucepan bring water, sugar and cinnamon to boil. Remove from heat and allow to cool. Remove cinnamon stick and stir in coffee extract.

### ASSEMBLY

1. Trim top of each pumpkin sponge layer.

2. Place one sponge layer in bottom of a 10" x 3" (25.4 x 7.6 cm)-high cake ring. Brush with coffee syrup.

3. Pour in 1/3 of the milk chocolate mousse.

4. Place another pumpkin sponge layer on top and brush with more coffee syrup.

5. Pour in another 1/3 of the milk chocolate mousse.

6. Top with the third pumpkin sponge layer; brush with syrup and pour on remaining mousse. Top with remaining pumpkin layer.

7. Freeze 8 hours or overnight until set.

### APPLE SAUCE

*24 liq oz/710 ml apple juice*
*1/2 vanilla bean*

1. In a saucepan, combine apple juice and vanilla bean; bring to a boil and simmer, uncovered, until the juice is reduced to 8 liq oz (237 ml).

2. Remove the vanilla bean and allow the sauce to cool.

### ASSEMBLY

*Confectioners' sugar*

Unmold the cake and allow to defrost. Slice; dust with confectioners' sugar. Place on dessert plate with a pool of apple sauce.

# PEANUT BUTTER AND JELLY BRIOCHE PUDDING

BRUNO FELDEISEN, FOUR SEASONS HOTEL, NEW YORK, NEW YORK

*Much like a bread pudding, but with brioche, this dessert sings with the American flavors of peanut butter and raspberry jelly.*

### YIELD: 12 SERVINGS

#### PUDDING

*32 oz/907 g brioche*
*8 oz/227 g granulated sugar*
*5.8 oz/166 g egg yolks*
*1 vanilla bean, split and scraped*
*32 liq oz/946 ml heavy cream*
*14 oz/397g peanut butter*
*12 oz/340 g raspberry jelly*

1. Trim the crust off of the brioche loaf. Cut the loaf into slices 1/2" (1.25 cm) thick. Lightly toast brioche slices in an oven until golden.

2. Preheat oven to 400°F ( 205°C).

3. In a bowl, whisk together sugar, egg yolks, and vanilla bean. Gradually whisk in cold cream.

4. Spread each slice of brioche liberally with peanut butter, then raspberry jelly. Soak each slice in the egg mixture and then arrange brioche slices in layers in a half hotel pan. Pour in remaining egg mixture.

5. Bake in a water bath  for 35–40 minutes. Cool slightly and cut pudding into 3" (7.6 cm) squares.

#### ASSEMBLY
*Chocolate sauce*

1. To serve, place 1 brioche pudding square on a soup plate. Place the plate in the oven until the pudding is warm.

2. Spoon some chocolate sauce around the pudding before serving.

*Following page: "This is a little 'thank you' to American cooking, with the flavors everyone here loved as a kid," says Bruno Feldeisen.*
*"The salt of the peanut butter when it blends with the crème brûlée produces an interesting flavor."*

# MOCHA PANNA COTTA WITH CARAMEL RUM SAUCE

EMILY LUCHETTI

*A completely smooth dessert experience, the mascarpone is flavored with mocha and sour cream, with the chocolate shavings as an accent.*

### YIELD: 6 SERVINGS

#### MOCHA PANNA COTTA

*1.25 tsp/5 g powdered gelatin*
*1 liq oz/30 ml cold water*
*7 liq oz/207 ml heavy cream*
*2.3 oz/65 g granulated sugar*
*10.7 oz/303 g sour cream*
*2.1 oz/60 g mascarpone cheese*
*1.25 tsp /5 g instant espresso powder*
*2 oz/57 g bittersweet chocolate, melted*

1. In a small saucepan, soften the gelatin in the water. Set aside.

2. In a large stainless steel bowl, whisk together the cream, sugar, sour cream, mascarpone and espresso powder until smooth.

3. Place the bowl over a pot of simmering water and heat the espresso cream mixture until hot. While the cream mixture is heating, dissolve the gelatin over low heat. Remove the espresso-cream mixture from the heat, and stir in the gelatin and melted chocolate. Pour the custard into six 6-oz (177-ml) ramekins. Refrigerate 6 hours or overnight.

#### CARAMEL RUM SAUCE

*10.5 oz/298 g granulated sugar*
*2 liq oz/59 ml water*
*4.2 liq oz/123 ml heavy cream*
*2 liq oz/59 ml dark rum*

1. Combine the sugar and water in a heavy-bottomed saucepan. Dissolve the sugar over medium heat. Increase to high heat and cook the mixture until it is golden amber in color.

*Following page: "This is a small serving because the dessert is so rich," says Emily Luchetti. "Chocolate and espresso are both very strong flavors, but when you combine them one doesn't overwhelm the other."*

2. Remove the saucepan from the heat and slowly stir in the cream. Stir until smooth. Let the sauce cool for 10 minutes and then stir in the rum. Refrigerate until ready to use.

### ASSEMBLY

*Whipped cream*
*Chocolate shavings*

1. Unmold each panna cotta onto a dessert plate and serve with the caramel rum sauce and whipped cream.

2. Garnish with chocolate shavings.

# CHOCOLATE CARAMEL HAZELNUT TART

EMILY LUCHETTI

*Of the white and dark chocolate, caramel and hazelnut flavors in this recipe, Emily Luchetti says, "Each of the flavors is recognized separately, even though they are all contained."*

## YIELD: 6 SERVINGS

### TART DOUGH
*.65 oz/18 g granulated sugar*
*9 oz/255 g all-purpose flour*
*pinch salt*
*9 oz/255 g unsalted butter, cut into 1/2 inch pieces*
*1 liq oz/30 ml cold water*

1. Combine the sugar, flour and salt in the bowl of an electric mixer. Using the paddle attachment, cut in the butter on low speed until the pieces are the size of small peas.

2. With the machine on low speed, add the water and mix just until the dough comes together and is no longer dry. Shape the dough into a disk, cover in plastic wrap and refrigerate for 30 minutes.

3. Preheat oven to 350°F (175°C).

4. Remove the dough from the refrigerator and roll into a 1/8" (.32 cm)-thick rectangle; line a 13 1/2" x 4" (34 x 10 cm) rectangular removable-bottom tart pan with the dough.

5. Refrigerate the shell for an hour, then bake at for 25–30 minutes or until golden brown.

### CHOCOLATE-CARAMEL-HAZELNUT FILLING
*10.5 oz/298 g granulated sugar*
*2.8 liq oz/82 ml water*
*10.36 liq oz/306 ml heavy cream, divided*
*1.75 oz/50 g whole egg*
*7.5 oz/213 g hazelnuts, toasted and skinned*
*4 oz/113 g bittersweet chocolate*
*1.06 liq oz/31 ml milk, divided*
*1 oz/28 g white chocolate*

*Facing page: "You have a lot of textures going on here," says Emily Luchetti. "The flakiness of the crust, the crunch of the hazelnuts, and the smoothness of the filling. For variety I did a rectangular tart. You do get tired of the wedge shape."*

1. Leave the oven preheated to 350°F (175°C). Combine the sugar and water in a heavy-bottomed saucepan. Dissolve the sugar over medium heat. Increase the heat and continue to cook until the sugar caramelizes and is amber-colored.

2. Remove the pot from the heat and slowly add 9 liq oz (266 ml) of the cream to the caramel mixture. Stir until smooth; cool slightly. Whisk the egg lightly in a medium bowl. Slowly whisk the caramel mixture into the beaten egg.

3. Put the hazelnuts in the bottom of the prebaked tart shell. Pour the caramel mixture over the hazelnuts. Bake the tart until set, 20–25 minutes. Let the tart cool to room temperature.

4. Melt the bittersweet chocolate with 1/2 of the milk and 1/2 of the remaining 1.36 liq oz (40 ml) cream in a bowl set over simmering water. Repeat this process in a separate bowl with the white chocolate and the remaining milk and cream.

5. Spread the melted bittersweet chocolate mixture over the tart. Drizzle the white chocolate mixture on top and swirl the 2 chocolates together in a decorative pattern. Refrigerate the tart until the chocolate is set, about 15 minutes.

# SWEET MELON CREAM

. . . . . . . . . . . . . . . . . . . . . . . . . . . . . . . . . . . . . . . . . . . . . . . . . . . .

MARY CECH, THE CULINARY INSTITUTE OF AMERICA AT GREYSTONE, ST. HELENA, CALIFORNIA

*It is important to use a ripe, ripe melon for this recipe, which complements the fruit with sweet melon cream and*
*a touch of lime juice. Sometimes it is served with mint syrup.*

### YIELD: 10 SERVINGS

#### MELON CREAM

*2 Tbs/24 g powdered gelatin*
*8 liq oz/237 ml skim milk or Reisling wine*
*2.5 lbs/1.13 kg ripe seasonal melon, peeled and cut into chunks*
*1.75–3.5 oz/50–99 g granulated sugar (depending on sweetness of melon)*
*lime juice, to taste*

1. In a small saucepan, sprinkle gelatin over skim milk or wine; set aside.

2. Place remaining ingredients in blender and process until smooth.

3. Cook gelatin mixture over low heat, stirring constantly until dissolved. Whisk gelatin mixture into melon cream.

4. Arrange ten 4 oz (118 ml) demi-sphere molds on a half sheet pan. Fill each mold completely with melon cream. Chill 6 hours or overnight until set.

#### DRIED MELON GARNISH

*2.5 lbs/1.13 kg ripe seasonal melon, peeled and cut into chunks*

*Following page: "I wanted to create a dessert from one ingredient, and I came up with this, a simple melon cream," says Mary Cech. "I*
*dry out the melon purée which becomes crispy chips; it adds another texture."*

*JUDY DOHERTY,*
*pastry chef at the*
*Hyatt Regency*
*Scottsdale at Gainey*
*Ranch, was born on*
*January 25, 1962,*
*in Washington, D.C.*
*She took her first job*
*in a restaurant only*
*as a means to buy a*
*car, but soon she was*
*passionately commit-*
*ted: she graduated*
*from the Culinary*
*Institute of America in 1982 and worked for a time as a line cook in*
*Florida, then was offered the pastry chef position at the Tucson Country*
*Club. While working in Tucson, she managed to study with Albert*
*Kumin at the International Pastry Arts Center in New York State*
*while also studying under various chefs in Switzerland for two months,*
*and "if I had a few days," Doherty recalls, "I would study with Ewald*
*Notter in Switzerland." After six years of this somewhat frantic self-*
*imposed work/study program, she took a job with Hyatt Hotels in*
*Florida; three years later she took the position in Scottsdale under*
*Executive Chef Anton Brunbauer. Doherty derives her visual inspira-*
*tion from books containing Native American and desert southwest art*
*and designs. Doherty is happy working in hotels because of the creative*
*freedom and the relatively generous budgets, staffing and facilities. She*
*and her husband are planning to start a family. "I just want to love*
*what I do and be creative and happy," she says.*

"**S**ee! What a beautiful frost-work of white sugar there is all over the top and sides! See, too, what characters there are, and made in sugar of all colours!" wrote Richard Horne in 1845. Horne, a well-traveled Victorian and a reliable diarist, is describing a lavish Twelfth Night cake: "Kings and Queens in their robes, and lions and dogs, and Jem Crow, and Swiss cottages in winter, and railway carriages, and girls with tambourines, and a village steeple with a cow looking in at the porch; and all these standing or walking, or dancing upon white sugar, surrounded with curling twists and true lover's knots in pink and green citron, with damson cheese and black currant paste between."

Horne, a dignified and sober fellow no doubt, seems positively giddy at the sight of food formed into resemblances of familiar objects, scaled-down in size yet heightened in color and sheen. Like Horne, we are more deeply stirred by distortion of reality than we are by attempts at reproduction of reality: a blown-sugar orange is more beautiful than an orange made of wax. What we — the audience, the customer, the gallery-goer — respond to, and what most artists aspire to, is not "real," but something ineffable: a crystallization, or distillation, or intentional distortion, of reality.

Hence the term "Illusionist" for the desserts presented here. *An Illusionist dessert* is one which *resembles a person, object or scene.* Resemblance, an echo, is all that is desired — and probably all that is possible, considering that pastry is involved.

It is this resemblance that makes Illusionist desserts fun, as dessert should be: from fuzzily-rendered ice cream cakes in the form of Fudgie the Whale and CookiePuss (not included in this volume) to the majesty of Judy Doherty's Native Drum, we experience a primal, childlike joy, seeing food crafted into a form we recognize. Here, more than any of the schools of plated desserts, the fine dining customer's experience is vivified; we spend a few moments admiring the form, beauty and craftsmanship on the plate before us, and then we gleefully reduce the artistry to a gooey shambles.

## YEOMAN'S WORK

The term "Illusionism," as applied to the discipline of plated desserts, is of recent vintage, but chefs had been reproducing human and animal forms, objects and scenes for a long time before Mr. Horne admired his Twelfth Night cake. In the 14th century, the European aristocracy enjoyed with each course a *sotelte* (subtlety): a jelly, pastry or other sweet dish, sculpted or molded by a kitchen artist into the forms of lions, eagles, crowns, heraldic devices and chessboards.

But it was pastry chefs of Milan in the 15th century, and their invention of marzipan, meringue and almond paste, that probably helped ignite a global passion for lifelike edibles. There are notes from that period of various "collations" of sugar and "marchpane" — thousands of items might be created to decorate a noble's dining hall for a single meal.

When the Medici queens were wedded to kings in France, they brought with them from Italy many artisans, some of whom worked in sugar and pastry. Italian confectioners of the time became famous the world over for their spun sugar sculptures, and the discipline quickly caught on elsewhere, particularly in England: notes of a "marchpane"-treated cake "garnysshed with dyverse fygures of aungellys" dates back to 1494.

As time went on, "Illusionist" works only became more elaborate. The wedding cake of Queen Victoria and Prince Albert in 1840 weighed 300 pounds and was liberally decorated with sugar figurines — the regal figure of Britannia, toga-garbed likenesses of the couple, turtle doves, dogs, gambolling cupids and flowers. Mr. Mawditt, the Queen's First Yeoman of the Confectionery in 1849, created a Christmas cake for Queen Victoria crowned with 16 figures gathered around a picnic repast, each plate, dish, bowl and glass as well as each item of food rendered in detail.

The plated desserts of today are, in one sense, very much like the elaborate Illusionist cakes and sweets of yore: they are labor-intensive, expensive propositions for people who can afford such entertainments.

In all other respects, however, an Illusionist plated dessert is distinct from the resemblances found in sculptures and celebration cakes. Cake stylists who create dazzling Victoriana or even sculptures with cakes employ marzipan, royal icing, edible paints and food colorings, fondant and buttercream, often with the support of dowel rods and foam boards. For pastry chefs in American restaurants and hotels, these items are not in great favor except as fleeting garnishes. The weight of the effects seen in this chapter must rely on perishable ingredients, and vertical structures must be self-supporting or aided only by pleasingly edible wafers and cookies. Although elements are crafted beforehand, the finished plates must be assembled to a customer's order.

## TOUCH THE HEART

No matter how serious the artist/chef may be toward his work, the reaction of the customer to an Illusionist dessert is almost always admiration, wonder and, inevitably, a smile. "I like to see a customer smile and hear them say 'yum,'" says Janet Rikala of Postrio in San Francisco. "I want their stomach and their brain to connect."

"A dessert should touch the heart," says Eric Girérd of San Domenico in New York City. "It is visual and sentimental. Anything that is beautiful has to touch people. When you

**DAN BUDD**
*Dan Budd, a pastry instructor at the Culinary Institute of America, was born on September 20, 1967, in West Rutland, Vermont. He was educated at the Culinary Institute of America, then immediately found work as a pastry cook at the River Café in New York City, an experience which he credits as a major influence on his approach to pastry, and as his "boot camp." "David Burke was very gung-ho on desserts," says Budd. "He hired Eric Gouteyron as pastry chef; I was thrown in as a liaison because Eric didn't speak English. We had this inspiration to change the world of desserts, to strive for something new." Budd was offered the position of Executive Pastry Chef of the Park Avenue Cafe in New York City, and years later opened the Park Avenue Cafe Chicago. He remains a consultant to the company. His ambitions for the future include slowing down. "I don't think I can sustain this pace for another ten years," he says. "I'd like to learn another craft. Maybe cabinet making, working with wood somehow. If I can make a park bench out of chocolate, maybe I can make one out of wood."*

**JANET RIKALA**
*Janet Rikala, pastry chef at Postrio in San Francisco, was born on November 23, 1958, in Aitkin, Minnesota. Although she grew up in a family that always baked and cooked, her first inspiration was the summer she spent in the bakery of a 105-year-old country inn. She went on to work at a small tea and pastry café in San Francisco, then Kuletos restaurant, then Rancho Valencia in Southern California before taking the job at Postrio, where she has been since 1989. "Much of my evolution as a pastry chef has occurred here," she says of Postrio. "Having the luxury of great equipment, quality ingredients and a supportive team — it's really a blast." Rikala notes that baking and pastry is an ongoing learning process, which is why it is such a great career. Plus: "You work with great people. We bounce ideas off each other and fight over plateware." As for the future, Rikala "can't imagine my life without being in a kitchen. It's part of what I am, and it makes me happy."*

*ERIC GIRÉRD*
*Eric Girérd, pastry chef at San Domenico in New York City, was born on May 18, 1952, in Annecy, France. As the third generation of a bakery/pastry family, he agreed, at age 14, to apprentice with his father ("He was a hard-headed man; I did it as a favor.").*

*At age 17, he entered a patisserie apprenticeship at Maison Armand in Lyon, then worked as pastry chef at Auberge de Père Bise in Talloires for ten years. He served as pastry chef at La Pyramide in Vienna and the Vista Hotel in Tokyo before he was contacted by a chef/friend in New York, who convinced him to come to America. Here, he quickly connected with David Ruggerio, Executive Chef at Le Chantilly. Girérd worked there until 1996. Eric credits as major influences on his approach to pastry Daniel Giraud (Maison Armand), Gabrielle Paillasson and François Bise ("He was a real artist in the kitchen. Attention to detail prevailed. He came from the old school where, above all, the client is king."). His ambition one day is to create a pastry school for children, and to write a children's pastry cookbook.*

*JACQUES TORRES*
*"Never compromise the quality of the produce you work with," says Jacques Torres. "If you start with good produce, it is possible that you will foul it up. But if you start with bad produce, you will automatically fail." Torres, pastry chef at Le Cirque in New York City, knows quality; he is considered by many to be one of the finest and most influential pastry chefs in the country. Torres was born on June 14, 1959, in North Algeria, but his family moved to the south of France when Jacques was three. He began his apprenticeship in pastry at age 15, then worked under Master Chef Jacques Maximin at the Hotel Negresco in Nice for eight years. He moved to the United States and, in 1989, joined the pastry kitchen at Le Cirque. "Technique is what interests me the most in this profession," says Torres. "Pastry is like mathematics. If you put things together in the right way, it will work, and you can know that by looking at the recipe." Torres hopes to someday write books, but in the meantime his ambition is to "be respected in my profession, known for my knowledge and technical skill."*

look at something beautiful, you understand that the person took the time to dream it, and produce it. It cannot be done with buttons, with computers. And it cannot be done beautifully unless you do it with your heart."

Such fanciful plates cannot be done at all if the restaurant's theme, or management, does not allow for it. Jacques Torres, pastry chef at Le Cirque in New York, points out that "Le Cirque, of course, means 'circus' in French, so I believe that I should do things that go with the spirit of the restaurant. It is a fun place, but we must create that fun. I help create it with my desserts."

The essential characteristics of an Illusionist dessert are resemblance, proportion and texture. The central component(s) of the dessert itself will bear a *resemblance* to a known person, object or scene, in form and in three dimensions. Resemblance means an attempt to be realistic; fanciful variations, artistic impressions and childlike simplifications may be encouraged in some settings, but they do not qualify a dessert for this school. The resemblance is supported by the re-creation of that object's *texture, color,* and an overall sense of *proportion* on the plate. In most cases, the dessert cannot be the actual size of the object being mimicked, but it should closely reproduce the original object's proportions. As to color, the desserts presented here follow the lead of their primary ingredient, chocolate, and complement with earth tones, using vibrant primary colors as accents. On plates in this school, there should be no jarring color elements to distract the viewer from the illusion.

Examples of skillful texture in these pages include the spun sugar that forms a snowbank around Jacques Torres' snowman — the sugar glistens yet conveys a fluffy quality, much like snow captured in bright sunlight. André Renard's Hussard and Eric Girérd's Humphrey Bogart's Hat are dusted with cocoa to give a "felt-like" texture to the hats. Meringue is the perfect medium with which Ann Amernick realizes the flourishes of a museum-worthy frame. And Christopher Gross uses milk and dark chocolate to recreate the tobacco wrap of a cigar, the impression reinforced with the precise cigar band made of cigarette paste.

In an Illusionist dessert, the garnish of the plate can support the illusion; however, if the illusion is maintained solely by the garnish, the dessert does not qualify as an Illusionist dessert. Jacques Torres' Chocolate Stove is, in essence, a garnish for the cake itself, but since the experience of eating the crisp stove so complements the experience of the moist cake, it qualifies. The same rule applies to the frame and box surrounding the mousse in Ann Amernick's Monet Painting. In general, a garnish should not overwhelm the dessert — a tenet which certainly holds for all good pastry making.

The visual schemes of these plates are sophisticated and playful. For example, Jacques Torres creates perspective with the tiles at the floor of his stove. Philippe Laurier draws the eye — and adds visual variety—to his Igloo with the "stone path" made of coulis. Eric Girérd could have used tempered dark chocolate for the surface of his piano — it would have been more sleek and "lifelike." But he has chosen to apply pâte à glacer with a sprayer simply because it looks more delicious. In his Humphrey Bogart's Hat, Girérd echoes the Bogart theme with playing card images, and frames them in art deco lines with chocolate and sauce. André Renard is free to create bolts of coulis along the field where his Hussard sits.

## BEAUTY IS BALANCE

The challenge for the chef conjuring an Illusionist dessert is two-fold, as Eric Girérd observes: "It is very difficult to create a visually pleasing dessert that also tastes good." The chefs represented here, for the most part, present mousses in artfully crafted enclosures of crunchy meringue and delicate chocolate cases. They create a literal thin line between flavor and visual beauty. For Jacques Torres and others, the beauty is in the flavor: "Beauty is balance, and good flavor," says Torres. "By balance, I would ideally like to include some softness, some crunch, some sweetness, some acidity, and if I can play with the temperature, so much the better. The dessert must talk to you while you eat it."

Eric Girérd agrees that much of the beauty of a dessert consists in the way it plays in the mouth. "A dessert should be lively," he says. "It must create magic in the mouth. Cookies and tuiles — which are essential to constructionist desserts — are too dry. After three main courses, you want something that is soft, sweet; above all, a soft texture. If it is only visual, it is sculpture. And sculpture is not delicious."

Balance is likewise important to Christopher Gross, both visually and in flavor. "I was taught to balance visual elements on the plate," he says. "If you put something on one side of a plate, don't leave the other half empty unless you're going for an effect. Make sure you have your picture framed. And there should be a sense of proportion," he continues. "I will not try to contrive something and sacrifice

**CHRISTOPHER GROSS**
*Christopher Gross, the chef and owner of Christopher's in Phoenix, was born on March 8, 1956, in Trenton, Missouri, though he grew up in the Phoenix area. He took his first job at a restaurant at age 14 to earn money to buy a dirt bike. Years later, he worked in a succession of hotels and small restaurants in Los Angeles, London and Paris, "doing everything, including pastry," he says. In 1982, he took a job as a sauce cook and fish cook at L'Orangerie in Los Angeles, while also learning from the pastry chef, Claude Koeberly. Gross went to France to study with Koeberly's father. In 1989, Gross opened his own restaurant, Christopher's, where he does his own pastry as well as savory cooking. "I always wanted to be in control of the pastry," Gross says. "I never wanted a pastry chef to put a gun to my head and say, 'I'm leaving.'" Gross envisions that someday he will live in the south of France, but otherwise he has no immediate plans for a change. "I'm not real aggressive," he says. "I believe that if I continue to work hard and do well, good things will happen."*

**ANDRÉ RENARD**
*André Renard, Executive Pastry Chef of the Essex House Hotel and its Les Célébrités restaurant in New York, was born on July 2, 1947, in Rambervillers, France. He began his apprenticeship at age 14 under Chef Valance in Luneville; after his three-year apprenticeship was over, he was asked to stay, and spent an additional seven years there. Renard then embarked on the life of the pastry chef/vagabond: he moved to Paris and found positions as pastry chef at Le Doyen and the Lido cabaret; he moved to Tunisia, acting as a consultant to various food service concerns; after one year, he moved to the United States as pastry chef/consultant for the Hotel Meridien in Newport Beach, California, followed by a similar position for the Queen Mary, on permanent display in Long Beach; he then returned to Paris and served as Executive Chef/pastry chef at Montmartre; he moved to Japan, then Morocco as a consultant. In 1991, he returned to New York to take the position at the Essex House. "Even with exotic fruits and spices there is really nothing new in pastry," he says.*

*ANN AMERNICK*
*As pastry chef and owner of Ann Amernick Pastry in Washington, D.C., Ann Amernick creates specialty cakes and fine pastries and candies. Born on September 15, 1943, in Baltimore, she worked in the kitchens of several restaurants in garde manger and pastry, but it was not until 1979 that she received any formal training, working for Yannick Cam at Le Pavillon. She went on to work with Patrick Musel at Palais de Friandises, at Place Vendôme, Jean-Louis at the Watergate and as Assistant Pastry Chef under Roland Mesnier at the White House. She is the author of* Special Desserts *(1992) and co-author of* Soufflés *(1992). "It's a real dilemma for me to create a recipe that is to be followed by someone else," she says. "In general, the more difficult one element is, the simpler other elements should be. And for professionals, I try to keep in mind as many do-ahead elements as possible." Amernick would like to return to writing some day, and perhaps to teach. "You have to stay true to what you like," she says. "Otherwise, what's the point?"*

taste. I remember going to a restaurant and seeing a chocolate pyramid — a good nine ounces of chocolate easily — and inside was about two ounces of mousse. You couldn't eat the chocolate, you'd be up all night. It was out of proportion."

Resemblance being the goal of Illusionist desserts, they have much in common with their counterparts in the Architectural school. In Architectural works, however, we begin to ease into abstraction as an end in itself; proportion takes an emphatic back seat.

In both Illusionist and Architectural desserts, however, we enjoy a moment of admiration. We admire the resemblance in one case, and wonder at the sheer daring of the other. And then that moment passes, and without hesitation, we swoop down with our forks and enjoy the destruction of these carefully crafted works like children on the beach, and castles in the sand.

# HUMPHREY BOGART'S HAT

ERIC GIRÉRD, SAN DOMENICO, NEW YORK, NEW YORK

*"White chocolate is neutral," Eric Girérd points out. "It takes on the flavor of the bourbon in the mousse, and orange sauce marries well with it." Girérd often serves the Hat with a ginger ale sorbet — further cementing the American hommage he is striving for and incorporating yet another flavor that blends well with bourbon.*

## YIELD: 14 SERVINGS

Special Equipment: Fourteen 3 oz/85 g pliable plastic oval-shaped molds
Aspic cutters

### BOURBON MOUSSE
*3.5 oz/99 g eggs*
*1.3 oz/37 g egg yolks*
*3 gelatin sheets, softened in cold water*
*12 oz/340 g white chocolate, melted (110°F/43°C)*
*12 liq oz/355 ml heavy cream, whipped to soft mounds*
*2 liq oz/59 ml bourbon*

1. Pinch the opposite ends of fourteen 3 oz (85 g) pliable plastic oval molds to form the two points of the hat. Line a half sheet pan with the molds and set aside.

2. Whisk eggs and yolks over a bain-marie until they are thick and register 160°F (71°C).

3. Drain the softened gelatin and whisk into egg mixture. Whisk in melted chocolate. Stir until the temperature is below 110°F (43°C).

4. Using a rubber spatula, fold in the whipped cream and bourbon. Pour into prepared molds. Place in freezer for 4 hours, or until set.

### ORANGE CARDAMOM SAUCE
*2 whole oranges*
*8 liq oz/237 ml water*
*8 oz/227 g granulated sugar*
*3 cardamom pods, crushed*

*Page 74: "I love America, and America is show business," says Eric Girérd. "Le Bogart is a celebration of that."*

### CHOCOLATE SPRAY COATING
*1 lb/454 g pâte à glacer, "brune"*

1. Unmold the pianos.

2. Place the pianos about 6" (15.2 cm) apart on two wire racks.

3. Melt the pâte à glacer.

4. Place in a Wagner airless sprayer. Spray a fine mist evenly across the surface of the chilled pianos.

5. Transfer the pianos to a parchment-lined sheet pan and refrigerate for 30 minutes.

*Pâte à glacer is available in brune, blonde, coffee, hazelnut and white. It has no cocoa butter; vegetable oil (35%) is used instead. It is much less expensive than chocolate, and is easier to use because it requires no tempering. Available from Cocoa Barry, it is sold in couverture form. Here it has been melted and applied with a Wagner airless sprayer.*

### CHOCOLATE PAINT
*17.6 oz/500 g bittersweet couverture, finely chopped*
*8.8 oz/250 g cocoa butter*

Melt the chocolate and cocoa butter together, stirring until smooth.

### ASSEMBLY

*Raspberries*
*Mint leaves*
*Coffee ice cream*

1. Using a small paintbrush, paint a design on 10 dessert plates with the chocolate paint.

2. Stand 3 ganache legs on each plate.

3. Place the chilled piano onto the legs.

4. Place a piano lid onto each piano, propping up the lid with a chocolate rectangle.

5. Place the keyboard across the bottom of the piano.

6. Garnish with a raspberry and mint leaf.

7. Sauce the plate with the coffee crème anglaise.

*The molds for Girérd's Hat and Piano are of Italian origin, and he bought them in France. Similar molds — including playing card cavity molds — are available from Tomric Plastics in Buffalo, New York.*

# MINIATURE CHOCOLATE STOVES

JACQUES TORRES, LE CIRQUE, NEW YORK, NEW YORK

*This opera cake is extremely moist, incorporating coffee buttercream and chocolate ganache. "It is very cakey,"*
*says Torres, partially because the use of bread flour gives it firm texture. Raspberry is a frequent choice for one*
*coulis, but Torres also uses passion fruit or mango.*

## YIELD: 4 SERVINGS

### SPONGE CAKE
*5.3 oz/150 g confectioners' sugar, divided*
*1.1 oz/32 g bread flour*
*1.25 oz/35.4 g hazelnuts, finely ground*
*5.25 oz/149 g egg whites, at room temperature*

1. Preheat oven to 400°F (204°C). Line a half sheet pan with parchment paper. Lightly butter the pan and dust with confectioners' sugar; set aside.

2. Sift together 1.3 oz (37 g) confectioners' sugar and bread flour; mix in ground hazelnuts.

3. In a mixer fitted with whisk attachment, beat the egg whites until frothy. Beat in remaining 4 oz (113 g) confectioners' sugar and continue beating until stiff and shiny.

4. Fold in dry ingredients in three additions. Spread evenly into prepared pan. Bake 7–9 minutes. Allow to cool on a wire rack.

### COFFEE BUTTERCREAM
*3.5 oz/99 g granulated sugar*
*3 Tbs/44 ml water*
*1.3 oz/37 g large egg yolks, at room temperature*
*7 oz/198 g unsalted butter, softened*
*2 tsp/8 g instant espresso powder, dissolved in 2 teaspoons hot water*

1. In saucepan, combine sugar and water; bring to a boil over medium-high heat, stirring until sugar dissolves.

2. In a mixer with a whisk attachment, beat egg yolks on medium-high speed.

3. Raise the heat under the syrup to high and bring the mixture to 210°F (94°C). Slowly pour the syrup over the whipped egg yolks and continue to beat until mixture is cool.

*Following page: "Even though we serve perhaps 400 people a day at the restaurant, this stove is still on the menu," says Jacques Torres.*

4. When the mixture is cool begin adding the softened butter and beat until creamy. Beat in the coffee mixture.

### GANACHE

*3.6 liq oz/106 ml heavy cream*
*4.5 oz/128 g Valrhona Guanaja chocolate, finely chopped*

In a saucepan, bring the cream to a boil over medium-high heat. Pour the boiling cream over the chocolate. Let sit 30 seconds; whisk until smooth.

### CAKE ASSEMBLY

1. Cut the cake into three 5" x 10" (12.7 x 25.4 cm) rectangles. Spread 2/3 of the coffee buttercream over the top of one of the layers. Place a second layer on top. Spread 2/3 of the ganache over this layer. Place the third layer on top of the ganache. Spread the remaining buttercream over this layer. Chill 30 minutes until buttercream is set.

2. Spread the remaining ganache over the buttercream. Chill 30 minutes until ganache is set.

### RASPBERRY COULIS

*12 oz/340 g frozen raspberries*
*4.6 oz/130 g granulated sugar*

1. In a saucepan, combine raspberries and sugar and bring to a boil.

2. Strain the mixture through a fine chinois.

### MINIATURE STOVES

*11 oz/312 g Valrhona Manjari chocolate, coarsely chopped*
*11 oz/312 g Valrhona Ivoire chocolate, coarsely chopped*

1. Melt and temper the dark chocolate.

2. Trace the templates (page 92) on sturdy paper. Cut out each template and label the pieces with their corresponding letters.

3. Place a rectangle of parchment paper on a work surface. Pour all but 3 Tbs (36 g) of dark chocolate on the paper. (Reserve this for gluing pieces together.) Spread the chocolate in an even layer. Let set for 10 minutes.

4. Using the templates as a guide, cut out the following pieces of each.:

8 pieces of A    8 pieces of C    4 pieces of H
4 pieces of B    4 pieces of D

Allow the chocolate pieces to set completely.

5. Melt and temper the white chocolate.

6. Place a rectangle of parchment paper on a work surface. Pour all but 3 Tbs (36g) of white chocolate on the paper. (Reserve this for gluing pieces together.) Spread the white chocolate in an even layer. Allow the chocolate to set for about 20 minutes, until somewhat soft but almost set.

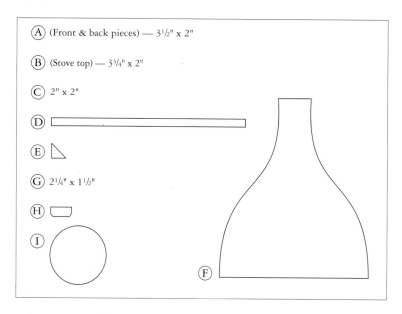

A (Front & back pieces) — 3½" x 2"

B (Stove top) — 3¾" x 2"

C 2" x 2"

D

E

G 2¼" x 1½"

H

I

F

7. Using the templates as a guide, cut out the following pieces of each:

8 pieces of E       8 pieces of G
4 pieces of F       8 pieces of I

Allow the white chocolate pieces to set completely.

8. Reheat the reserved dark and white chocolate separately. Fill two small paper cones with each of the melted chocolates.

9. Place an "A" piece standing upright with a long side against the parchment paper. Place a "C" piece adjacent to it at a right angle, touching it. Using the dark melted chocolate, pipe a line of chocolate along the seam to "glue" the two pieces together. Glue another "C" with the dark chocolate to the opposite end of the "A" piece. Glue another "A" piece to the two open ends of the "C" pieces, forming a rectangular hollow box. Glue a "B" piece on top of the box (this will be the top of the stove).

10. Using the melted white chocolate, glue two "I" pieces next to each other on the stove top (these are the burners). With the white chocolate, glue piece "G" in the center of the front of the stove (this is the stove door). Now glue two triangular supports, piece "E," in the upper corners of the front of the stove (refer to the photo of this dessert on page 90). When supports have set, place the oven bar, piece "D," on top of the triangles. Carefully glue piece "F" along the top back edge of the stove to form the chimney. Use the melted dark chocolate to glue piece "H" to the top of the oven door (piece "G") to form a handle for the door. Allow the stove to set completely before moving it. Repeat to make 4 miniature stoves.

### ASSEMBLY

*Melted bittersweet chocolate*
*Raspberry coulis*

1. Place stove on a dessert plate. Use melted chocolate to pipe a tiled floor design in front of stove. Fill in every other tile with raspberry coulis.

2. Place a 2 1/2" x 1" (6.35 x 2.54 cm) rectangle of cake at the opening of the oven. Garnish with little chocolate pots filled with coulis, if desired.

*Torres uses chocolate to secure the seams of the stove panels. But be sure to make the panels of the stove thick enough to ensure that it will stand.*

# CHOCOLATE CIGAR WITH VANILLA-ARMAGNAC ICE CREAM

CHRISTOPHER GROSS, CHRISTOPHER'S, PHOENIX, ARIZONA

*A sheath of milk chocolate and dark chocolate encloses a chocolate mousse, with an accompanying vanilla armagnac/prune ice cream.*

## YIELD: 12 SERVINGS

Special equipment: 1" (2.54 cm) wooden dowel

### CHOCOLATE MOUSSE FILLING
*5 .5 oz/156 g bittersweet chocolate*
*1.5 oz/43 g unsalted butter*
*10 oz/283 g egg whites*
*1.75 oz/50 g superfine sugar*
*4 liq oz/118 ml heavy cream, beaten to soft peaks*

1. Cut out twelve 8" x 6" (20.3 x 15.25 cm) rectangles of parchment paper.

2. In a bain-marie, melt bittersweet chocolate with the butter.

3. In a mixer with the whisk attachment, beat the egg whites with the sugar to stiff peaks.

4. Fold the warm chocolate mixture into the egg whites, then fold in the whipped cream.

5. Roll the parchment strips into tubes 6" long and 1" in diameter (15.25 x 2.54 cm), and tape them securely.

6. Fill a pastry bag with the mousse; stand the parchment tubes in a coffee can, and fill the tubes with mousse. Place the mousse tubes upright in the freezer until the mousse is solid.

### CIGAR "PAPER"
*4 oz/113 g bittersweet chocolate, melted*
*10 oz/283 g white chocolate, melted*
*melted bittersweet chocolate, for dipping cigar tips*
*chocolate shavings*

*Following page: "It was always our intention to take a traditional chocolate mousse dessert and make it slimmer," says Christopher Gross. "In the first version, we made the cigar actual size, but there was too much chocolate; it threw the balance off. The mousse was supposed to shine through. So we reduced the size. Armagnac goes with cigars, so the prune-soaked armagnac ice cream made sense."*

1. Cut out twelve 4" x 6" (10 x 15 cm) rectangles of parchment paper.

2. Mix together the chocolates just enough to achieve a subtle wood-grain effect that simulates the shades of color in a tobacco leaf.

3. Spread the mixture thinly over the parchment paper. While chocolate is still melted, unwrap the frozen mousse cigars, and wrap the strips of chocolate around them. Refrigerate until the chocolate sets up.

4. Unwrap the cigars and place them in the refrigerator to allow the frozen mousse to soften.

5. Finish the cigars by dipping the tips in melted chocolate, then into chocolate shavings.

### TUILE (CIGAR BAND)

*2.25 oz/64 g unsalted butter, melted*
*4 oz/113 g granulated sugar*
*3 liq oz/89 ml egg whites*
*2.25 oz/64 g all-purpose flour*

1. Preheat oven to 425°F (218°C). Line a sheet pan with a piece of buttered parchment paper or silicon baking mat. Cut out a cigar band stencil from plastic. Make sure the stencil allows for a circumference slightly larger than that of the cigar.

2. In a mixer using the paddle attachment, mix together the butter and sugar. Add the egg whites; beat until combined. Fold in the flour.

3. Place the stencil on the prepared sheet pan. With a small offset spatula, spread a small amount of the batter over the stencil. Lift the stencil and repeat to form 4–6 cigar band-shaped cookies.

4. On each band, make a design with a parchment cone filled with melted chocolate.

5. Bake the bands until the cookies are brown around the edges and their middles are set, about 5 minutes.

6. Wrap each cookie around a 1" (2.54 cm) dowel until they hold their shape.

7. Repeat steps 2–5 to form 12 tuile cigar bands.

### VANILLA-ARMAGNAC ICE CREAM

*16 liq oz/473 ml milk*
*16 liq oz/473 ml half-and-half*
*1 vanilla bean, split lengthwise*
*5.25 oz/149 g egg yolks*
*7 oz/198 g granulated sugar*
*1.6 oz/ 45 g prunes, chopped and soaked overnight in Armagnac*

1. In a saucepan, slowly bring milk, half-and-half and vanilla bean to a boil.

2. Whisk the yolks with the sugar; temper the yolks with the hot milk mixture. Return to heat. Cook until the mixture reaches the custard stage. Remove from heat, strain and cool over an ice bath to 40°F (4°C). Add the marinated prunes.

3. Process mixture in a commercial ice cream machine.

### ESPRESSO SAUCE

*16 liq oz/473 g half-and-half*
*1/2 vanilla bean, split lengthwise*
*.5 liq oz/15 ml vanilla extract*
*5.25 oz/149 g egg yolks*
*3.5 oz/99 g granulated sugar*
*3 oz/85 g espresso beans*

1. In a saucepan, simmer the half-and-half with the vanilla bean and extract.

2. In a medium bowl, whisk together the yolks and sugar until combined.

3. Temper the hot milk mixture into the yolks. Return the mixture to the saucepan and add the espresso beans. Cook until the mixture reaches the custard stage; strain and cool.

### ASSEMBLY

*Fresh fruits or seasonal berries*
*Mint leaves*

1. Place a tuile cigar "band" around the end of each mousse cigar.

2. Spoon espresso sauce onto the bottom of a plate or bowl. (At Christopher's Restaurant a crystal ash-tray is used as a serving dish.)

3. Top the sauce with berries, and position the cigar in the dish. Garnish with vanilla-armagnac ice cream and mint leaves.

# NATIVE DRUM

. . . . . . . . . . . . . . . . . . . . . . . . . . . . . . . . . . . . . . . . . . . . .

JUDY DOHERTY, HYATT REGENCY, SCOTTSDALE, ARIZONA

*A crispy wafer cylinder surrounds rich white chocolate ice cream, with sautéed berries and chocolates*
*finishing the plate.*

### YIELD: 10 SERVINGS

Special Equipment: One 5/8"-(1.5 cm)-diameter dowel or PVC tubing, at least 3 3/4" (1.8 cm) long

#### HIPPENMASSE FOR DRUM

*8 oz/227 g granulated sugar*
*2 oz/57 g almond paste*
*6.7 oz/190 g eggs, divided*
*6 oz/170 g bread flour*
*.5 liq oz/15 ml heavy cream*
*.5 oz/14 g cocoa powder*

1. Preheat oven to 350°F (175°C).

2. In a mixer with paddle attachment, cream together sugar, almond paste and 1.7 oz (48 g) eggs. Add remaining 5 oz (142 g) eggs; mix until combined. Add bread flour and heavy cream, and mix until combined.

3. Divide mixture in half; sift cocoa powder into one-half of the batch; mix until combined.

4. Cut stencils from a cake box (see illustration to the right). On a silicon baking mat-lined sheet pan, spread dark hippenmasse batter into the drum cylinder stencil. Fill a parchment cone with the light hippenmasse batter and pipe a design on the dark batter. Bake until just set, about 7–10 minutes. Using an offset metal spatula, lift the pattern from the baking mat and wrap it around the tubing or dowel to form a cylinder 2 1/4" (5.7 cm) tall and 1 5/8" (4.1 cm) in diameter. Hold until set. Return cylinder to oven to harden, if necessary.

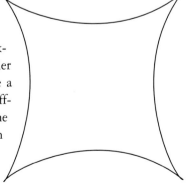

*Following page: "The Native Drum was originally created for the World Pastry Cup competitions," Doherty says. "The theme was enter-*
*tainment, and I knew I wanted to do something different. I thought of the native dancers in this region (Arizona). More than entertain-*
*ment, rain was life or death to these people. I did a lot of research to get the look right."*

5. On a silicon baking mat-lined sheet pan, spread the light hippenmasse batter into the drumhead stencil. Bake shape until just set. Using an offset metal spatula, lift the pattern from the baking mat and drape it over the top of the dowel or tubing until set. Return drumheads to the oven to harden, if necessary. (Note: If draping the drumhead hippenmasse over the top of a PVC tube, invert the tube and allow the hippenmasse to set up on a flat surface. Otherwise, the drumhead may sag into the tube's opening.)

## WHITE CHOCOLATE ICE CREAM

*1.3 oz/37 g egg yolks*
*8 liq oz/237 ml milk*
*8 liq oz/237 ml heavy cream*
*3 oz/85 g granulated sugar*
*4 oz/113 g white chocolate, finely chopped*
*1 liq oz/30 ml white chocolate liqueur*

1. In a medium bowl, whisk yolks until smooth.

2. In a saucepan, bring milk, cream and sugar to a boil. Temper yolks with cream mixture. Return to the saucepan and cook until thickened.

3. Place white chocolate in a large bowl. Strain crème anglaise over chocolate; mix until smooth.

4. Add liqueur; cool and chill.

5. Freeze in an ice cream machine.

## SAUTÉED BERRIES

*2 liq oz/59 ml simple syrup*
*1 liq oz/30 ml Chambord (black raspberry liqueur)*
*zest of one lemon*
*zest of one orange*
*20 oz/567 g assorted berries*

In sauté pan, bring simple syrup, Chambord and zests to a boil. Remove from heat and add berries.

## ASSEMBLY

*Assorted fruit coulis*
*Chocolate feathers and tom-tom garnishes*

1. Place a drumhead hippen upside-down on the plate, and top with the drum cylinder. Fill a tipless pastry bag with the white chocolate ice cream, and pipe the ice cream into the drum. Top with another drumhead.

2. Garnish plate with assorted fruit coulis, chocolate feather garnish and tom-tom garnish.

*Doherty "borrowed" some small marble slabs from the hotel and put them in her freezer. "The white chocolate on the frozen slab is malleable for about a minute," she says. It allows her time to roll the chocolate and wrap it around a chocolate cigarette, for the Native Drum.*

# MONET PAINTING

ANN AMERNICK, ANN AMERNICK PASTRY, WASHINGTON D.C.

*A dacquoise is alternately layered with hazelnut and mocha buttercreams and garnished with a pastillage frame
which is flecked with 23K gold powder.*

*A company called Lloyd Harbor carries hazelnut and cashew butters. Amernick then grinds in fresh nuts.*

## YIELD: 6 SERVINGS

### DACQUOISE
*3.75 oz/106 g almond meal*
*7.5 oz/213 g granulated sugar, divided*
*.26 oz/7.4 g cornstarch*
*4.2 oz/119 g egg whites*

1. Preheat oven to 325°F (165°C). Line 3 half sheet pans with parchment paper.

2. Mix the almond meal with 5.25 oz (149 g) of the sugar and cornstarch until thoroughly blended.

3. In a mixer with whisk attachment, whip the egg whites until foamy, then add the remaining 2.3 oz/65 g sugar and continue whipping until stiff peaks form. Quickly fold in the almond/sugar mixture.

4. Fill a pastry bag fitted with a 1/4" (.63 cm) plain tip with the meringue. Pipe eighteen 3 1/2" x 2 1/4" (8.9 x 5.7 cm) rectangles onto the prepared pans. Bake for 30 minutes or until lightly browned. Trim with a serrated knife to uniform size.

### BUTTERCREAM
*7.8 oz/221 g egg yolks*
*7 oz/198 g granulated sugar*
*2.08 liq oz/61 ml water*
*1 lb/454 g unsalted butter, at room temperature*
*10 oz/283 g hazelnut or cashew butter*
*2 liq oz/59 ml dark rum, divided*
*2 oz/57 g bittersweet chocolate, melted*
*.97 oz/27.5 g instant espresso powder*

1. In a mixer with the whip attachment, whip egg yolks to ribbon stage.

2. In a saucepan, cook sugar and water to 240°F (117°C). Slowly add the sugar syrup to the yolks and whip until cooled. Add the butter piece by piece until incorporated.

3. Divide the buttercream in half. Mix the nut butter and 1/2 of the rum into 1/2 of the buttercream.

*Facing page: Amernick, who collects antiques and miniatures, paints free-hand, using food coloring. "Doing it by hand gives it some movement,"
she says. She points out that food coloring is a medium that most people can work with effectively, whether or not they are skilled painters.*

4. Mix together the melted chocolate, espresso powder and the remaining rum and add to the other 1/2 of the buttercream.

### PASTILLAGE FRAME

*.37 oz/10.5 g powdered gelatin, softened and clarified*
*18 oz/510 g confectioners' sugar*
*gin or vodka, as needed*

1. In a mixer with paddle attachment, combine clarified gelatin and confectioners' sugar and mix until smooth. If the mixture is dry, add a little water until it forms a ball. Turn out onto a board sprinkled with confectioners' sugar. Knead until smooth. Wrap in plastic wrap, place in a plastic container with a lid and refrigerate for 30 minutes until firm.

2. On a work surface sprinkled with confectioners' sugar,  roll the pastillage out to 1/16" (.15 cm) and cut out twelve 3 1/2" x 2 1/4" (8.9 x 5.7 cm) rectangles. From 6 of the rectangles, cut out a center rectangle measuring 2 1/2" x 1 1/4" (6.3 x 3.2 cm), to make a  1/2" (1.25 cm) thick  frame. Place one pastillage frame over each of the rectangles and glue in place with water.

3. Allow frame bases to dry for several days. Coat the dried pastillage frames with gin or vodka and allow to dry.

### ROYAL ICING

*8 oz/227 g confectioners' sugar*
*.52 oz/15 g egg white*
*23 carat gold powder*
*lemon extract*
*assorted paste food coloring*

1. In a medium bowl, mix confectioners' sugar with egg white until blended.  (Add additional egg white if mixture is too dry). Place the royal icing in a parchment cone.

2. Pipe the royal icing onto the frame border base in any desired design. Allow to set several hours until hard.  Paint the frame border with 23 carat gold powder mixed with lemon extract to taste.

3. Using the assorted paste food coloring and a fine artists' brush, paint a Monet scene on the pastillage "canvas." Allow to dry.

### ASSEMBLY

1. Spread a thin layer of nut buttercream on a dacquoise rectangle and top with another layer of dacquoise. Spread a thin layer of mocha buttercream over the second dacquoise layer and top with a third dacquoise rectangle, placing the smooth side up.  Frost the sides and the top with a thin layer of mocha buttercream. Repeat to form 5 more dacquoise stacks.

2. Place the framed pastillage picture on top of each dacquoise stack and serve on dessert plate.

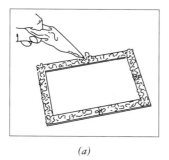
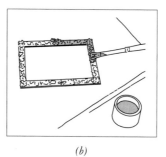

(a)                                    (b)                                    (c)

# IGLOO WITH FIREPLACE

PHILIPPE LAURIER, PATISFRANCE USA, EAST RUTHERFORD, NEW JERSEY

*Smooth pistachio ice cream and tart mixed berry sorbet provide the flavor, meringue and biscuit provide the texture, and kirsch sparks the flame in this retro dessert.*

### YIELD: 16 SERVINGS

Special Equipment: Sixteen 3" (7.6 cm) demisphere molds

#### MIXED BERRY SORBET

*7 oz /198 g raspberry purée*
*8 oz/227 g strawberry purée*
*4 oz/113 g red currant purée*
*3 oz/85 g black currant purée*
*1 lb/454 g granulated sugar*
*14 liq oz/414 ml water*
*1 oz/28 g glucose*
*1 oz/28 g trimoline*
*.088 oz/2.5 g Gelglace stabilizer*
*2 liq oz/59 ml lemon juice*

1. In saucepan, bring all ingredients to a boil; chill.

2. Process in an ice cream machine until nearly firm.

#### PISTACHIO ICE CREAM

*32 liq oz/946 ml milk*
*4 liq oz/118 ml heavy cream*
*4 oz/113 g unsweetened pistachio paste*
*7.8 oz/221 g egg yolks*
*10 oz/283 g granulated sugar*
*1 liq oz/30 ml kirsch*

1. In a saucepan, bring milk, heavy cream and pistachio paste to a boil.

*Following page: Philippe Laurier foresees the return of show business pizzazz to the restaurant business, as desserts like his Igloo are designed to be brought to the customer aflame.*

2. In a mixer with whisk attachment, beat yolks with sugar until fluffy. Temper the hot milk mixture into the yolks. Return to the stove and cook until mixture reaches the custard stage. Strain into a bowl and cool over ice bath. Stir in kirsch. Let chill.

3. Process in an ice cream machine.

### BISCUIT SACHER

*10 oz/283 g almond paste*
*3 oz/85 g confectioners' sugar*
*3.5 oz/99 g eggs*
*6.5 oz/184 g egg yolks*
*1 tsp/4 ml vanilla extract*
*3 oz/85 g all-purpose flour*
*3 oz/85 g cocoa powder, sifted*
*3 oz/85 g unsalted butter, melted*
*10.5 oz/298 g egg whites*
*4 oz/113 g granulated sugar*

1. Preheat oven to 375°F (190°C). Line a sheet pan with parchment paper.

2. In a mixer with whisk attachment, beat together almond paste, confectioners' sugar, eggs, yolks and vanilla until light and fluffy.

3. Add flour, cocoa and melted butter.

4. In a mixer with whisk attachment, whip egg whites with granulated sugar to stiff peaks; fold into cake batter.

5. Scrape batter onto prepared sheet pan and bake 18–20 minutes or until set.

### ITALIAN MERINGUE

*8 oz/227 g granulated sugar*
*3 liq oz/89 ml water*
*10.5 oz/298 g egg whites*

1. In a saucepan, cook sugar and water to the soft ball stage, 238°F–240°F (114°C–116°C).

2. In a mixer with whisk attachment, whip egg whites to a soft peak and slowly add the hot sugar mixture in a steady stream. Continue whipping until cool.

### RASPBERRY/BLACK CURRANT COULIS

*32 oz/907 g raspberry or black currant purée*
*5 oz/142 g glucose*

In a saucepan cook together purée and glucose until reduced by 1/4. Cool.

### KIRSCH SIMPLE SYRUP

*30 liq oz/887 ml water*
*24 oz/680 g granulated sugar*
*2 liq oz/59 ml kirsch*

In a saucepan, cook water and sugar until reduced by 1/3. Cool and stir in kirsch.

ASSEMBLY

*12 egg shells halves*

1. Take sixteen 3" demi-sphere molds and turn them upside down in metal dessert rings to steady them while filling.

2. Lightly soak biscuit sacher sponge cake with kirsch syrup and cut into sixteen  2" (4.9 cm) circles and sixteen 3" (7.6 cm) circles.

3. Fill molds 1/3 with mixed berry sorbet.

4. Place a 2" cake sponge circle over sorbet. Fill remainder of the mold with pistachio ice cream, leaving a 1/8" (.32 cm) gap at the top. Place a 3" cake circle on top of the ice cream.

5. Freeze for at least 3 hours.

6. Unmold dome onto dessert plate and spread meringue evenly over it in a 1/2" (1.25 cm) layer. Using a small knife, score the meringue in a brick pattern, making a small doorway.

7. Pipe a circle of meringue onto the plate and press an egg shell halfway into it, to form a "fireplace."

8. Using a propane torch, brown the meringue igloo and fireplace.

9. With a small plain tip, pipe meringue onto the plate in a brick pattern to form a "pathway" leading to the door. Spoon the 2 fruit coulis into the brick outlines.

10. Pour kirsch inside the egg shell and ignite.

# CHOCOLATE COFFEE CUP CAKE

Janet Rikala, Postrio, San Francisco

*A chocolate cup and chocolate liqueur add texture and flavor to a traditional tiramisù, which is already enhanced with a marsala sabayon.*

**YIELD: 36 SERVINGS**

Special Equipment: Thirty-six 3" (7.6 cm) ring molds

### WHITE LADYFINGER SHEET
*8 oz/227 g egg yolks*
*1 lb/454 g granulated sugar, divided*
*4 oz/113 g pastry flour*
*5 oz/142 g cornstarch*
*12.5 oz/354 g egg whites*

### ESPRESSO LADYFINGER SHEET
*8 oz/227 g egg yolks*
*1 lb/454 g granulated sugar, divided*
*.5 oz/14 g espresso powder*
*4 oz/113 g pastry flour*
*5 oz/142 g cornstarch*
*12.5 oz/354 g egg whites*

### CHOCOLATE LADYFINGER SHEET
*8 oz/227 g egg yolks*
*1 lb/454 g granulated sugar, divided*
*1 oz/28 g cocoa powder*
*4 oz/113 g pastry flour*
*5 oz/142 g cornstarch*
*12.5 oz/354 g egg whites*

*Following page: "We were looking for a more sophisticated look for tiramisù," Rikala says of the genesis of her Chocolate Coffee Cup Cake. "We talked about the ingredients — especially the coffee — and came up with this design. Fooling around with the ingredients, we added the marsala sabayon and the Godiva liqueur."*

1. Preheat oven to 350°F (175°C). Butter and flour 3 sheet pans.

2. For each flavor of ladyfinger sheet: In a mixer with whisk attachment, whip yolks and half of the sugar until light.

3. Sift together flour and cornstarch with espresso powder or cocoa. Fold into whipped egg yolk mixture.

4. In mixer with whisk attachment, whip whites to soft peaks. Add remaining sugar and whip until stiff and shiny but not dry. Fold meringue into yolk mixture. Spread batter onto prepared baking sheet. Bake for 25–30 minutes until dry in center. Cool on wire rack. (Repeat with espresso and chocolate ladyfinger mixtures.)

### TIRAMISÙ CREAM

*12 oz/340 g egg yolks*
*16 liq oz/473 ml sweet Marsala wine*
*7 oz/198 g granulated sugar*
*10 lbs/4.5 k mascarpone cheese*
*8 oz/227 g confectioners' sugar, sifted*

1. Combine egg yolks, Marsala and sugar in mixing bowl. Whisk over a hot water bath until light and mixture reaches 160°F (71°C). Place in mixer stand and whip until cool.

2. Blend mascarpone and confectioners' sugar until smooth. Fold cooled sabayon into mascarpone mixture. Refrigerate.

### SOAKING SYRUPS
## Simple syrup base

*17 oz/482 g granulated sugar*
*1 qt 12 liq oz/1.3 L water*

1. In large pot, combine sugar and water and bring to a boil; cool.

2. Divide syrup into thirds, and use one part for each flavor syrup below.

### TUACO SYRUP

*8 liq oz/237 ml orange juice*
*4 liq oz/118 ml Tuaco liqueur*

Add orange juice and Tuaco to simple syrup.

### ESPRESSO/RUM SYRUP

*8 liq oz/237 ml brewed espresso*
*4 liq oz/118 ml Meyer's dark rum*

Add espresso and rum to simple syrup.

### GODIVA SYRUP

*6 liq oz/177 ml water*
*6 liq oz/177 ml Godiva liqueur*

Add water and Godiva liqueur to simple syrup.

### CANDIED LEMON STRIPS

*julienned zest of 12 lemons*
*2 lbs 10 oz/1.19 k granulated sugar*
*1 qt 16 liq oz/1.4 L water*
*4 oz/113 g superfine sugar*

1. Blanch lemon zests 3 times in fresh changes of cold water.

2. Combine sugar, water, and blanched zests. Cook until tender. Strain and let air-dry on parchment paper-lined sheet pan. Toss in superfine sugar.

### CHOCOLATE SPOONS

*31.5 oz/893 g granulated sugar*
*19 oz/539 g egg whites*
*9 oz/255 g pastry flour, sifted*
*3.3 oz/94 g cocoa powder, sifted*
*.5 liq oz/15 ml vanilla extract*
*1 lb/454 g unsalted butter, melted*

1. Preheat oven to 350°F (175°C). Line a sheet pan with a silicon baking mat. Cut a demitasse spoon stencil from a plastic lid.

2. In a mixer with the paddle attachment, combine sugar and egg whites. Add flour and cocoa powder, scraping down the bowl as necessary. Add vanilla and warm butter.

3. Place stencil on prepared pan and spread a small amount of batter over it in a thin, even layer. Use template to make 8 spoon cookies.

4. Bake until edges begin to brown. Lift cookies off pan and place between 2 demitasse spoons to form spoon shape. Repeat to make a total of 36 spoon cookies. Store in airtight container.

### BEGIN TO ASSEMBLE CAKES

1. Using a 3" (7.4 cm) cutter, cut each cake layer into 36 rounds. Line a sheet pan with parchment and line with thirty-six 3" ring molds.

2. Place a white ladyfinger round in the bottom of each mold and soak with the orange syrup.

3. Pipe 1/2 of the mascarpone filling evenly over the 36 molds.

4. Place espresso ladyfinger rounds in molds; brush with coffee/rum syrup. Pipe over remaining mascarpone filling.

5. Top with chocolate ladyfinger rounds. Brush with Godiva syrup. Refrigerate for 4 hours or overnight. Unmold.

CHOCOLATE COFFEE CUP CAKE

**CHOCOLATE BANDS**

*3 lbs/1.36 kg bittersweet chocolate, melted and tempered*

1. Cut out thirty-six 2 1/2" x 12" (6.3 x 30.5 cm) strips of butcher paper; 3" (7.6 cm) from one end of each strip, cut each strip at a 45° angle. Spread chocolate on each strip. Let set a few minutes.

2. Wrap one strip, chocolate-side in, around each cake. Return to refrigerator. Chill until set.

3. Unwrap, and using a warm pastry tip, press a hole in the extension to resemble a coffee cup handle.

**PLATING**

*Whipped cream*
*Cocoa powder*

Top each cake with whipped cream and sprinkle with cocoa powder. Garnish with cookie spoon and lemon zests.

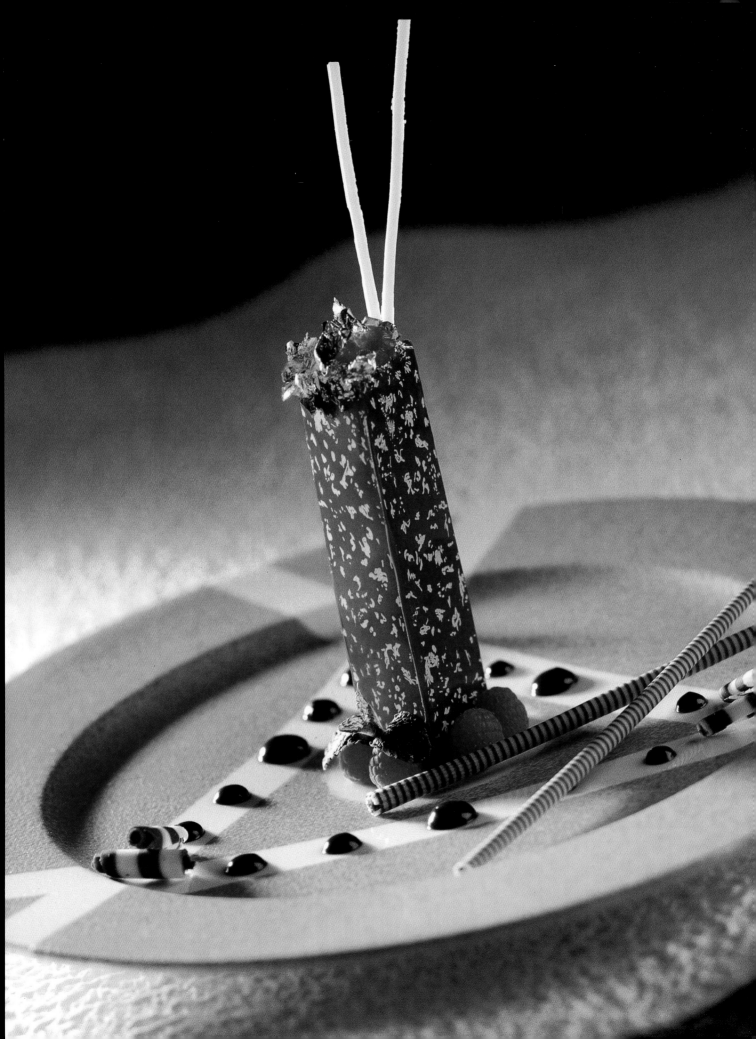

# A R C H I T E C T U R A L I S M

*"...if the joy produced by a work of beauty proceeds from some*

*truth...it proceeds from the perfection with which the work*

*expresses or manifests form."*

JACQUES MARITAIN


*"Whether I put my mousse in a bowl or stand it straight up, it's*

*still the same recipe. The question is, can the guy cook*

*in the first place?"*

RICHARD LEACH

2. Spread with the milk chocolate, coating the entire surface. Allow to set completely.

3. Cut out 4" ( 10 cm) triangles, 2 1/2" (6.3 cm) circles and 1 1/4" (3.1 cm) elongated triangles from the stenciled chocolate. Using metal cutters, cut out 2" (5 cm) circles from inside the 4" (10 cm) triangles, and 1" (2.54 cm) circles from inside the 2 1/2" (6.3 cm) circles. Save the circles to build up the pyramids.

## MORELLO SAUCE

*17.6 liq oz/520 ml Morello cherry purée*
*3.5 oz/99 g granulated sugar*
*3 liq oz/89 ml lemon juice*
*.26 oz/7.4 g arrowroot*

In a saucepan, bring Morello purée, sugar and lemon juice to a boil and reduce by 1/3. Dissolve arrowroot in a small amount of cold water and add to saucepan. Cook just until thickened. Cool.

## SPRAY MIXTURE

*4 oz/113 g bittersweet couverture chocolate, melted*
*4 oz/113 g cocoa butter, melted*

In a bowl, combine melted chocolate and cocoa butter. Set aside.

## ASSEMBLY

*Bittersweet chocolate, melted*

1. Remove the pyramids from the freezer and unmold.

2. Using a Wagner aireless paint sprayer, spray each pyramid with the chocolate mixture until evenly coated.

3. Place one 4" triangle on a plate. Place some of the melted chocolate on the triangle and stand two of the 1" circles on their edges in the chocolate. Place some of the melted chocolate on top of the circles and place one of the 2" circles on top. Place the pistachio pyramid on top of the circle. Place one of the 2 1/2" circles through the top of the pyramid and top with an elongated triangle.

4. Place a few drops of the Morello sauce on the plate.

# CHOCOLATE PASSION FRUIT MOUSSE

RUBEN FOSTER, ARIZONA BILTMORE, PHOENIX, ARIZONA

*Crunchy almond-scented hippenmasse adds texture to the smooth chocolate passion fruit mousse.*

## YIELD: 25 SERVINGS

Special Equipment: Plastic cone molds, 3 1/8" base and 4 1/4" high (7.9 cm x 10.8 cm)

### CHOCOLATE PASSION FRUIT MOUSSE

*1.12 lbs/508 g egg yolks*
*12 oz/340 g granulated sugar*
*8 oz/227 g passion fruit purée*
*2.12 lbs/962 g bittersweet chocolate, melted*
*1.5 qts/1.4 L heavy cream, whipped to soft peaks*

1. In a mixer with whisk attachment, beat yolks and sugar until light. Add passion fruit purée and mix until combined. Remove from mixer stand and add melted chocolate all at once; blend thoroughly.

2. Fold in whipped cream 1/3 at a time.

### PASSION FRUIT SAUCE

*1 qt/.95 L orange juice*
*4 liq oz/118 ml passion fruit purée*
*10 oz/283 g granulated sugar*
*1.5 Tbs/18 g cornstarch*
*2 liq oz/59 ml water*

1. In a saucepan, bring orange juice, passion fruit purée and sugar to a boil.

2. Dissolve cornstarch in water. Add to orange juice mixture and boil for 1 minute, until thickened. Cool over an ice bath.

### HIPPENMASSE TRIANGLES

*12 oz/340 g almond paste*
*6 oz/170 g granulated sugar*
*8 oz/227 g egg whites*
*4 liq oz/118 ml heavy cream*
*5.12 oz/145 g high-gluten flour*

*Following page: "Ideas come from anywhere," says Ruben Foster, "and then I sketch very rough, first forms. But it never ends up being what I drew."*

1. In a mixer with paddle attachment, mix together almond paste and sugar. Add egg whites gradually, scraping down the bowl often. Mix in heavy cream. Add the flour all at once and mix just until incorporated.

2. Strain the batter through a fine chinois. Let stand 30 minutes before baking.

3. Preheat oven to 350°F (175°C). Line a sheet pan with parchment paper.

4. Cut triangle stencil 8 3/4" x 2" (22 x 5cm) at widest point out of light cardboard (see pattern; a cake box is perfect for this). Place the stencil on the prepared sheet pan and spread a thin layer of batter over it. Remove stencil and repeat with remaining batter. Bake until golden brown, 10–12 minutes. Cool.

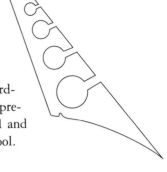

### CHOCOLATE CONES

*8 oz/227 g white chocolate, melted and tempered*
*1.5 lbs/680 g bittersweet chocolate, melted and tempered*

1. Place white chocolate in parchment cone and pipe thin lines around interior of cone molds. Allow to set completely.

2. Ladle about 3 oz (85 g) of the melted chocolate into each cone. Turn upside down and allow excess chocolate to drip out. Allow to set. Repeat with another layer of bittersweet chocolate. Refrigerate cone molds until completely set.

3. Fill molds with chocolate passion fruit mousse and chill until serving.

### CARAMEL SPIRALS

*8 oz/227 g granulated sugar*
*8 liq oz/237 ml water*
*pinch cream of tartar*

1. Lightly oil a parchment-lined sheet pan. In a heavy-bottomed saucepan, cook sugar, water and cream of tartar to caramel stage. Remove from heat and cool bottom of pot in ice bath until slightly thickened.

2. Put on thick rubber gloves. Very carefully, pour the caramel into a parchment cone. Pipe the hot caramel out into spiral shapes onto the prepared sheet pan. Make at least 30 spirals to allow for breakage. Allow the spirals to set.

### ASSEMBLY

*Orange segments*

1. Unmold chocolate passion fruit cones and place on a dessert plate. Heat a knife with a torch and place it vertically against one side of the dessert to create a space for the hippenmasse triangle. Place the triangle into the cone.

2. Garnish plate with passion fruit sauce and orange segments. Warm the caramel spiral briefly in the oven to soften. Place the caramel spiral on the hippenmasse, letting it dangle toward the plate.

# HAWAIIAN KAHLUA POT DE CRÈME

DAN RUNDELL, AUREOLE, NEW YORK, NEW YORK

*Tuiles add crunch and playfulness to chocolate boxes filled with rich chocolate mousse and silky Kahlua-spiked chocolate pot de crème.*

## YIELD: 6 SERVINGS

Special Equipment: Twelve 1.5"x 1.5"x 1.5" (3.8 x 3.8 x 3.8 cm) plastic boxes
(available at office supply stores)

### CHOCOLATE BOXES

*1.5 lbs/680 g Cocoa Barry pâte à glacer "brune" chocolate (or Valrhona Bittersweet chocolate, tempered )*

1. Coat inside of plastic boxes with thin layer of chocolate. Chill for 5–15 minutes; coat with an additional layer of chocolate. (Be sure chocolate coating is not too hot, or it will melt the first layer.) The chocolate should be 1/16"–1/8" (.16 x .32 cm) thick.

2. Set boxes on a parchment-lined sheet pan and allow to set.

### HAWAIIAN KAHLUA POT DE CRÈME

*4 oz/113 g egg yolks*
*12 oz/340 g Hawaiian Vintage chocolate, melted*
*8 liq oz/237 ml heavy cream*
*2 liq oz/59 ml Kahlua liqueur*

1. Whisk egg yolks into slightly cooled chocolate.

2. Bring cream to boil; pour over chocolate-egg mixture and whisk until smooth. Add Kahlua.

3. Cool in an ice bath. Pour into 6 of the prepared chocolate boxes and chill for 3–6 hours.

*Facing page: "This is like a sculpture you might find in a garden," says Dan Rundell. "I might have seen something similar in a museum. Stacking the boxes like that, it all happened at the last minute. And the shape of the tuiles, they just happened. It's not something I thought a lot about."*

# BITTERSWEET CHOCOLATE MOUSSE WITH CHOCOLATE TEA ICE CREAM

RICHARD LEACH, PARK AVENUE CAFE, NEW YORK, NEW YORK

*"The bitter properties of tea and chocolate complement each other so well," says Richard Leach. All shades of texture are found in chocolate cake, chocolate mousse, chocolate tea ice cream, and chocolate cookies.*

## YIELD: 6 SERVINGS

Special Equipment: Six 3" x 1 1/2" (7.6 x 3.8 cm) high ring molds

### CHOCOLATE TEA ICE CREAM
*1 qt/946 ml heavy cream*
*17 liq oz/502 ml milk*
*8 Earl Grey tea bags*
*10.5 oz/298 g granulated sugar, divided*
*7.8 oz/221 g large egg yolks*
*8 oz/227 g Valrhona Extra-Bitter chocolate, finely chopped*

1. In a saucepan combine cream, milk, tea bags and 7 oz (198 g) sugar. Cook, stirring, until scalding. Remove from heat, cover, and allow to infuse for 20 minutes.

2. In bowl, whisk together egg yolks and remaining sugar until light.

3. Strain milk mixture and return to boil. Temper milk mixture with yolks. Add chocolate and whisk until smooth; strain. Chill in ice bath. Freeze in ice cream machine.

### CHOCOLATE TUILE COOKIES
*5 oz/142 g confectioners' sugar*
*2.8 oz/80 g all-purpose flour*
*.81 oz/23 g alkalized cocoa powder*
*4 oz/113 g unsalted butter*
*2.9 oz/82 g honey*
*2.1 oz/60 g egg whites*

1. Preheat oven to 300°F (149°C). Line a sheet pan with parchment paper.

2. Sift together confectioners' sugar, flour and cocoa powder.

*Facing page: "A collection of shapes, and all things chocolate," is the way Richard Leach describes this plate. "I've always used tea as an accent," he continues, "often without telling anyone. Earl Grey complements chocolate very well, but I've tried all kinds."*

# PYRAMID OF COFFEE MOUSSE

PAT COSTON

*Chocolate and coffee are the stars here: rich chocolate-coffee mousse atop crunchy chocolate shortbread accompanied by coffee and chocolate sauces.*

### YIELD: 8 SERVINGS

Special Equipment: Eight 4 oz (113 g) pyramid molds

#### SHORTBREAD

*2.25 oz/64 g cake flour*
*3.75 oz/106 g all-purpose flour*
*2 oz/57 g confectioners' sugar*
*1 Tbs/12 g cocoa powder*
*.5 tsp/2 g salt*
*6 oz/170 g unsalted butter*

1. Preheat oven to 350°F (175°C). Line a sheet pan with parchment paper.

2. In a mixer with paddle attachment, mix the first 5 ingredients on low speed. Add the butter in 2 parts. Continue mixing at low speed until a mass forms (this will take 2–3 minutes).

3. Roll dough on lightly floured board to 1/4" (.63 cm) thickness and cut 3" x 3" (7.6 x 7.6 cm) squares. Place the squares on a prepared sheet pan and bake for 12–14 minutes. Cool and reserve.

#### COFFEE MOUSSE

*3.9 oz/110 g egg yolks*
*2 Tbs/30 ml coffee extract*
*5.25 oz/149 g granulated sugar*
*3 Tbs/44 ml water*
*8 oz/227 g bittersweet chocolate, melted*
*4 oz/113 g unsalted butter, slightly softened*
*32.5 liq oz/961 ml heavy cream*

1. In a mixer with whisk attachment, whip the egg yolks and coffee extract to the ribbon stage.

*Facing page: "I like working with chocolate, and a pyramid is a good shape for it," says Pat Coston. "The piped sugar cage drapes down over it and adds another dimension."*

2. In a saucepan, cook sugar and water to 240°F (117°C) on a candy thermometer and add in a steady stream to the yolks. Continue whipping at high speed until almost cool. Add the melted chocolate and the butter.

3. Whip cream until soft peaks form and fold into the chocolate-coffee mixture. Refrigerate.

### ASSEMBLY

*8 oz/227 g milk chocolate, melted and tempered*
*1 lb/454 g bittersweet chocolate, melted and tempered*

*Coffee crème anglaise*
*Caramel stencils*
*Chocolate sauce*
*Cocoa powder*

1. Place milk chocolate in small parchment cone. Pipe thin lines of chocolate in interior of each mold. (See illustrations below.) Allow to set. Pour bittersweet chocolate into each mold, turning the molds to coat the interiors completely and evenly. Turn the molds upright to allow the excess chocolate to drip out. Allow to set completely at room temperature.

2. Fill each mold with coffee mousse and cover with more of the tempered bittersweet chocolate. Refrigerate for 15 minutes.

3. Place a chocolate shortbread square on a dessert plate. Unmold a pyramid and place at an angle on the chocolate shortbread square. Place a caramel stencil on top of the pyramid. Sprinkle plate with cocoa powder. Garnish plate with coffee crème anglaise and chocolate sauce.

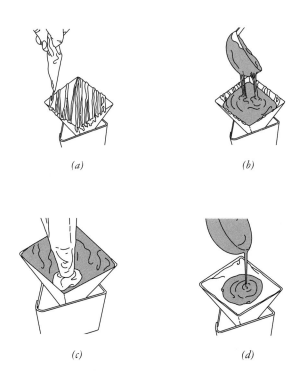

*(a)*          *(b)*

*(c)*          *(d)*

# DARK CHOCOLATE AND PRALINE MOUSSE TOWER

PAT COSTON

*Chocolate-soaked chocolate-bitter-almond sponge cake is layered with mango mousse, passion fruit-chocolate sabayon and crunchy praline ganache. Mango-saffron coulis and chocolate sauce finish this flavorful plate.*

### YIELD: 8 SERVINGS

Special Equipment : Eight 2" diameter x 3" high (5 x 7.6 cm) stainless steel cylinder molds
Eight 7" x 3" (17.8 x 7.6 cm) acetate strips

### PRALINE MOUSSE
*20 oz/567 g semisweet chocolate*
*8 oz/227 g unsalted butter*
*12 oz/340 g granulated sugar*
*8.3 liq oz/245 ml water*
*7.8 oz/221 g egg yolks*
*8 oz/227 g praline paste*
*16.2 liq oz/479 ml heavy cream, whipped to soft mounds*

1. Melt chocolate with butter over a double boiler.

2. Boil sugar and water to 240°F (117°C).

3. In a mixer with whisk attachment, beat egg yolks to ribbon stage.

4. Slowly pour syrup over yolks and whip until cool.

5. Add chocolate-butter mixture and mix until smooth.

6. Fold in praline paste and whipped cream.

### FLOURLESS CHOCOLATE CAKE
*1 lb/454 g semisweet chocolate*
*8 oz/227 g unsalted butter*
*17.5 oz/496 g eggs, separated*
*4.5 oz/128 g granulated sugar, divided*

1. Preheat oven to 375°F (190°C). Line a sheet pan with parchment paper and brush with butter.

2. Melt chocolate and butter over double boiler.

*Following page: "I wanted to stay mainly with chocolate," says Pat Coston, "and I was going for a color effect: polka dots with a layer of dark chocolate, plus three colors of cigarettes."*

3. Beat egg yolks and 4 oz (113 g) sugar until pale and doubled in volume. Fold in melted chocolate.

4. Whip the whites with the remaining sugar to soft peaks. Fold into the chocolate.

5. Spread evenly into pan and bake 10–15 minutes.

6. Cool and cut out 2" (5 cm) diameter circles using cylinder mold.

## HAZELNUT ANGLAISE

*2.6 oz/74 g egg yolks*
*2 oz/57 g granulated sugar*
*4 oz/113 g praline paste*
*16.4 liq oz/485 ml heavy cream*
*4.25 liq oz/126 ml milk*

1. Whisk egg yolks with sugar and praline paste.

2. Combine cream and milk and bring to a boil. Temper yolks with hot cream. Return to saucepan and cook until thickened. Strain and cool.

## DARK CHOCOLATE SAUCE

*16.24 liq oz/480 ml heavy cream*
*3 oz/85 g unsalted butter*
*6 oz/170 g bittersweet chocolate, chopped*

In a saucepan, bring cream and butter to a boil. Pour over chocolate and mix until smooth. Cool.

## CARAMELIZED HAZELNUTS

*1 oz/28g hazelnuts, skins removed*
*14 oz/397 g granulated sugar*
*4 liq oz/118 ml water*

1. Spread hazelnuts on a sheet pan and place in oven to warm.

2. In a saucepan, combine sugar and water. Cook to 320°F (160°C). Stir in hazelnuts and remove with a fork onto a greased marble slab. Let cool and crush.

## CAKE ASSEMBLY

1. Place cake circles in the bottom of each cylinder mold.

2. Pipe mousse on top and continue to alternate with chocolate cake until mold is full. Finish the top with a cake circle. Refrigerate until completely set; unmold.

## CHOCOLATE BANDS

*2 oz/57 g white chocolate, melted and tempered*
*6 oz/170g milk chocolate, melted and tempered*
*6 oz/170 g bittersweet chocolate, melted*

1. Randomly dot the white chocolate on each acetate strip and let set. Spread with milk chocolate, coating the entire strip. When set but still supple, coat with a layer of the dark chocolate.

2. Wrap around each cake/mousse cylinder and refrigerate until completely set.

3. Remove acetate and serve with sauces and crushed nuts.

# TOWER OF CHOCOLATE

. . . . . . . . . . . . . . . . . . . . . . . . . . . . . . . . . . . . . . . . . . . . . . . . . . . . . .

MARTIN HOWARD, HUDSON RIVER CLUB, NEW YORK, NEW YORK

*Two chocolate cakes—a rich, dense brownie and a light, sponge-like cake—are layered together with crisp choco-late meringue and milk chocolate mousse. Chocolate-almond spears add crispness and flavor.*

### YIELD: 6 SERVINGS

#### MILK CHOCOLATE MOUSSE

*7 oz/198 g milk chocolate*
*.25 oz/7 g powdered gelatin*
*2.4 liq oz/71 ml coffee liqueur*
*16.2 liq oz/479 ml heavy cream*
*1.95 oz/55 g egg yolks*
*1.25 oz/35.4 g granulated sugar*
*2 liq oz/59 ml white wine*

1. Melt chocolate over double boiler.

2. In a small bowl, soften gelatin in coffee liqueur.

3. Whip the heavy cream to soft peaks.

4. Clarify the gelatin mixture over simmering water.

5. In a large bowl over simmering water, whisk together egg yolks, sugar and white wine until light and thick. Whisk in melted chocolate, then whisk in the gelatin mixture.

6. Fold in the whipped cream. Chill 2 hours or overnight.

#### CHOCOLATE MERINGUE

*2.1 oz/60 g egg whites*
*4 oz/113 g superfine sugar, divided*
*1 Tbs/12 g cocoa powder*

1. In a mixer with whisk attachment, beat whites until stiff. Add half of the sugar and whip until glossy, about 30 seconds. Fold in the remaining sugar and cocoa.

*Facing page: "I started this recipe when I was working down in Key West," says Martin Howard. "The mousse, meringue, brownie and cake—I brought it with me when I took the job in New York City, but we decided it should have more of a New York look. It needed height."*

2. Line a sheet pan with parchment. Fill a pastry bag fitted with a medium plain tip with the meringue. Pipe out 2" (5 cm) circles of meringue and bake at 250°F (121°C) for two hours until dry.

### CHOCOLATE SPEARS

*16 oz/454 g bittersweet chocolate, melted and tempered*
*4 oz/113 g toasted sliced almonds*

1. Spread the chocolate thinly on the parchment lined sheet. Sprinkle surface of wet chocolate with almonds. Allow to set.

2. Cut chocolate into triangular spear shapes, measuring 6"x 6" x 1" (15.2 x 15.2 x 2.54 cm).

### CHOCOLATE CAKE

*2.75 oz/78 g unsalted butter, softened*
*2 oz/57 g granulated sugar*
*1.95 oz/55 g egg yolks*
*2 oz/57 g almond flour*
*4 oz/113 g semisweet chocolate, melted*
*.5 tsp/2 ml vanilla extract*
*3.15 oz/89 g egg whites, whipped to soft peaks*

1. Preheat oven to 350°F (175°C). In a mixer with paddle attachment, cream together butter and sugar. Beat in egg yolks until well combined. Blend in almond flour, chocolate and vanilla.

2. Fold in whipped egg whites.

3. Line a 13" x 9" (33 x 23 cm) baking pan with parchment. Butter and flour the pan. Scrape batter into prepared pan and bake 15 minutes. Let cool completely.

### GANACHE

*4 oz/113 g semisweet chocolate, finely chopped*
*3 liq oz/89 ml heavy cream*
*.5 oz/14 g unsalted butter*

1. Place the chocolate in a medium bowl. Place the cream and butter in a small saucepan and bring to a boil.

2. Pour cream mixure over chocolate. Mix with a spatula until combined.

3. Cover the cooled cake with the melted ganache.

### BROWNIE LAYER

*2.5 oz/71 g unsweetened chocolate*
*4 oz/113 g unsalted butter*
*8 oz/227 g granulated sugar*
*3.5 oz/99 g whole eggs*
*1 tsp/4 ml vanilla extract*
*3.5 oz/99 g all-purpose flour*
*3.5 oz/99 g chopped walnuts*

1. In a double boiler, melt together chocolate and butter. Remove from heat and stir in sugar. Vigorously stir in eggs and vanilla until blended. Stir in flour and walnuts.

2. Line a 13" x 9" (33 x 23 cm) pan with parchment, and butter and flour the pan. Bake at 350°F (175°C) for 15 minutes. Let cool completely.

### ASSEMBLY

*Chocolate sauce*
*Crème anglaise*
*Sliced almonds*

1. Cut chocolate cake tops and brownies into 3" (7.6 cm) circles with a cutter.

2. Fill a pastry bag fitted with a medium star tip with mousse. Place a spoonful of mousse onto the center of plate. Place a brownie circle over mousse. Pipe a layer of mousse over the brownie, and top with a meringue circle. Pipe another layer of mousse on the meringue, and top with a chocolate cake round.

3. Arrange four of the chocolate spears around the "tower" using the mousse as "glue."

4. Garnish the plate with chocolate sauce, crème anglaise and sliced almonds, if desired.

*Assembling these right at service time will keep the meringue disks from losing their crispness. The brownie and chocolate cake circles may be cut ahead of time.*

# CHOCOLATE PYRAMID

. . . . . . . . . . . . . . . . . . . . . . . . . . . . . . . . . . . . . . . . . . . . . . . . . .

FRANÇOIS PAYARD, RESTAURANT DANIEL, NEW YORK, NEW YORK

*A rich dessert experience—hazelnut in the biscuit adds flavor and crunch to the smooth crème brûlée custard*
*and airy chocolate mousse, all contained in a pâte à glacer shell.*

## YIELD: 15 SERVINGS

Special Equipment:  Fifteen 3" x 3" (7.6 x 7.6 cm) polyurethane pyramid molds
Wagner airless paint sprayer

### CHOCOLATE MOUSSE

*8.8 oz/250 g egg yolks*
*7.7 oz/218 g egg whites*
*8.8 oz/250 g granulated sugar*
*24 oz/680 g extra-bitter chocolate, coarsely chopped*
*34 liq oz/1 L heavy cream, whipped to soft peaks*

1.  In a mixer with whisk attachment, beat egg yolks and whites together on medium-high speed until light and pale.

2.  Meanwhile, in a saucepan, combine sugar with enough water to form the consistency of wet sand. Cook the sugar mixture to 250°F (121°C). While continuing to beat the eggs on low speed, slowly pour the hot sugar syrup down the side of the bowl. Continue to beat on medium speed until cool.

3.  Melt the chocolate. Quickly fold the chocolate into the cream; fold in the egg mixture.

### HAZELNUT BISCUIT

*9.9 oz/280 g hazelnut flour*
*9.9 oz/280 g confectioners' sugar*
*12.7 oz/360 g egg whites*
*4.2 oz/119 g granulated sugar, divided*
*4 liq oz/118 ml lemon juice, divided*
*1.9 oz/54 g chopped hazelnuts*

*Facing page: François Payard was not interested in creating a chocolate pyramid until he discovered a particular, distinctive polyurethane*
*mold while in France.*

146

1. Preheat oven to 400°F (205°C). Place a silicon baking mat on a sheet pan.

2. In  bowl, combine the hazelnut flour and confectioners' sugar.

3. In a mixer with whisk attachment, beat together the egg whites, 1/3 of the granulated sugar and the lemon juice. Beat in the remaining sugar 1/3 at a time and beat until stiff peaks form.

4. Fold the flour mixture into the egg whites. Scrape the batter into the prepared pan and sprinkle with the chopped hazelnuts. Bake until center springs back when lightly touched, 8–10 minutes. Cool and cut into fifteen 1" (2.54 cm) and fifteen 1 1/2" (3.8 cm) disks. Set aside.

### CRÈME BRÛLÉE

*34 liq oz/1 L heavy cream*
*3 vanilla beans, split and scraped*
*5.2 oz/147 g egg yolks*
*5.6 oz/160 g granulated sugar*

1. Preheat oven to 250°F (121°C).  In saucepan, bring the cream and vanilla beans to a simmer.

2. Meanwhile, in a mixer with whisk attachment, beat yolks and sugar to ribbon stage. Add some of the hot cream to the yolk mixture to temper. Add all of the cream; pour the mixture through a strainer into a silicon baking mat-lined half sheet pan. Bake in a water bath for 10 minutes; lower heat to 210°F (100°C) and bake until set in the center, about 45 minutes. Cool and freeze several hours.

3. Cut frozen brûlée into 1" (2.54 cm) rounds and place in freezer.

### ASSEMBLY

*1 lb/454 g pâte à glacer brune, melted*

1. With a pastry brush, coat the interior of the pyramid molds with pâte à glacer. Allow to set and repeat 2 times, allowing each coat to set.

2. Fill a pastry bag fitted with a plain tip with chocolate mousse. Pipe a small amount of the mousse into the prepared pyramid molds. Top with the small biscuit disks. Pipe on more mousse and top with the brûlée rounds. End with the large biscuit rounds, pressing them into the molds. Unmold the pyramids and place in freezer for at least 30 minutes.

3. Fill a Wagner airless paint sprayer with pâte à glacer. Spray a fine mist evenly over the pyramids.

### SERVICE

*Chocolate sauce*
*Chocolate cigarettes*
*Roasted cocoa beans, dusted with confectioners' sugar*

Make a 4" (10 cm) round stencil and place on dessert plate, centering it. Spray with mist of pâte à glacer. Place pyramid toward back of plate. Garnish plate with chocolate sauce, chocolate cigarettes and roasted cocoa beans.

*KURT WALRATH*
*Kurt Walrath is Executive Pastry Chef of Rainbow! in New York City, the organization which encompasses three restaurants, including the Rainbow Room and Rainbow Suites. Walrath was born on April 27, 1962, in Flint, Michigan. He started working in restaurants at age 14 as a cook and baker in an Italian restaurant, then worked in a series of restaurants while learning pastry. His first job as a pastry chef was at Sweet Endings in Bloomfield Hills, Michigan. Walrath then moved to New York and got a job as a sous chef at Le Cirque by requesting an interview/demo with Jacques Torres. "I showed him what I could do and he said okay." Walrath's next move was to Nashville, where he opened four restaurants for a wholesale/retail restaurant group. Returning to New York, he worked at the River Café and the Essex House Hotel while finding time to earn a spot on the United States team to the World Pastry Cup. In 1995, he took the position at Rainbow!. Walrath would like to continue honing his skills, and someday would like to teach.*

*THOMAS WORHACH*
*Thomas Worhach, Executive Pastry Chef at the Four Seasons Ocean Grand in Palm Beach, Florida, was born on March 21, 1952, in Danville, Pennsylvania, though he grew up in Binghamton, New York. He worked both as manager and chef in a bistro while obtaining his college degree in marketing. He went to the Culinary Institute of America in 1977, intending to become an executive chef, but through his association with the Baker's Club, he worked closely with Albert Kumin. "He was a tremendous, tremendous influence on me," says Worhach. Worhach worked at the Hotel Bel Air in Los Angeles (where a labor strike was called on his first day and his entire kitchen staff disappeared), at Ritz-Carlton hotels in Houston and Philadelphia, and at the Mansion on Turtle Creek before longtime friend and professional associate, Executive Chef Hubert Keller, asked him to take the reins of the pastry kitchens of the Ocean Grand. "As long as I'm having fun I'll keep doing what I'm doing."*

If you were making a movie about a 19th-century French Impressionist painter, you would do well to cast André Renard in the lead. Renard, Executive Pastry Chef of the Essex House Hotel and Les Célébrités restaurant in New York City, is Gallic, handsome, charming...and roguish. "I design a lot of desserts," he says. "It comes to me quickly, like in a dream. I sketch it quickly. Sometimes the dessert has a theme, sometimes it's just crazy. We put it on the plate; usually it follows the sketch. Ten minutes later, I've forgotten it." It's difficult to know how much of this is truth, and how much is tweak. But Renard, like many pastry chefs, possesses the soul of an artist, as his Impressionist plate, Autumn Fantasy, attests.

An Impressionist dessert is one which *communicates a theme or mood*. This theme can be presented in one of two ways: *either* the entire plate — dessert components and garnish — can suggest the theme *entirely through abstract forms*, with no attempt to recreate that theme literally, or the plate can include *one or more literal forms* among abstract components to convey the theme. An Impressionist dessert's title labels, or at least reinforces, the theme.

## PIZZAZZ

The 19th-century French artists we refer to as Impressionists presented a stark challenge to the academic traditions in French painting. In fact, the term "Impressionist" was first used in a negative way. The established artists and patrons of the salons dismissed the new style as generating nothing more than quick impressions, sketchwork not worthy of serious attention. The movement is generally dated from about 1866, when Edouard Manet first began to produce his controversial canvases.

Impressionists broke away from the tradition of continuous brush strokes; their discontinuous and quite visible brush strokes were to be combined by the eye of the beholder. They resisted the representation of clearly outlined objects and previous formulations of the colors that depict objects in nature; they sought bolder colors and to break light into its components and to render the way it plays on various surfaces. They chose outdoor subjects and people at their leisure, which at the time was a new subject dismissed by the establishment as irrelevant, unworthy. Claude Monet, Pierre Auguste Renoir, Edgar Degas, Camille Pissarro and Alfred Sisley are the names prominently associated with the movement. But Edouard Manet most accurately codified the changes he was seeking. Before, painters had relied on modeling and shading to make their shapes look round and solid, and the spaces around them deep and hollow. But Manet decided that this could be accomplished by color changes alone, rather than shades of light and dark. He used "color patches" to denote either an object or an empty space. For Manet, "the picture has become more important than the thing it represents," he said. The world of the canvas has its own "natural laws": namely that each brush stroke and every color patch is equally "real," regardless of what it stands for in nature.

What the Impressionists proved, in part, was that a free and imprecise final product can demand careful planning and meticulous craft. This is likewise true of the chefs who offer Impressionist desserts. Less-dedicated chefs who plate carelessly offer the customer a slipshod product. The chefs showcased here plan and plate carefully, and what they offer are desserts with startling colors, carefully composed images, a sense of motion, unified themes and unforgettable flavor.

Just as quick brush strokes can confer a feeling of motion in Impressionist paintings, chefs can create motion in their plates: the scissor kicks of Kurt Walrath's Rockettes, the windy upsweep of Renard's Autumn Fantasy, and the coil and snap of Thomas Worhach's Hurricane, created by the whorling sauces and the lightning bolt cookies above. Both the circular sweep of Didier Berlioz' Au Claire de la Lune, Mon Ami Pierrot, and the nebular revolution of Martin Howard's Chocolate

**SHANE GORRINGE**
*Shane Gorringe, chef and owner of Zöe's Bakery in the New Orleans area, was born on February 29, 1960, in South London, England. After working in an Austrian bakery, Gorringe was motivated to go to Munich, where he trained under pastry chef Helmut Mock in a hotel setting. "He was very old and quite sick, and I was more or less his hands," recalls Gorringe. "Everything he'd learned I made for him. In those two years I probably learned more than I would have in ten years elsewhere." Gorringe went on to work in hotels in Amsterdam, in Qatar on the Persian Gulf, Oklahoma City and Caracas. Eventually he wound up in New Orleans at the Meridien Hotel, and then at the Windsor Court. Now, as owner of his own bakery, Gorringe creates wedding cakes and specialty cakes — "We make whatever we can sell," he says, noting that many people are shocked when they sample, say, a wedding cake that is made with fresh ingredients. "We did a cake a few weeks ago and we must have gotten 12 orders from that one cake," he says. Someday, Gorringe would like to teach. "That's what I enjoy the most, showing people what I know. It seems that today everyone wants to make the money, nobody wants to learn. 'I'm out of school, now pay me.' That's not the way it is. There's still plenty to learn. I would like to teach someone, and see that person do something with what I've learned."*

Planet are created, not just by scudding fruit sauces, but by images at center (a fan of fruit, a Saturn-like ring) reinforced by images on the fringe (white chocolate moon phases, dabs of crème fraîche).

And just as Impressionist paintings suggest rather than fully render figures and scenes, these plates suggest a theme through one literal figure in a field of more abstract forms, or through an overall composition of abstract forms. The literal Pierrot and crescent moons placed by Didier Berlioz on his Au Claire de la Lune is enough to bewitch any French child, as the plate is based on a classic French children's rhyme. The show-biz pizzazz of Kurt Walrath's Rockettes is evoked by the high-kicking legs and billowing skirt. (One wonders whether the dappled texture of the dome was intended to simulate goose-bumped skin.) The props in Walrath's Matisse — the canvas, palette and brushes — are supported by colors of fruit arranged like paint dabs, and the fruits are arranged in such a way as to suggest that they are the object of the painting in progress. More inferential — because of their lack of dominant, literal forms — are André Renard's Autumn Fantasy, with its mere suggestion of leaves in the jagged forms, their arrangement into a conical heap, the clever use of white and dark chocolate for autumn color, the "twigs" of chocolate and the colors lent by the fruit arrangement; Tom Worhach's Chocolate Banana Rum Bread Pudding, with the front-and-center circus colors in the sauce painting and the collar around the clown-like "hat" (truth be told, Worhach himself never intended this theme in the original plating, and only introduced the collar when people conveyed to him what the plate represented to them); Dan Budd's meringue clouds with that looming sugar moon; and Worhach's Hurricane.

Some desserts shown here might qualify as Illusionist, except that there are nonliteral touches (Shane Gorringe's Chocolate Butterfly) or, in the case of Ann Amernick's Meringue Basket, the image is an impression of a recognizable work of art. It is Amernick's impression of a basket that was a common visual element in Claude Monet's paintings, especially the ones painted in the vicinity of Giverny, Monet's home. "Various of his paintings include baskets filled with fruit," says Amernick. "I've chosen a lime-flavored dessert topped with grapes, recreating a basket of grapes in a specific painting." She has squared what is commonly a cylindrical basket in the Monet works.

## DOUBLE WHAMMY

"Beauty is looking through a dessert into the thought behind its preparation," says Mary Cech of the Culinary Institute of America, at Greystone, St. Helena, California. There is no question that much thought has gone into these presentations, but for many of the chefs who create Impressionist plates, the visual presentation is inextricably linked with the flavor payoff. The beauty lies in both. Didier Berlioz says he strives for "harmony in colors and precise set-up so that everyone can appreciate the details. Visual appeal is very important," he continues. "I like the customer to catch the humor in some of the detail, then hesitate before digging in and enjoying all of the flavor. It creates a memory."

"It has to have harmony in terms of flavor and look," agrees Kurt Walrath. He is particularly concerned with how rich a dessert should be: "I want something that blends well with the meal and won't finish me off, something that will stimulate me, not put me in a wheelchair."

Dan Budd feels that it is compelling presentation that helps the customer fully enjoy flavor. "When something doesn't capture the eye, the person will just eat it and not take a moment to say 'wow' — then it doesn't taste as good," he says. "If he or she does take that moment, it's a whole experience. It's a double whammy.

"What makes a beautiful dessert?" muses Budd. "What I'm popular for are desserts that are like a fantasy. They are objects. There is beauty in that...but there is also beauty in a streusel crumb with ice cream melting through it. Maybe you can smell the cinnamon and butter, and that's the beauty in the dessert. There's beauty in a simple apple tart. Things don't have to be constructed to be beautiful. Sometimes a chocolate pudding with a chocolate sauce is beautiful to a chocolate lover."

## GOING OVERBOARD

In a medium where flavor and presentation are mutually dependent it is no surprise that a good number of the chefs in this book were born into families of pastry chefs or visual artists. "My mother was an artist," says Ruben Foster of the Arizona Biltmore, "prolifically and intensely an artist. That's how she made her living. I was always surrounded by it. She helped me develop a sense of taste, of design. She would point things out to us — 'look at that house, look at this sketch' — and so as kids, we had things to consider that other kids didn't. I think that's where my sense of design comes from. It's not conscious. It's just part of my makeup."

Judy Doherty's mother was also an artist. "She was always giving us drawing lessons and teaching us basic elements of design and color," says Doherty, pastry chef at the Hyatt

Regency Scottsdale at Gainey Ranch. "She always told us to keep it simple. She taught us complementary colors and contrast in shapes — if you have round berries, you might want to work with triangles."

Philippe Laurier's father was not a visual artist. He was a pastry chef. "I just got three weeks 'training' with him," recalls Laurier. "He wanted me to quit so he gave me the worst part of the job to make me realize how hard it was."

Many chefs, of course, come from backgrounds neither artistic nor pastry-oriented; they find their way to the professional pastry kitchen somehow. "When I was young I wanted to be a sculptor, but I was never encouraged," says Kurt Walrath of Rainbow! in New York City. "There was no sense that you could earn a living by the arts. All I ever heard was the phrase 'starving artist.' When I got into pastry I found an outlet for my interest in sculpting. Pastry is a very sensual thing." Walrath studied sculpting at the Art Students League in New York City. "We worked with nudes," he says. "I was trying to find a way to incorporate more organic forms into my work."

"Part of the fun of this business is that you don't know what to expect anymore," says Thomas Worhach,

**PHILIPPE LAURIER**
*Philippe Laurier, Executive Pastry Chef of Patisfrance USA, was born on August 31, 1941, in Paris. "My father was one of the best pastry chefs I ever met," Laurier says, "but he wouldn't teach me the profession. He felt the job was so hard for him, he didn't want his son to follow." So, at age 14, Laurier began his apprenticeship at St. Horer, the famous pastry shop in Paris, then continued his studies under Chefs Bisson (a master chocolatier) and Tuscherer (pastry). In 1976, he came to America as the Executive Pastry Chef for La Grenouille in New York, after which he opened La Délices de la Côte Basque and the Tavern on the Green. He then toured the country teaching classes before taking positions as instructor at Fairfax College and the Culinary Art Institute of Washington, D.C. In 1985, he joined Patisfrance USA. "I am a lucky guy," he says. "I work for a company whose future is based on the success of this profession. Ten years from now? Who knows? I will be on the Riviera enjoying the sun, the flowers and the good food."*

Executive Pastry Chef of the Four Seasons Ocean Grand in Palm Beach. Worhach is referring to the many different styles chefs are free to pursue in terms of ingredients and presentation; but he could also be talking about the the arc of his pastry career. Worhach was already an accomplished pastry chef when he discovered the medium in which he would take particular joy: he got started in sauce painting when he was at the Mansion on Turtle Creek in Dallas. "In 1983, some chefs from Germany were visiting us," he recalls. "One of them did a presentation with various vegetable coulis. So I started doing it. Back then people who did this were limited to chocolate, crème anglaise and caramel, but I started using fruit coulis. From there I started going farther and farther. It's so eye appealing. You start with one or two and the next thing you know you have four or five. Sometimes you can go a little too far, but I don't just throw sauces on the plate. I might go overboard on one dessert, and simpler on the next. You think about which sauces will go best with the main dessert." Reflecting on this abrupt turn in his style, Worhach adds: "I think that once you reach a certain level, it is your own desire that determines how good you are going to be."

## FINDING A NICHE

Many of the chefs who appear in this book create centerpieces for special parties as well as intricate works for competitions. They sculpt in chocolate or sugar or both. Centerpieces are not expected to startle or provoke, but rather are to be admired, and thus the chefs creating them must adhere to classic principles of harmony, symmetry, balance, proportion and contrast. But when it comes to plated desserts, these pastry chefs do as artists in all disciplines eventually must do if they are to make an impression: they take the rules and use them as a basis to go their own way. All that remains are the three essentials to quality in the visual arts: feeling, order and imagination.

"The beauty of a plated dessert is like a painting," says Philippe Laurier. "You look at it and let your imagination go. It could be abstract or modern, architectural or very simple, using color and finesse." The unique facet of pastry-as-art is that it is inevitably joyous in feeling: it is hard to imagine a searing indictment of fascist cruelty or a blistering visual essay on the darkness of man's heart being formed out of sugar, chocolate, fruit coulis and puff pastry.

"We will find a niche for ourselves, just as artists do," says Didier Berlioz. "We give a lot of what is inside to create a dessert." Certainly, chefs who create Modernist desserts do so; as we will see in the next chapter, many of them harness their classical training to evoke forms that seem to spring from their unconscious.

But when Freud is drawn into a discussion of food, you know it's growing far too serious. Let Dan Budd bring us back to earth: "It's fun. I love it when the desserts go down on the table and what you see is a smile," he says. "A smile is a beautiful thing. Even before they eat it, the customer is having a nice feeling. That's a gift in itself to a pastry chef."

# MERINGUE BASKET

ANN AMERNICK, ANN AMERNICK PASTRY, WASHINGTON, D.C.

*Tart lime cream is complemented by grapes and a sweet meringue, which add a crunchy/chewy texture.*

### YIELD: 6 SERVINGS

#### BASKET
*8.4 oz/238 g egg whites*
*13.2 oz/375 g granulated sugar*
*4.4 oz/124 g confectioners' sugar*

1. In a mixer with whisk attachment, whip the egg whites until foamy. Slowly add the granulated sugar and beat until stiff.

2. Sift the confectioners' sugar over the whites and gently fold in.

3. Line six half sheet pans with parchment paper. Fill a pastry bag fitted with an Ateco #2B tip; pipe three 2 1/2" x 3" (6.3 x 7.6 cm) lines next to each other to form the floor of the box. Again using the Ateco #2B tip, pipe two 2 1/2" lines next to each other to make the side walls. Make 2 more 2-stroke lines for the front and back, about 3 1/2" (8.9 cm) in length. If you want to make a lid for the basket, make a 4-stroke square about 3 3/4" (9.5 cm) so that it is larger than the base and sides. (Remember, these will be trimmed as will the lid).

4. Use a Wilton #5 tip to pipe vertical lines about 1/2" (1.25 cm) apart, over the sides and lids (but not the base). Then, using the Wilton #48 tip, pipe horizontal strokes, alternating the placement to simulate a basket. Bake the basket in a 150°F (66°C) oven overnight. (The meringues should not color at all, but should dry so that when trimmed, they are firm and dry as chalk.)

#### ASSEMBLY
*Royal icing*

1. Trim the front and back of the box to fit, and glue together with royal icing.

2. Trim the sides of the box just to slide in and stand flush with the base. Shave the flat side of the front, back and sides at the bottom where they will meet the base to ensure a smooth fit. Glue together with royal icing.

---

*Page 150: "This basket is based on various fruit-filled baskets seen in Monet's paintings," says Ann Amernick. "I've chosen a lime-cream filling, but it can be filled with anything — ice creams, frozen soufflés, fruits or even chocolate truffles."*

### YELLOW GENOISE

*10.5 oz/298 g whole eggs*
*7 oz/198 g granulated sugar*
*.17 liq. oz/5 ml vanilla extract*
*3.5 oz/99 g cake flour, sifted*
*4 oz/113 g unsalted butter, clarified and lukewarm*

1. Preheat the oven to 350°F (175°C). Butter and flour 1 half sheet pan.

2. In a large stainless steel mixing bowl set over a pot of simmering water, whisk together the eggs, sugar and vanilla; continue to whisk until the mixture triples in volume.

3. Remove the bowl from the pot and fold in 1/3 of the flour, followed by 1/3 of the butter. Fold in the remaining flour and butter in 2 additions.

4. Pour the batter into the prepared pan and bake for 20–25 minutes or until the top is lightly browned and the cake pulls away slightly from the sides of the pan. Let cool for 5 minutes, then invert the cake onto a rack to cool completely.

### LIME CREAM

*8.75 liq oz/259 ml fresh lime juice (5 large limes)*
*4 oz/113 g unsalted butter*
*5.25 oz/149 g whole eggs*
*1.95 oz/55 g egg yolks*
*5.25 oz/149 g granulated sugar*

1. Finely grate the rind of the limes before juicing. Place the zest, juice and butter in a 4-qt (3.78 L) heavy-bottomed enamel or stainless steel saucepan. Bring to a boil over medium heat.

2. In a medium bowl, mix the eggs, yolks and sugar together until well combined. Temper in the hot butter mixture and return the mixture to the pan on the stove. Whisk over medium-high heat until thick and smooth, about 5–8 minutes. Strain into a stainless steel or glass bowl. Place a layer of plastic wrap directly on top of the cream and chill.

### ASSEMBLY

*5 liq oz/148 ml lime juice*
*Berries or grapes*

1. Cut a layer of genoise to fit inside each box and lightly soak with lime juice.

2. Add a layer of lime cream, then top with fresh berries or grapes.

# CHOCOLATE PLANET

MARTIN HOWARD, HUDSON RIVER CLUB, NEW YORK, NEW YORK

*Layers of chocolate and caramel mousse are glazed in chocolate, rolled in chocolate cake crumbs and accompanied by raspberry and blueberry coulis. Red sour cherries add a touch of tart.*

### YIELD: 10 SERVINGS

#### CHOCOLATE CAKE

*7.8 oz/221 g egg yolks*
*2 Tbs/30 ml vanilla extract*
*10 oz/283 g bittersweet chocolate, melted*
*12.6 oz/357 g egg whites*
*9 oz/255 g granulated sugar*
*.25 tsp/.1.25 g salt*

1. Preheat oven to 350°F (175°C).

2. In a medium bowl, whisk egg yolks, vanilla and melted chocolate until combined.

3. In a mixer with whisk attachment, beat whites to soft peaks. Add the sugar and salt and whip until stiff.

4. Carefully fold yolk mixture into whites.

5. Divide and spread onto 2 buttered and floured half sheet pans. Bake for 15 minutes or until the cakes just begin to spring back from the edges of the pans.

6. Cool the cakes in the pans set on a wire rack.

#### CHOCOLATE MOUSSE

*2.6 oz/74 g egg yolks*
*2 oz/57 g granulated sugar*
*6 liq oz/177 ml brewed espresso*
*3 gelatin sheets, softened in water*
*1 pt/59 ml brandy*
*8 oz/227 g bittersweet chocolate, melted*
*1 pt/473 ml heavy cream*
*4.2 oz/119 g egg whites*
*1 oz/28 g granulated sugar*

*Following page "Some friends and I were once planning to open a shop, and we were going to call it Chocolate Planet," says Martin Howard. "The name was inspired by a song by the B-52s, 'Planet Clare.'"*

1. Whisk together egg yolks, sugar and espresso in a bowl and cook over simmering water, whisking constantly, to sabayon.

2. Bloom gelatin and combine with brandy and chocolate.

3. Whisk chocolate into yolk mixture. Cool.

4. Whip cream to soft mounds.

5. In a mixer with whisk attachment, beat whites to soft peaks. Add sugar and whip until stiff.

6. Fold cream into chocolate mixture and then fold in whites.

7. Spread over chocolate cake in 1 of the half sheet pans. Freeze until firm.

## CARAMEL MOUSSE

*1 lb/454 g granulated sugar*
*1 Tbs/15 ml lemon juice*
*24 liq oz/710 ml heavy cream*
*3 gelatin sheets, softened in water*
*2 liq oz/59 ml brandy*
*2 tsp/10 ml vanilla extract*

1. In a saucepan over high heat, caramelize the sugar and the lemon juice. Cook, stirring until golden brown.

2. Remove saucepan from heat and slowly whisk in 8 liq oz (237 ml) heavy cream; cool.

3. Drain gelatin. Combine with brandy and vanilla. Whisk into the caramel.

4. Whip remaining 1 pt (473 ml) of cream to soft mound stage and fold into caramel and vanilla. Spread in an even layer over chocolate mousse.

5. Remove the remaining chocolate cake layer from the half sheet pan and carefully stack on top of caramel layer. Refrigerate. When firm, using 4" (10 cm) ring molds, cut the dessert to fit the molds, reserving the excess cake to coat the planets. Freeze the molds thoroughly.

## CHOCOLATE GLAZE

*12 liq oz/355 ml heavy cream*
*1 oz/28 g unsalted butter*
*1 lb/454 g bittersweet chocolate, chopped*

Bring cream and butter to a boil and pour over chopped chocolate. Stir until smooth.

## CAKE CRUMBS

In a food processor fitted with the metal chopping blade, process the cake pieces until crumb-like. Set aside.

### PASSION FRUIT AND STRAWBERRY MOUSSE

*24 oz/680g strawberries, stemmed*
*14 oz/397 g passion fruit purée*
*27 oz/765 g granulated sugar, divided*
*5 oz/142 g dessert gelée ** 
*1 lb/454 g egg whites*
*1 qt/.946 L heavy cream, whipped to soft peaks*

1. Heat strawberries, passion fruit purée and 7 oz (198 g) sugar until warm. Purée mixture and add gelatin while still warm. Cool mixture slightly.

2. Make Swiss meringue by heating the remaining 20 oz (567 g) sugar with egg whites until sugar dissolves and mixture is warm to touch. In a mixer with whisk attachment, beat whites at high speed until stiff peaks form and the whites are cool.

3. Fold meringue and then whipped cream into purée.

4. Spread mousse onto reserved angel food cake and freeze.

### PASSION FRUIT SAUCE

*1 lb /454 g passion fruit purée*
*8 oz/227 g granulated sugar*
*2 Tbs/30 ml water*
*1 Tbs/12 g cornstarch*

In a saucepan, bring purée and sugar to boil. Blend cornstarch and water and whisk into purée mixture. Boil to thicken. Cool in water bath.

### VANILLA SYRUP

*25.3 liq oz/748 ml dry white wine*
*1 lb/454 g granulated sugar*
*10/10 vanilla beans, split and scraped*

In a saucepan, boil together wine, sugar and vanilla beans to a boil; simmer for 15 minutes. Cool.

### CLOUD MERINGUE

*8 oz/227 g egg whites*
*2 liq oz/59 ml lemon juice*
*1 Tbs/12 g dried egg white powder*
*1 lb /454 g confectioners' sugar*

Whisk ingredients together and make Swiss meringue by heating mixture until warm to touch. In a mixer with whisk attachment, whip on high speed to stiff peaks.

*\* Available from Gourmand, Herndon, Va. (800) 627–7272*

ASSEMBLY

*Strawberries*
*Mint*
*Poured sugar moon*
*Blown sugar angels*

1. Cut frozen mousse-angel food cake with various-sized round cutters. Place rounds on end into curved portion of angel food cakes.

2. Pipe meringue onto mousse in cloud-like pattern. Torch lightly to brown.

3. Drizzle passion fruit sauce and vanilla syrup on plate. Place cake on cut strawberries for support. Garnish with mint. Decorate with poured sugar moon and blown sugar angels.

# CHOCOLATE BUTTERFLY

SHANE GORRINGE, ZÖE'S BAKERY, COVINGTON, LOUISIANA

*"This can be used as an intermezzo because it's so light — just sorbet and fruit," says Shane Gorringe.*
*Chocolate wings give it flight.*

### YIELD: 6 SERVINGS

#### RASPBERRY SORBET

*8 liq oz/237 ml water*
*7 oz/198 g granulated sugar*
*12 liq oz/355 ml raspberry purée*
*2 liq oz/59 ml lemon juice*

1. In a saucepan bring water and sugar to boil. Remove from heat and stir in raspberry purée and lemon juice. Chill over ice bath.

2. Process sorbet in ice cream machine and freeze until serving.

#### BUTTERFLY OUTLINE

*12 oz /340 g bittersweet chocolate, melted and tempered*

1. Make a butterfly template out of cardboard or plastic, making sure the wings of the butterfly extend beyond the edge of the dessert plate.

2. Place a dessert plate on a work surface. Place a piece of foil over the plate, cutting it larger than the size of the template. Place a piece of parchment, the same size as the foil, on top. Place another dessert plate on top of parchment. Place template on plate.

3. Place some of the tempered chocolate in a parchment cone. On a parchment-lined baking sheet, pipe out 6 sets of antennae and allow to set.

4. Pipe chocolate around the template onto the plate and onto the parchment paper, going over the area off the plate with additional chocolate so that it can support itself. Pipe a small mound of chocolate at the head of the butterfly and stick the antennae in it. Allow the chocolate to set completely.

5. Carefully remove the top plate from the bottom plate. Gently peel away the parchment paper from the chocolate. Store in a cool place until service.

*Following page: "This was originally created for the then-president of Caracas," says Shane Gorringe. "He was having a private dinner party for 12, and since he collected butterflies I was asked to do something with that, something that would leave an impression. What I like about it is it comes off the plate."*

### ASSEMBLY

*Crème anglaise*
*3 assorted fruit purées (such as raspberry, blackberry and mango)*
*Assorted fresh fruit*

1. Place crème anglaise and fruit purées in squeeze bottles and squeeze out in concentric ovals in each quadrant of the plate, within the outline of the butterfly. Drag a knife or toothpick through the sauces to create a "feathered" effect.

2. Place a scoop of the sorbet just below the antennae. Garnish with fresh fruit.

# HURRICANE

THOMAS WORHACH, THE FOUR SEASONS OCEAN GRAND, CORAL GABLES, FLORIDA

*An unexpected flavor combination in a familiar guise: warm chocolate cake with a molten chocolate center and Jack Daniels ice cream.*

### YIELD: 16 SERVINGS

Special Equipment: Sixteen 6 oz/170 cm ramekins

#### CHOCOLATE JACK DANIELS ICE CREAM

*10 oz/283 g semisweet chocolate*
*1 pt/473 ml heavy cream*
*6.5 oz/184 g egg yolks*
*8 oz/227 g granulated sugar*
*4 liq oz/118 ml Jack Daniels bourbon*
*26 liq oz/769 ml milk*

1. Melt chocolate; set aside.

2. In a medium saucepan, bring heavy cream to a boil. In a bowl, whisk together egg yolks and sugar and slowly temper in cream. Return entire mixture to saucepan and stir in the melted chocolate and Jack Daniels. Remove from heat; cool 5 minutes and stir in milk. Chill.

3. Run mixture through an ice cream machine and freeze.

#### CHOCOLATE TRUFFLE CAKE

*10 oz/283 g semisweet Venezuelan chocolate, such as El Rey*
*10 oz/283 g unsalted butter*
*4.6 oz/130 g egg yolks*
*10.5 oz/298 g whole eggs*
*8 oz/227 g granulated sugar*
*4 oz/113 g all-purpose flour, sifted*

1. Melt chocolate and butter together; cool slightly.

2. In a mixer with whisk attachment, whip egg yolks and sugar to the ribbon stage. Add melted chocolate at low speed until combined. Gently fold in the sifted flour.

3. Pour batter into lightly greased 6 oz ramekins until 3/4 full. Refrigerate until ready to bake. (Bake cakes to order.)

*Facing page: "They advertise Jack Daniels as being a smooth whiskey," says Thomas Worhach, "but you should taste it in ice cream, in combination with chocolate."*

## ASSEMBLY
*16 chocolate truffles*
*Assorted fruit coulis*

1. Preheat oven to 325°F (165°C). Remove chocolate-filled ramekins from refrigerator and place 1 chocolate truffle on top of each cake. Bake cakes for 12 minutes.

2. Remove the cakes from the oven and allow to cool for 1 minute. Unmold cake and place on a plate painted with assorted fruit coulis, chocolate garnishes and a scoop of Jack Daniels ice cream.

# CHOCOLATE BANANA RUM BREAD PUDDING

THOMAS WORHACH, THE FOUR SEASONS OCEAN GRAND, CORAL GABLES, FLORIDA

*A custardy chocolate banana bread pudding spiked with rum is topped by a chocolate cone enclosing a tart pineapple-coconut sorbet. Assorted fruit coulis finish the experience.*

### YIELD: 7 SERVINGS

Special Equipment: Seven 4 oz/113 g ramekins

#### BREAD PUDDING

*4.5 oz/128 g bread, cut into 1/4" (.63 cm) cubes*
*2 oz/57 g dried banana chips*
*17 liq oz/502 ml milk*
*3 oz/85 g semisweet chocolate, finely chopped*
*7 oz/198 g whole eggs*
*5.25 oz/149 g granulated sugar*
*2 oz/57 g butter, melted*
*1 tsp/4 ml vanilla extract*
*.5 tsp/2 g ground cinnamon*
*.25 tsp/1.25 g salt*
*7.8 liq oz/231 ml heavy cream*
*2 liq oz/59 ml Meyer's dark rum*
*2 liq oz/59 ml banana liqueur*

1. Preheat oven to 325°F (165°C). Toss bread cubes with banana chips and divide evenly among 7 buttered 4 oz ramekins.

2. Scald milk; add chocolate and let stand 30 seconds. Whisk until smooth.

3. Whisk in remaining ingredients and pour custard into prepared ramekins. Bake in water bath 45 minutes or until set.

#### CHOCOLATE CONE

*8 oz/227 g white chocolate, melted*
*8 oz/227 g milk chocolate, melted*
*8 oz/227 g semisweet chocolate, melted*

*Following page: Thomas Worhach thought of this as a chocolate banana rum pudding until people started commenting about its clownish, circus look. "So recently I added the banana tuile, wrapped it around so it looks like a clown outfit," he says.*

1. Form 7 parchment cones with a 3" (7.6 cm) diameter at opening.

2. Swirl the 3 chocolates into each cone to create a marbled effect. Turn cones upside down on baking sheet and chill until chocolate sets completely.

### PINEAPPLE COCONUT SORBET

*1 qt/.95 L pineapple juice*
*8 liq oz/237 ml simple syrup*
*4.5 liq oz/133 ml cream of coconut, such as Coco Lopez*
*1.05 oz/30 g egg whites*
*2 oz/57 g toasted coconut*

1. Combine all ingredients except coconut; chill.

2. Freeze in ice cream machine, adding toasted coconut at the end.

### ASSEMBLY

*Assorted fruit coulis*
*Mint*

1. Unmold bread puddings.

2. Remove paper from chocolate cones and fill with sorbet. Place 1 sorbet-filled cone upside down on each bread pudding.

3. Garnish with assorted fruit coulis and mint.

# MATISSE

. . . . . . . . . . . . . . . . . . . . . . . . . . . . . . . . . . . . . . . . . . . . . . . . .

KURT WALRATH, RAINBOW!, NEW YORK, NEW YORK

*Almond-flavored joconde is moistened and cooled by a succession of flavorful fruit sorbets.*

### YIELD: 36 SERVINGS

Special Equipment: Wood grain decorating tool
3 Silpat sheets
Dough divider
Ruler or yardstick
Airbrush
5" x 7" (12.7 x 17.8 cm)  sheet of acetate

#### JOCONDE
*1.5 lbs/680 g chocolate cigarette paste*
*17.6 oz/500 g almond flour*
*17.6 oz/500 g confectioners' sugar*
*22.7 oz/645 g whole eggs*
*.5 tsp/2.5 g salt*
*5.5 oz/156 g all-purpose flour*
*3.5 oz/99 g whole butter, melted*
*23 oz/652 g egg whites*
*4 oz/113 g granulated sugar*
*2 Tbs/24 g dried egg whites*
*1 tsp/4 g cream of tartar*

1.  Using chocolate cigarette paste and a wood grain decorating tool, create a wood grain design on 3 silpat sheets fit into sheet pans.

2.  In a mixing bowl using the whisk attachment, combine the almond flour, confectioners' sugar, eggs and salt. Beat to a pale ribbon, about 15 minutes.

3.  Add the flour to the egg mixture and begin folding it in. As you fold in the flour, gradually add the melted butter.

4.  In another mixing bowl using the whisk attachment, combine the remaining ingredients and whip to stiff peaks. Fold the meringue into the egg mixture.

*Facing page: "Putting sorbet on a palette is nothing new," says Kurt Walrath. "The painting is an afterthought. To me, it's great when the sorbet melts into the biscuit joconde. The chocolate completes it."*

5. Spread mixture onto the wood grain-decorated silpat sheet, and bake at 425°F (218°C) for 8–10 minutes. Allow to cool, then cut the sponge into 5 1/2" x 4 1/2" (13.9 x 11.4 cm) palette shapes. Cut four 1/2" (1.25 cm) holes from each palette to accommodate scoops of sorbet.

### SORBET SYRUP

*1 gal/3.7 L water*
*8 lbs/3.6 kg granulated sugar*
*1.25 oz/35.4 g stabilizer, such as Gelglace from Patisfrance*
*8 oz/227 g trimoline*

Mix all ingredients together and bring to a boil. Cool.

### APRICOT SORBET

*34 liq oz/1 L apricot purée*
*2 Tbs/30 ml lemon juice*
*9 liq oz/266 ml sorbet syrup*

Combine all ingredients, then process the mixture in an ice cream machine.

### RASPBERRY SORBET

*34 liq oz/1 L raspberry purée*
*2 Tbs/30 ml lemon juice*
*16 liq oz/473 ml sorbet syrup*

Combine all ingredients, then process the mixture in an ice cream machine.

### WHITE PEACH SORBET

*34 liq oz/1 L white peach sorbet*
*2 Tbs/30 ml lemon juice*
*7 liq oz/207 ml sorbet syrup*

Combine all ingredients, then process the mixture in an ice cream machine.

### YOGURT SORBET

*5 lbs/2.3 kg plain yogurt*
*2 Tbs/30 ml lemon juice*
*30 liq oz/887 ml sorbet syrup*

Combine all ingredients, then process the mixture in an ice cream machine.

### CANVAS

*5 lbs/2.27 K white chocolate, tempered and melted*

1. Spread enough chocolate into a sheet pan fitted with parchment paper to make a layer 1/8" (.32 cm) thick. Allow to set.

2. With a dough divider, cut the set chocolate into 4" x 3" (10 x 7.6 cm) rectangles.

### E A S E L

*7.5 lbs/3.4 K semisweet chocolate, melted and tempered.*

1.  Spread enough chocolate into a sheet pan fitted with parchment paper to make a layer 1/8" (.32 cm) thick. Allow to set.

2.  Remove set chocolate from the full sheet pan, and place the sheet horizontally in front of you. From left to right, score the sheet every 4" (10 cm); from top to bottom, score the sheet every 3" (7.6 cm). With a ruler and a paring knife, cut triangles measuring 4" (10 cm) high and 3" (7.6 cm) wide. (See illustrations.)

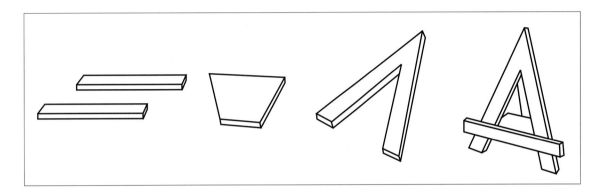

3.  From the base of the triangles, cut a smaller, equally proportioned triangle with a base of 2 1/2" (6.3 cm). Reserve the remaining portion of the larger triangle.

4.  From the tops of the smaller triangles, trim the top 1/2" (1.25 cm). Reserve the bottom, trapezoid-shaped portions.

5.  Remove set chocolate from the half sheet pan. With a dough divider, cut several 3" x 1/4" (7.6 x .63 cm) strips from the chocolate sheet. Reserve.

6.  To assemble, using a parchment bag filled with melted chocolate as glue, attach a 3" (7.6 cm) strip of the chocolate horizontally across the larger triangle, about 1/4" (.63 cm) above its base. Allow to set facedown on a parchment-lined sheet pan.

7.  Stand the wide end of one of the chocolate trapezoids straight up behind the 3" (7.6 cm) strip, and glue it into place. To form the third leg of the easel, glue a 3" (7.6 cm) strip of chocolate at the top of the larger triangle and the middle of the narrow side of the trapezoid. Hold pieces in place until they set enough to stay together. Dry completely.

### B R U S H E S

1.  Fill two parchment pastry bags, one with tempered white melted chocolate, the other with tempered dark melted chocolate.

2.  On a sheet pan lined with parchment paper, pipe out a 5" (12.7 cm) dagger of dark chocolate that starts out thick and tapers to a pointed end.

3.  At the thick end of the dagger, pipe out a 1/2" (1.25 cm) long dollop of white chocolate that quickly tapers to a point.

STENCIL

2 liq oz/59 ml coffee extract

1. Center a 5" x 7" (12.7 x 17.8 cm) piece of acetate over the "Matisse" pattern (below) and, with a paring or exacto knife, create a stencil.

2. Fill an airbrush with coffee extract.

3. Place acetate stencil over a rectangle of white chocolate, and airbrush the pattern onto the chocolate. Allow to dry, and place the chocolate canvas onto the easel.

ASSEMBLY

*Assortment of fresh fruit and berries*
*Raspberry coulis*
*Apricot coulis*

Position an easel on a dessert plate, and place a joconde palette in front of it. Fill the palette with a small scoop of each sorbet, and arrange paint brushes over the palette. Decorate plate with fruit, berries and the coulis.

# ROCKETTES

. . . . . . . . . . . . . . . . . . . . . . . . . . . . . . . . . . . . . . . . .

KURT WALRATH, RAINBOW!, NEW YORK, NEW YORK

*"Banana gianduja mousse, caramelized and hazelnut cake," says Kurt Walrath. "When I tasted it, I just thought it was a very interesting combinaton."*

YIELD: 12 SERVINGS

Special Equipment: 4" (10 cm) bowl
Twelve 3 1/2" (8.9 cm) demi-sphere molds

### BANANA MOUSSE

*26 oz/737 g banana purée*
*1 liq oz/30 ml lemon juice*
*3 liq oz/89 ml rum*
*7 gelatin sheets*
*6.3 oz/179 g egg whites*
*7 oz/198 g granulated sugar*
*3.5 liq oz/103 ml light corn syrup*
*17.5 liq oz/517 ml heavy cream, whipped to stiff peaks*

1. In a saucepan, heat banana purée over medium heat. Stir in lemon juice and rum.

2. Soften gelatin sheets in cold water; drain and add to warm banana purée. Cool over ice bath.

3. In a mixer with whisk attachment, beat egg whites until frothy. Meanwhile, in a small saucepan bring sugar and corn syrup to a boil. Cook to 248°F (120°C).

4. Slowly pour sugar syrup into egg whites and continue to beat until whites form stiff peaks and are cool.

5. Fold whipped cream into cooled banana purée mixture. Fold in egg whites. Refrigerate.

### GIANDUJA MOUSSE

*8.8 liq oz/260 ml milk*
*5.2 oz/147 g egg yolks*
*3.5 oz/99 g granulated sugar*
*9 gelatin sheets, softened in cold water*
*23 oz/652 g gianduja chocolate, chopped*
*1 qt/.95 L heavy cream, whipped to stiff peaks*

*Following page: "I passed a lingerie store and saw a row of mechanized legs, kicking," Kurt Walrath says, recalling the inspiration for this dessert. "I used the design for the tryouts for the World Cup. At the time it was called Can-Can."*

1. In a saucepan over medium heat, bring milk to a boil.

2. In a mixer with whip attachment, beat egg yolks and sugar together to ribbon stage. Temper in the hot milk. Return to pot and cook until mixture coats the back of a spoon.

3. Remove from heat. Drain gelatin and stir into hot mixture.

4. Place the chopped gianduja chocolate in a bowl and pour the hot milk mixture over the chocolate. Stir well until chocolate is melted and mixtures are completely combined. Cool over ice bath.

5. Fold in whipped cream. Refrigerate.

### HAZELNUT DACQUOISE
*9.7 oz/275 g hazelnut flour*
*7 oz/198 g confectioners' sugar*
*1.2 oz/34 g cake flour*
*.88 oz/25 g salt*
*10.5 oz/298 g egg whites*
*.5 tsp/2 g cream of tartar*
*2.8 oz/79 g granulated sugar*

1. Preheat oven to 400°F (205°C). Line 2 half sheet pans with parchment paper.

2. Sift together hazelnut flour, confectioners' sugar, cake flour and salt.

3. In a mixer with whisk attachment, beat egg whites and cream of tartar to soft peaks. Add sugar and continue to whip to stiff peaks.

4. Spread mixture onto prepared pans and bake about 12 minutes until lightly browned. Cool completely.

5. Cut into twenty-four 2 1/2" (6.3 cm) circles.

### SKIRT TUILES
*7.4 oz/210 g hazelnut flour*
*10.5 oz/298 g granulated sugar*
*1 tsp/4 g salt*
*1.75 oz/50 g bread flour*
*5.3 liq oz/157 ml milk*
*1 tsp/4 ml vanilla extract*
*5.2 oz/147 g unsalted butter, melted*

1. In a medium bowl, combine hazelnut flour, sugar, salt, and bread flour.

2. Add milk and vanilla to flour mixture while stirring slowly.

3. Add melted butter and mix until combined. Refrigerate.

4. Preheat oven to 350°F (175°C). Using a 3 1/2" (8.9 cm) round template, spread a thin layer of the tuile batter onto a buttered pan or silicon mat. Bake until golden brown, about 12 minutes.

5. Immediately place tuile in a 4" bowl, pressing the sides slightly to form pleats of the skirt.

### CARAMELIZED BANANAS
*4 bananas*
*8 oz/227 g granulated sugar*
*3 liq oz/89 ml cold water*

1. Peel bananas, cut into 3/8" (.95 cm) slices and place in bowl.

2. Place the sugar in a medium saucepan. Cook over medium heat, stirring constantly until sugar caramelizes.

3. Carefully pour in cold water. Stir until combined.

4. Pour mixture over sliced bananas and cool.

5. When cool, strain bananas and reserve caramel liquid for sauce.

### COCOA TUILE LEGS

*19 oz/539g all-purpose flour*
*5 oz/142 g cocoa powder, sifted*
*2 lbs/907 g unsalted butter, melted*
*2 lbs/907 g confectioners' sugar*
*.5 oz/14 g salt*
*.5 oz/14 g vanilla extract*
*2 lbs, 12 oz/1.24 kg egg whites*

1. Preheat oven to 350°F. Line a sheet pan with parchment paper. In a bowl, combine flour and cocoa powder; set aside.

2. In a mixer with paddle attachment, combine butter and sugar and mix until smooth. Mix in vanilla and salt; alternately add the egg whites and flour mixture in 4 additions and mix until smooth. Chill for at least 2 hours.

3. Cut out a stencil for the kicking legs, extended leg 7 3/4" (19.5 cm), bent leg 5" (12.5 cm), and each 1" (2.54 cm) wide (see pattern). Place the stencil on the prepared sheet pan and spread the cocoa tuile batter thinly over it. Repeat, making 24 sets of legs.

4. Bake the tuiles until set, 10–12 minutes. Cool.

### ASSEMBLY

*8 oz/227 g white chocolate, melted*
*8 oz/227 g bittersweet chocolate, melted*
*Caramel sauce*
*Fruit coulis*

1. Using a pastry bag, fill twelve 3 1/2" demi-sphere molds half full with banana mousse.

2. With the back of a spoon, spread the mousse over the entire interior of the mold.

3. Place a 2 1/2" (6.3 cm) round of hazelnut dacquoise on top of the banana mousse.

4. Using a pastry bag, pipe a layer of gianduja mousse on top of the banana mousse.

5. Place 3 or 4 caramelized banana slices on top of the gianduja mousse.

6. Place a second layer of hazelnut dacquoise on top of bananas.

7. Finish with a thin layer of banana mousse. Smooth over the top with an offset spatula. Freeze until set.

8. Unmold the domes.

9. Using a Wagner paint sprayer, spray one side with melted white chocolate. Spray the other side with melted bittersweet chocolate.

10. Place on a plate and dot the top of the mold with melted chocolate. Place the tuile skirt on top of the mold. Using melted chocolate, arrange the cocoa tuile legs inside the tuile.

11. Serve with fruit coulis and caramel sauce.

# AU CLAIRE DE LA LUNE, MON AMI PIERROT

DIDIER BERLIOZ, LA PANETIÉRE, RYE, NEW YORK

*The delicate flavorings of peach and hazelnut are enhanced by a light genoise and a milk chocolate mousse.*

## YIELD: 18 SERVINGS

Special Equipment:
Pierrot face mold
Clay or Play-Doh
Porcelain "Pierrot" face, 2.25" high x 1.5" (5.7 x 3.8 cm) wide, lightly oiled
Silicon gel and hardener*

### PIERROT FACE MOLD

1. Using a very flat metal full or half sheet pan as a bottom, use the clay to form 4 walls of a box measuring 2 1/2" wide by 3 1/4" long, and approximately 1 1/4" deep (6.3 x 8.2 x 3.2 cm). Lightly oil the inside of the walls with cooking oil.

2. Place the Pierrot mold face up in the center of the box, making sure that the figure's "nose" is not higher than the clay walls. (If it is, build the walls higher until they exceed the tip of the figure by 1/8" [3.2 cm].)

3. Mix together the silicon gel and hardener according to the manufacturer's directions. Pour the mixture over the face mold. Allow the gel to harden for 24 hours at room temperature.

4. Carefully remove the walls and the face from the mold. At this point, the mold is ready for use.

### PIERROT FACE

*8 oz /227 g white chocolate, melted and tempered*

Line the mold with melted white chocolate and freeze until the chocolate sets up.

*Food-safe silicon gel and hardener are available from Albert Uster Imports Inc. Gaithersburg, Md.
(800) 231–8154 (Item #S00004).*

*Following page: "When I design a dessert, I think about what I want for a few days," says Didier Berlioz. "I might envision the base, a round shape, something falling out of it...I don't know the flavors until I start putting it together."*

CLAIR DE LU[...]

Claude Debu[...]

## GIANDUJA MOUSSE

*1.9 oz/54 g egg yolks*
*4.4 oz/124 g granulated sugar*
*1.75 oz/50 g whole eggs*
*10.6 oz/300 g gianduja chocolate, melted*
*3.5 oz/99 g milk chocolate, melted*
*23 liq oz/680 ml heavy cream, whipped to soft peaks*

1. In a mixer, using the whip attachment, whip the egg yolks to the ribbon stage.

2. Place the sugar in a stainless steel saucepan and cook to 240°F (117°C). With the mixer running at high speed, slowly add the sugar syrup to the egg yolks. Whip for about 2 minutes until the mixture has cooled down but is still warm.

3. Warm the melted chocolates and fold them into the whipped cream.

4. Fold the chocolate whipped cream mixture into the whipped egg yolks.

5. Without removing the white chocolate from the Pierrot mold, fill the mold with the mousse. Freeze until set.

6. Once the mousse sets up, carefully unmold the Pierrot face. Dip the top of the head in melted dark chocolate, and store faceup on a parchment-lined sheet pan in the refrigerator. Repeat steps 5 and 6 until you've made the desired number of Pierrot faces.

## WHITE PEACH ICING

*14.1 oz/400 g apricot glaze*
*7 oz/198 g white peach purée*
*6 gelatin sheets, softened in cold water*
*7 liq oz/207 ml peach liqueur*

1. In a saucepan, bring the glaze and purée to a boil. Squeeze the water from the gelatin sheets and add the sheets and the peach liqueur to the purée.

2. When the gelatin dissolves, remove the pan from the heat and allow icing to cool at room temperature; don't allow the icing to set up.

## HAZELNUT PRALINE

*8.8 oz/250 g granulated sugar*
*10.6 oz/300 g blanched hazelnuts*
*.88 oz/25 g unsalted butter*

Cook the sugar to 240°F (117°C). Add the hazelnuts and stir until the mixture begins to caramelize. Remove from heat, and mix in the butter to stop the cooking process. Cool.

## CHOCOLATE GENOISE

*8.75 oz/248 g whole eggs*
*5.3 oz/150 g granulated sugar*
*4.4 oz/124 g all-purpose flour*
*.88 oz/25 g cocoa powder*

1. Preheat oven to 375°F (190°C). Line the bottom of a sheet pan with parchment paper and butter the sides.

2. In a mixing bowl over a hot water bath, whisk together eggs and sugar until the mixture reaches 105°F (41°C). Place the bowl in a mixer fitted with the whisk attachment and whip until tripled in volume.

3. Sift flour and cocoa powder together and fold into egg mixture.

4. With an offset spatula, spread the batter over the bottom of the sheet pan to a thickness of 1/8" (.31 cm). Bake for five minutes. Allow genoise to cool.

### WHITE PEACH PARFAIT

*5.2 oz/147 g egg yolks*
*8.8 oz/250 g granulated sugar*
*24.7 oz/700 g white peach purée*
*20.3 liq oz/600 ml heavy cream, whipped to medium peaks*

1. In a mixer using the whisk attachment, whip the egg yolks to the ribbon stage.

2. Place sugar in a stainless steel saucepan and cook to 240°F (117°C). With the mixer running at high speed, slowly add the sugar to the egg yolks and whip for about two minutes, until the mixture has cooled but is still warm.

3. Fold the purée into the whipped cream.

4. Fold the whipped cream mixture into the whipped egg yolks.

### WHITE PEACH SAUCE

*35.2 oz/1 kg white peach purée*
*.88 oz/25 g cornstarch*
*5.3 oz/150 g granulated sugar*

In a small bowl, thoroughly mix a little of the peach purée into the cornstarch. In a medium saucepan, combine the sugar and the remaining purée, and mix in the moistened cornstarch. Bring to a boil; cool.

### ASSEMBLY

*Raspberry coulis*
*Chantilly cream*
*Fresh peach slices, about 1/8" (.32 cm) thick*

1. Cut the genoise sheet in half. Cover 1/2 with the parfait, using most of it but reserving some. Cover the parfait with the other half sheet of chocolate genoise. With an offset spatula, seal the top of the genoise with a thin layer of the remaining parfait, then cover the cake with the cooled icing.

2. Cut crescent shapes 3" tall x 2 1/2" wide (7.6 x 6.3 cm) out of the genoise. Flatten the bottoms of the crescents so they'll stand up on the plate.

3. Cover the plate with a layer of sauce and decorate with a raspberry coulis. At one corner of the plate, place a drop of chantilly. Arrange thin slices of fresh peaches around the cream, and stand the Pierrot at the center of the slices. At the opposite end of the plate, stand the crescent moon. Sprinkle some of the hazelnut praline on the plate.

# AUTUMN FANTASY

. . . . . . . . . . . . . . . . . . . . . . . . . . . . . . . . . . . . . . . . . . . . . . . . . . .

ANDRÉ RENARD, ESSEX HOUSE, NEW YORK, NEW YORK

*The fall flavors of ginger and chocolate with a cranberry accent: a ginger bavarian is placed on a ginger-soaked biscuit which is piped with chocolate mousse. A scoop of cranberry compote and chocolate leaves complete the experience.*

## YIELD: 8 SERVINGS

### GINGER BAVARIAN

*10.6 liq oz/313 ml milk*
*3.5 oz/99 g granulated sugar, divided*
*.5 oz/14 g candied ginger, finely chopped*
*.14 oz/4 g salt*
*2.6 oz/74 g egg yolks*
*.3 oz/8.5 g unflavored powdered gelatin, softened*
*1.95 liq oz/58 ml ginger liqueur*
*.08 liq oz/2.4 ml vanilla extract*
*6.08 liq oz/180 ml heavy cream*

1. Brush a 13" x 9" (33 x 23 cm) pan with butter. Line the pan with plastic wrap. Set aside.

2. In a saucepan, bring the milk, 1.75 oz (49.5 g) sugar, ginger and salt to a boil. Remove from heat and infuse for 15 minutes.

3. Whisk yolks and remaining sugar together.

4. Bring milk mixture back to the boil and temper yolk mixture with the ginger milk. Return to heat and cook until mixture thickens and coats the back of a spoon. Remove from heat and whisk in softened gelatin, vanilla extract and ginger liqueur.

5. Pass through a chinois. Cool completely. Whip cream to medium peaks. Fold into ginger anglaise.

6. Pour the ginger Bavarian into the prepared pan. Cover with plastic wrap and chill 4 hours or overnight.

*Following page: "Sometimes I create something tangible, other times it's abstract," says André Renard. "This is about the colors of Fall and creating an image of Fall that's somewhat intangible."*

### BISCUIT ROUNDS
*1.95 oz/55 g egg yolks*
*3.5 oz/99 g granulated sugar, divided*
*2.1 oz/60 g egg whites*
*2.6 oz/74 g all-purpose flour*
*1 oz/28 g confectioners' sugar*

1. Preheat oven to 375°F (190° C). Line an 11" x 17" (28 x 43 cm) baking sheet with parchment paper. Lightly butter the pan and set aside.

2. In a mixer fitted with the whisk attachment, whip the egg yolks and 1.75 oz (49.5 g) of sugar to the ribbon stage.

3. In a separate bowl fitted with the whip attachment, whip the egg whites until soft peaks form. Add the remaining 1.75 oz (49.5 g) of sugar and continue to whip until stiff and shiny.

4. Fold the meringue into the yolk mixture. Sift the flour into the egg mixture.

5. Pipe 8 each of 2 1/2", 2", and 1" (6.3 x 5, 2.54 cm) circles onto baking sheets lined with parchment paper. Dust the tops of each circle with confectioners' sugar and bake for 18–22 minutes or until golden. Cool.

### GINGER SOAKING SYRUP
*2.7 liq oz/80 ml water*
*1.6 oz/45 g granulated sugar*
*.3 oz/8.5 g candied ginger, finely chopped*
*1 liq oz/30 ml ginger liqueur*

Bring the water, sugar and ginger to a boil in a saucepan. Remove from heat and cool completely. Add the ginger liqueur and strain through a fine mesh strainer. Set aside.

### CHOCOLATE MOUSSE
*8 oz/227 g bittersweet chocolate, coarsely chopped*
*1 oz/28 g unsalted butter, cut into small cubes*
*1.95 oz/55 g egg yolks*
*3.5 oz/99 g whole eggs*
*4.7 oz/135 g granulated sugar*
*1.5 liq oz/44 ml light rum*
*.16 liq oz/4.73 ml vanilla extract*
*10 liq oz/296 ml heavy cream*

1. Melt chocolate and butter over a double boiler.

2. Whisk yolks, eggs, sugar, rum and vanilla over a double boiler until the mixture reaches 160°F (71°C) Remove from heat and continue whipping with an electric mixer to the ribbon stage.

3. Whip the heavy cream to soft peaks.

4. Fold the melted chocolate into the egg mixture until combined.

5. Fold the whipped cream into the chocolate-egg mixture. Chill 3 hours or overnight.

### CRANBERRY COMPOTE

*3.5 oz/99 g granulated sugar*
*4.25 liq oz/126 ml orange juice*
*.088 oz/2.5 g grated lemon zest*
*6 oz/170 g fresh cranberries*

Bring sugar, orange juice and lemon zest to a boil. Reduce heat and add the cranberries. Cook for 10 minutes without stirring. Remove from heat and transfer to a bowl. Cover with plastic and refrigerate until assembly.

### MARBLED CHOCOLATE BARK

*3 oz/85 g white chocolate, melted*
*3 oz/85 g semisweet chocolate, melted*

Line a large baking sheet with parchment paper. Drizzle the white chocolate across the parchment paper and allow to set up about 1 minute. Using an offset spatula, evenly spread the semisweet chocolate over the white chocolate to create a marbling effect.

### FANTASY LEAVES

*2 oz/57 g unsalted butter*
*3.5 oz/99 g granulated sugar*
*2.1 oz/60 g egg whites*
*.04 liq oz/1.2 ml vanilla extract*
*4 drops green food coloring*
*2.1 oz/60 g all-purpose flour*

1. Cut a maple leaf stencil 4" (10 cm) wide out of heavy plastic. Set aside.

2. Preheat oven to 350°F (175°C). In a mixer with paddle attachment, cream together butter and sugar; gradually add egg whites and mix until smooth. Add the vanilla, food coloring and flour; mix until smooth.

3. Place the maple leaf stencil on a nonstick baking sheet. Spread the tuile batter over the stencil in a thin, even layer. Remove and repeat to form 8 leaves. Bake 5–8 minutes, until edges begin to turn golden. Remove the leaves from the oven and immediately place in bowl to form cupped shape. Allow to set.

4. Spread some of the remaining batter onto the baking sheet in an irregular rectangular shape. Spread into a 1/8" (.32 cm) thickness. With your finger, randomly touch spots in the batter to form holes. Bake 3 minutes until batter is opaque. Randomly tear the half-baked batter into irregular pieces. Return the sheet to the oven and bake 3–5 minutes, until golden. Cool.

ASSEMBLY

*Orange sorbet*
*Chocolate twigs*

1. Invert the chilled ginger Bavarian onto a sheet pan. Freeze 1 hour to firm up Bavarian.

2. Using 2 1/2", 2", and 1" (6.3, 5, and 2.54 cm) round cutters, trim the biscuit rounds into even circles. Brush the surface of the 2 1/2"(6.1 cm) rounds with ginger syrup.

3. Cut eight 2 1/2" (6.3 cm) disks from the frozen Bavarian. Place the 2 1/2" (6.3 cm) Bavarian disks on the moistened biscuit rounds. Place the 2" (5 cm) biscuit rounds on top of the Bavarian discs and brush with syrup. Place the 1" (2.54 cm) biscuit rounds on top and moisten with syrup.

4. Fill a pastry bag fitted with a medium star tip (Ateco #4) with the chocolate mousse. Pipe adjacent lines of mousse up the sides of the stacked rounds. Cover loosely with plastic wrap and freeze 30 minutes.

5. Place a mousse round on dessert plate. Place several pieces of chocolate bark into the surface of the mousse. Place a maple leaf on the plate and fill with a scoop of orange sorbet. Garnish with chocolate twigs and cranberry compote.

Martin Howard trained with chef Albert Kumin. Classic preparation is something he respects and incorporates into his work as pastry chef at the Hudson River Club in New York City. But sometimes he can't help himself. For a major national wedding cake competition a few years back, he created a cake with the theme "Madonna Marries the Devil." "It had flames and pitchfork flowers," Howard recalls. "Madonna and the Devil were peering out from underneath rather than on top." It was a delicious cake and, in its way, beautifully crafted. "When Chef Kumin sees some of the things I do, he just says to me, 'You're getting too far away.' So I make sure I try something a little more sedate next time," says Howard.

In Modernist desserts, there is a tension between outrageousness and classic purity. Rebellion and conformity. Order and chaos. Chefs who create in this school are versed in the classics. Their skills are well honed. This knowledge and skill gives them the confidence to create way out there, way up there, where the air is very, very thin.

## HOW DROLL!

In a Modernist plated dessert, the components are *carefully crafted forms* arranged in such a way that they *do not represent anything outside themselves;* that is, they do not compose an architectural construct, or conjure either a literal or poetic image, nor do they mimick a known object unless there is also a deliberate effort to undermine or subtly satirize the image being reproduced. *Colors* in this school are often *bold*, even garish; the *forms* are often *completely abstracted, neither geometric nor organic.*

*JIM GRAHAM*
*Jim Graham is currently pastry chef at Le Français restaurant and chocolatier of Chocolats Le Français, both in Wheeling, Illinois. Graham was born in Houston, Texas, in January, 1958. He studied pastry at Le Cordon Bleu in Paris in 1982, and quickly found work in the pastry kitchens of Taillevent, a restaurant in Paris. There, he worked under chef Gilles Bajolle. "I very much admired his unique combination of professionalism and lack of pretension," says Graham. "On the other hand, I've learned a great deal from all of the 'lousy' chefs and cooks to whom I've been exposed, too. We have to remain open to influences from all quarters." Graham returned to Houston to work at the new Houston facility of Lenôtre. Returning to Paris, Graham worked as a patissier, then approached Robert Linxe of La Maison du Chocolat. "Chocolate appeals to my technical curiosity and fondness for precision," says Graham. "I was again fortunate to be hired by M. Linxe." During his three-year stint at La Maison, Graham met Mary Beth Liccioni; in 1989, when Liccioni and her husband Roland opened Le Français, they invited Graham aboard. "With all due respect to my mentors, the best learning experience I've had has been the self-reliance and creative freedom of this current position," says Graham. "Ultimately, we have to teach ourselves."*

A patron strolling the Modernist Plated Dessert Museum might stop before Mary Cech's Bittersweet Espresso Mousse Cones and pronounce them pure Modernism: the base is not quite an artist's palette nor is it an industrial gear, and the chocolate strands which seem to be offering the cones are utterly haywire. ("It's a cruel comment on industrialized baking and chain restaurants. You can feel the agony of their death throes.") But Jim Graham's art deco Stratus expresses no such ambiguity or mood: it is a simple horizontal sweep, sleek as can be, with cream and gold contrasted against chocolate in a soothing, almost meditative way. Other forms the patron would take particular note of are the flamboyant sugar bush of Roxsand Scocos' Le Cirque Flora and the deep-fried fusilli which rises quietly from it ("Like a religious symbol in an alternate universe"), the egg and cracked shell suggestion of Jim Graham's White Coffee Ice Cream ("It speaks to me of rebirth"), and the cookie unfurling so luxuriantly from Sebastien Canonne's White Chocolate Delight ("Is it just me, or is that sexy?").

The sudden omnipresence of the color pink — found nowhere else in this volume — is a clear sign that we are in Modernist territory. It's found in Martin Howard's Strawberry Rhubarb Betty Bouffant, Roxsand Scocos' Le Cirque Flora and Ruben Foster's Lemon Tart. The tart is a medley of odd color alliances — cream and gold, red and pink. More familiar are the vivid reds pooling at the base of Canonne's White Chocolate Delight. Most startling of all, arguably, is the non-color of Graham's White Coffee Ice Cream: pure white and cream, no mint leaf, no kiwi slice, no apologies.

The humor to be found in Modernist desserts is exemplified in Martin Howard's Strawberry-Rhubarb Betty Bouffant — the face is quickly rendered on a tuile flanking the Brown Betty. And the Modernist's trick of undermining or winking at conventions of form can be seen in the warped triangular cookies which Philippe Laurier has arranged to surround, and distort, his more conventional pyramid; they seem to be opening, like petals, to reveal the mystery within. Ruben Foster's Lemon Tart is contained in a cone which seems to sink sadly into the plate, while a fan of sugar rises perkily behind.

## ATTITUDE

In a sense, then, "Modernism" in pastry is an attitude more than a visual philosophy. This is also true of Modernism in the fine arts.

The term "Modernist" was first applied to artists in the 1880s who were determined to continue the work begun by the Impressionist painters — to continue to pull away from salon traditions that determined style, materials and subjects. Modernists were consciously striving to create dissenting, dissonant, deliberately provocative work. The attitude was (and is): anything against the dominant view, the dominant aesthetic. Individualism is the ideal, originality the goal.

Abstraction (which is defined as "having only intrinsic form with little or no attempt at pictorial representation") stands at the center of Modernist desserts. In the visual arts, abstraction has been a means of communication as far back as prehistoric times. Certain artists of long-ago periods discovered that forms found in nature were sometimes easier for the eye to apprehend if they were reworked in terms of the simpler forms found in geometry. Cézanne and Georges Seurat, painters of the late 19th century, are generally credited with taking this use of abstraction further into the territory we now recognize as Modernism. The term is applied to art that contains no recognizable imagery but uses the formal building blocks of the pictorial and sculptural arts — lines, shapes, colors, forms, textures — as well as the inherent properties of the materials at hand, to create a reality of its own, referring to no single source. "Nonfigurative," "nonobjective" and "nonrepresentational" are terms that relate to abstraction.

*ROXSAND SCOCOS*
*Roxsand Scocos, chef/owner of RoxSand restaurant in Phoenix, was born on September 6, 1957, in Tacoma, Washington, and raised in Lake Orion, Michigan. She studied art and cooking simultaneously, studying at La Varenne in Paris for a short time.*
*When she was only 24 years old, she moved to Hawaii and opened a French restaurant in Honolulu. "I've had an unusual career—I owned my own business too early," she says. "Obviously, I was in the fledgling stage of my abilities as a chef." The restaurant was a success, and Scocos opened a catering business and a nightclub. After six years, however, she moved to Phoenix for personal reasons. "I started from square one," she says. "I'd always owned my own businesses. I'd never needed a job before." She became the pastry chef at the Boulders until 1985, when she again opened her own restaurant. "That's when I really started cooking and developing my own style," she says. "I called it 'trans-continental' cooking, but once I lifted my face from the cutting board I realized that other people were doing it too. Global cooking, fusion cooking." Scocos has always done her own pastry in her restaurants. "Pastry has always been my first love," she says.*

*SEBASTIEN CANONNE*
*Sebastien Canonne, Executive Pastry Chef at the Ritz-Carlton Chicago, was born on October 9, 1968, in Amiens, France. At age 15, he apprenticed at the École Hotelière de Rouen in Normandy, followed by an apprenticeship in Paris, at the pastry shop of Gaston Lenôtre. He found a position at La Côte St. Jacques in Burgundy, then continued his training in Switzerland, at the Beau Rivage Palace in Geneva and the Hotel Palace Euler in Basel. Canonne then met his military obligation by cooking for then French President François Mitterand. After his discharge, Canonne spent more time in Switzerland honing his skills, then moved to Chicago to take a position at St. Germain, a French restaurant and pastry shop. Just as his one-year work visa was about to expire, he was offered the position at the Ritz-Carlton. "Someday I would like to teach," he says. "That's what I do here most of the time anyway. And I hope to have kids, to make cakes for my kids at home."*

Modernists anticipated the diverse, melting-pot world we now live in: a global village. According to Philip Yenawine, abstraction is also "an attempt to find vocabularies that are so generalized that they are universally understandable."

Modernism is an attitude, not a formal set of rules. This is made even more clear when contrasted with post-modern, the term we might expect to apply to a discipline that post-dates the advent of Modernism. The fact that these chefs produce work in the mid-1990s does not make them post-modern. Post-modern is the term applied to the many schools of art and thought that proliferated around the 1970s — pop art, minimalism, performance art — in reaction to Modernism, which, as we've said, was conceived in reaction to strict adherence to received rules of art. Modernists generally throw off the past and strive for individualism and innovation, while post-modernists embrace the past, using its images as cornerstones in creating the new. The post-modern attitude is one of freely borrowing images of pop art and the past in a very eclectic stew; it is skeptical and cynical, ironic about politics and the potential of change and society. Where Modernists tend to adhere to one style, one medium, post-modernists jump from painting to video to sculpture and combine them in new ways.

## Shake and Bake

We associate wildly imaginative plates — plates with daring and imagination — with youth, with reckless inexperience, with romantic, tumultuous emotion. But in fact, these plates are the work of people who respect classic training — and who, at the same time, enjoy the play and possibilities of the human imagination.

Philippe Laurier, Executive Chef of Patisfrance New York, received quintessential, classic training in pastry. He was submerged in that world from the time he was a child; his father was a pastry chef. "The person who influenced me most was my father," says Laurier. "I will never forget seeing him finish sixty cakes in one afternoon. Not one was the same." As a result of his father's creativity, Laurier is a staunch seeker of the new and unusual. "The creativity is the most valuable part of our profession," he says. "Pastry is an art. You can never make too much effort on the look. Every day you can come up with new ideas and a new concept. It is endless. When I teach, I often say that I never follow a recipe. I will always change something at the last minute." Laurier always knew that he would do a pyramidal dessert for Patisfrance, but, he says, "reproduction of a building is not creation. You need more abstraction." So he added the gold flakes and the surrounding tuile cookies. "What I want to see is a 'Whoahhh!' from the customer before he even tastes it," says Laurier.

"Beauty is something you want to eat," agrees Sebastien Canonne of the Ritz-Carlton Chicago, yet another chef with classic training but an entertainer's sensibility. "In this country they expect a certain look," he says. To achieve that look, Canonne is inspired by art deco and the elegant shapes he sees at exhibitions, museums and libraries. He then goes to the kitchen and starts "playing with the materials. It starts with flavor," he says. "First you get the taste right, then textures and colors. Then you think about whether you can refine its look with chocolate or sugar."

"I like to take classical things and make them fun," says Martin Howard of the Hudson River Club in New York. "I like to start with something that's a specific dessert and flavor. Get the flavor before you get too carried away with the look." This is one chef who does get carried away, and admits it. Not surprising, considering that he takes his inspira-

S

• • • • •

tion from the pulsing lights, glittery clothes and *au courant* hairstyles of the "crazy people" of New York City's club scene. "A weekly dose of dancing, drinks and drag queens helps keep the creative juices flowing," maintains Howard, "a technique I call 'shake and bake.'"

It's a long way from New York to Phoenix, and Martin Howard's "shake and bake" approach is a far cry from the serene methodology of Roxsand Scocos, chef and owner of Roxsand's. "We're such a noisy society, sometimes our food gets noisy," says Scocos. "I don't like a lot of noise. I like simplicity. I like form and balance. My building blocks are classical, but what I do with them is not traditional."

Scocos is dubious about the meticulously arranged plates of many of her classically trained peers. "I don't like a manhandled plate. Anything that looks like eight guys worked over a plate, it's gaggy to me," says Scocos. "I like an organic look, like there's still dew on it. Delicate. A gentle quality to it." To achieve this, Scocos "casts" her food. "I like it cast on the plate rather than tweezered onto the plate," she says. "It's beautiful, like a stone skipping on a lake. The ripples have their own expression rather than being forced on the water by design." Scocos is quick to add that her technique is different than that espoused by Wayne Brachman, who, along with chef Bobby Flay, drops his food (see Minimalism). "I'm not a thrower, I'm a caster," says Scocos. "Bobby Flay is a friend, I like what he does, but my plates don't look anything like his."

Scocos has a few rules she follows as she casts her desserts in the kitchen. "If an item has a point, you never put the point in," she says. "It looks off to me. I take the reference from ballet — points out. And I'm into floral design, where you never show the base of what you do," she continues. "You have to hide the mechanics in flower arranging. And you should never show the mechanics of how you do things on a plate. You want the customer delighted and surprised and 'how did they do that?'; but you never want the customer to feel that he or she is part of an experiment."

Jim Graham of Le Français and Chocolats Le Français in Wheeling, Illinois, has developed a succesful non-method over the years. "Whatever progression has occured in my professional development has been the result of letting go of philosophies, missions and systems of belief," says Graham. "All of them act as blinders to the full range of possibilities afforded by each unique set of ingredients and circumstances. I have a long way to go in this regard, and creativity is still a painful process for me, but the process seems easier when I can go into a project with a minimum of preconceptions. From there, the properties of the ingredients, my past experiences, and influences from other fields sometimes synthesize, independently of my control, to suggest the dessert."

Graham's plates — the sleek Stratus and the delicate White Coffee Ice Cream — do seem to spring from the unconscious. There is nothing in them to suggest that they were born of committee or taught in a school. "The best desserts seem to make themselves," says Graham. "The more I try to impose my will to achieve a certain outcome, the less pleased I usually am with the results. This is leading me to experiment with decorative techniques which are less precise and manipulative, in which I have less control over the result, and the materials composing the dessert look and behave according to their potential. This is scary territory, though: there are no guarantees that I'll like what comes out of this process, and I have to fight the urge to retreat to safer, more controlled approaches. The synthesis I mention above at its best creates a dessert which has an undefinable yet recognizable spark of life, an honesty."

3. Bake in a convection oven at 325°F (165°C) for 45 minutes, or until browned and bubbling around the edges. Allow to cool; chill several hours.

4. Using a 3" ring mold, cut out rounds of the Brown Betty.

### TUILE BATTER (FOR FACE)

*4.2 oz/119 g egg whites*
*5 oz/142 g confectioners' sugar, sifted*
*3 oz/85 g all-purpose flour*
*.25 tsp/1.25 g salt*
*2.5 oz/71 g butter, melted*
*1 tsp/5 ml vanilla extract*
*1 tsp/5 g cocoa powder*

1. Using a piece of acetate, cut out a face-shaped stencil.

2. In a mixer with whip attachment, beat egg whites to soft peaks. Blend in confectioners' sugar, flour and salt. At low speed, blend in butter and vanilla.

3. Stencil the tuile batter onto a nonstick baking sheet.

4. Mix a small amount of the tuile batter with some cocoa powder and pour into a parchment cone. Pipe features onto the face-shaped tuiles. Bake the tuiles at 325°F (165°C) for 8 minutes. Immediately after removing the tuiles from the oven, place them over a can to form a curved shape.

### SPUN SUGAR (FOR HAIR)

*1 lb/454 g granulated sugar*
*16.7 liq oz/494 ml water*
*.25 tsp/1.25 g cream of tartar*

1. Place all ingredients in a saucepan and bring to boil. Cook until temperature reaches 315°F (157°C). Remove from heat and add red paste food coloring to desired shade of pink.

2. Use a cut-off whisk to form spun sugar "hair."

### ASSEMBLY

*Raspberry coulis*
*Crème anglaise*
*Sliced strawberries*
*Mint leaves*

Before service, warm a Brown Betty round in oven. Place on dessert plate. Place tuile "face" on the side of the round. Pile some of the spun sugar "hair" on top of the round. Garnish the plate with the sauces, strawberries and mint.

# PYRAMID

PHILIPPE LAURIER, PATISFRANCE USA, EAST RUTHERFORD, NEW JERSEY

*Chocolate sponge is layered with praline ganache, passion fruit chocolate sabayon and mango mousse, then encased in a gold flecked chocolate glaze.*

### YIELD: 24 SERVINGS

Special Equipment: Flexipan pyramid molds (24 size) or twenty-four 3" x 3" x 3"
(7.6 x 7.6 x 7.6 cm) triangle molds
Brick stencil design
Silicon baking mat
Chocolate comb

### CHOCOLATE BITTER-ALMOND SPONGE

*14 oz/397 g almond paste (50%)*
*5 oz/142 g confectioners' sugar*
*3.5 oz/99 g whole eggs*
*5.9 oz/167 g egg yolks*
*4 oz/113 g whole butter, softened*
*.5 liq oz/15 ml vanilla extract*
*4.5 oz/128 g all-purpose flour*
*4.5 oz/128 g cocoa powder*
*12.6 oz/357 g egg whites*
*5 oz/142 g granulated sugar*

1. Preheat oven to 375°F (190°C).

2. In a mixer using the paddle attachment, cream together the almond paste and confectioners' sugar. Slowly add eggs and yolks, and beat until mixture is pale yellow. Add butter and vanilla extract; paddle until combined.

3. Sift together flour and cocoa powder; add to mixture and paddle until combined.

4. In a mixer with the wire whip attachment, whip the egg whites with the sugar to stiff peaks. Fold 1/3 of the meringue into cake batter to lighten the mixture; fold in remaining meringue.

5. In a greased sheet pan lined with parchment paper, spread batter to cover whole pan. Bake until set.

*Following page: "This is like a temple so I added the gold, as sort of a treasure," says Philippe Laurier. "And I take the form in a new direction with the tuiles. They add visual dimension and crunch."*

### PASSION CHOCOLATE SABAYON

*13 oz/369 g bittersweet chocolate, chopped*
*8 liq oz/227 ml heavy cream*
*8 oz/227 g frozen passion fruit purée, thawed*
*5 oz/142 g granulated sugar*
*3.25 oz/92 g egg yolks*
*3.5 oz/99 g whole eggs*
*12 liq oz/355 ml heavy cream, whipped to soft peaks*

1. Place chocolate in a bowl.

2. Bring cream and passion fruit purée to a boil in a saucepan; pour over chocolate. Let stand 2 minutes; whisk until smooth. Allow mixture to cool until just warm.

3. In a mixer fitted with the paddle attachment, beat together the sugar and egg yolks until pale yellow; beat in eggs until incorporated.

4. Fold the beaten yolks into the chocolate mixture; fold in the whipped cream.

### PRALINE GANACHE

*2 oz/57 g smooth praline paste*
*4 liq oz/118 ml heavy cream*
*4 oz/113 g bittersweet chocolate (60% mi-amere), finely chopped*
*1 gaufrette or similar wafer, crumbled*

1. Place chocolate in a bowl.

2. Bring praline paste and heavy cream to a boil.

3. Pour cream mixture over chocolate. Let stand for 2 minutes; mix until smooth. Cool; mix in crumbled wafer.

### CHOCOLATE SOAKING SYRUP

*2 oz/57g granulated sugar*
*2.5 liq oz/74 ml water*
*1.5 oz/42 g cocoa powder*

Place chocolate in a bowl. In a saucepan, bring sugar and water to a boil, pour over cocoa powder and whisk until smooth. Cool.

### DARK CHOCOLATE GLAZE

*10 oz/283 g pâté à glacer, chopped*
*6 oz/170 g semisweet chocolate couverture, chopped*
*2 liq oz/59 ml milk*
*3 liq oz/89 ml heavy cream*
*2 oz/57 g granulated sugar*
*2 liq oz/59 ml water*
*2 oz/57 g glucose*

1. Place chopped coating and couverture in a bowl.

2. Bring milk, cream, sugar, water and glucose to a boil. Pour cream mixture over the coating and couverture. Let stand 2 minutes; whisk together until smooth. Cool until slightly warm and still pourable.

### MANGO SAFFRON COULIS

*32 oz/907 g frozen mango purée, thawed*
*5 oz/142 g glucose*
*pinch saffron*

Reduce mango purée and glucose in a saucepan until thickened. Add the pinch of saffron; cool.

### CHOCOLATE SAUCE

*6 liq oz/177 ml milk*
*4 oz/113 g granulated sugar, divided*
*3.25 oz/92 g egg yolks*
*4 oz/113 g bittersweet chocolate, finely chopped*

1. In a small saucepan, bring milk and 1 oz (28 g) sugar to a boil.

2. In a mixer using the wire whip attachment, beat egg yolks and remaining 3 oz (85 g) sugar until light and fluffy. Temper yolks with hot milk; return to saucepan, and bring back to 180°F (82°C). Remove from heat and pour over chopped chocolate. Whisk until smooth.

### MANGO MOUSSE

*7 gelatin sheets, softened in cold water*
*18 oz/510 g frozen mango purée, thawed*
*2 oz/57 g granulated sugar*
*14 liq oz/414 ml heavy cream, whipped to soft peaks*
*3 oz/85 g mango, chopped into 1/4"/.63 cm pieces*

1. Squeeze the water from the gelatin sheets and melt in a double boiler.

2. In a bowl, combine mango purée and sugar.

3. Add 1 oz (28 g) of the purée mixture to the gelatin; mix until smooth. Add the rest of the purée mixture and mix completely.

4. Fold in the whipped cream and mango pieces. Use mousse before it sets up.

### COOKIES FOR PYRAMID SIDES

*2 oz/57g cocoa "stencil" paste*
*8 oz/227 g confectioners' sugar*
*8 oz/227 g unsalted butter, softened*
*8 oz/227 g egg whites*
*8 oz/227 g all-purpose flour*

1. Preheat oven to 350°F (175°C). From a cake box, cut a triangular stencil to fit the side of the pyramid molds.

2. Place a "brick" silicon baking mat over a silpat. Using a straight-sided comb or spatula, carefully spread the cocoa paste evenly over the stencil, removing the excess.

3. Carefully remove the stencil from the mat. Transfer the silicon mat to a sheet pan and freeze for 1 hour or until set.

4. In an electric mixer with the paddle attachment, cream together the sugar and butter. Add egg whites and mix until combined. Add flour and mix until just combined.

5. Remove the brick stencil from the freezer. With an offset spatula, spread the cigarette paste into the triangle stencil placed over the brick-stenciled silicon mat. Bake at 350°F (175°C) for 6-7 minutes, or until just brown.

6. Carefully remove cookies from the silicon mat and drape over a dowel until set.

### ASSEMBLY
*Edible gold leaf*

1. Prepare twenty-four 3" x 3" x 3" (7.6 x 7.6 x 7.6 cm) triangle molds by oiling and dusting with sugar, or by lining each with custom-fitted film. Or, place Flexipan pyramid sheet on a sheet pan. If using triangle molds, fit them in metal dessert rings to steady them during filling.

2. Lightly soak chocolate sponge with chocolate syrup; cut out twenty-four 1 1/4" (3.1 cm) squares. Spread a thin layer of praline ganache over the remaining chocolate sponge. Cut twenty-four 3" (7.6 cm) squares from the sheet.

3. Fill the triangle molds to 1/3 full with mango mousse. Place a chocolate sponge square over mousse.

4. Fill remainder of mold with passion-chocolate sabayon, leaving a little room to fit the 3" (7.6 cm) sponge. Position the chocolate sponge squares with the ganache side against the sabayon.

5. Chill pyramids a minimum of 5 hours. Unmold onto wire rack and coat with chocolate glaze. While the glaze is still soft, apply the gold leaf.

6. Place pyramid at the center top of the plate, attach cookies and decorate plate with mango-saffron coulis.

# WHITE COFFEE ICE CREAM

JIM GRAHAM, LE FRANÇAIS, WHEELING, ILLINOIS

*"This grew out of some experiments I was doing, exploiting the capacity of chocolate to absorb odors," says Jim Graham. "I was intrigued by these ethereal flavors, detected only in the nose, that came from enclosing chocolate with aromatics like coffee or cinnamon. It's as if the chocolate has a memory."*

## YIELD: 6 SERVINGS

### WHITE COFFEE ICE CREAM
*10.6 oz/300 g white chocolate, chopped*
*3.5 oz/99 g whole coffee beans*
*37 liq oz/1.1 L milk*
*3.9 oz/110 g egg yolks*
*2.5 oz/71 g granulated sugar*

1. Melt white chocolate and place in an airtight container with coffee beans. Stir to mix; seal and place in a warm area (e.g., in oven with pilot light or proofing cabinet) overnight or longer.

2. In a saucepan, bring milk to a boil. Whisk egg yolks and sugar until smooth. Gradually whisk hot milk into yolks; transfer mixture back to saucepan. Cook over medium heat, stirring constantly, until mixture thickens slightly and coats the back of the spoon. Plunge bottom of pan in cold water to stop cooking process.

3. Transfer white chocolate and coffee beans to a mixing bowl. Pour about 1/4 of the milk mixture onto the white chocolate and whisk vigorously. Whisk in remaining milk; pass the mixture through a very fine mesh strainer. Process in ice cream machine.

*Chef Graham uses a knee-high stocking (which he reserves for food use!) to strain the ice cream mixture before processing.*

### WHITE CHOCOLATE SHELLS
*1 lb/454 g white chocolate, melted and tempered*

1. Spread a ladleful of the tempered chocolate in a 1/8" (.32 cm) layer on a marble slab or other hard, cool surface.

*Facing page: Jim Graham points out that the absence of a coffee color in the ice cream "seems to reinforce psychologically the disembodied nature of the flavor. The decor was a 'no-brainer,' flowing easily from the color theme."*

2. When set but not hard, take a 4" (10 cm) round cutter and draw it through the chocolate at a low angle to create cupped curls. (This may take practice; if the chocolate piles up inside cutter, it is too soft. If the curls crumble, it is too hard.) Repeat to form 18 cups.

### MERINGUE STRAWS

*3.15 oz/89 g egg whites*
*4.2 oz/119 g granulated sugar*
*4.2 oz/119 g confectioners' sugar, sifted*

1. Line a sheet pan with a silicon baking mat. Preheat oven to 200°F (95°C).

2. In a mixer with whip attachment, beat egg whites at high speed to soft peaks. Gradually beat in granulated sugar 1 Tbs (12 g) at a time until stiff peaks form. Fold in confectioners' sugar in thirds.

3. Fill a pastry bag fitted with a medium plain tip with meringue. Pipe lines of meringue of various lengths (some long and some short) onto sheet. Bake 45 minutes or until dry.

### ASSEMBLY

1. Place 3 white chocolate shells on a dessert plate. Fill each shell with a scoop of the white coffee ice cream.

2. Garnish plate with meringue straws.

# STRATUS

· · · · · · · · · · · · · · · · · · · · · · · · · · · · · · · · · · · · · · · · · · · · · · · · · ·

JIM GRAHAM, LE FRANÇAIS, WHEELING, ILLINOIS

*"The satisfying but familiar flavors," says Jim Graham, allow the diner to concentrate on the three textures:*
*"smooth, amorphous custard, the delicately brittle chocolate, and crunchy hazelnuts."*

### YIELD: 6 SERVINGS

Special equipment: Several 6" x 6" (15.25 x 15.25 cm) sheets plastic sheeting (such as the plastic
used to wrap gift baskets) or acetate
Plexiglass sheet
Silicon baking mat

### CUSTARD

*1.05 oz/30 g hazelnuts, blanched and roasted*
*4.6 oz/130 g granulated sugar*
*9.12 liq oz/270 ml heavy cream*
*7.77 liq oz/230 ml milk*
*3.9 oz/110 g egg yolks*

1. Preheat oven to 300°F (149° C). Line a quarter sheet pan with heavy-duty aluminum foil; brush
foil lightly with butter.

2. Using the bottom of a heavy pan, crush the roasted hazelnuts.

3. In a heavy saucepan, cook the sugar over high heat, stirring constantly. When the sugar caramelizes
and a light smoke begins to rise from it, remove from heat and carefully add the cream (the mixture
will bubble violently). Return the pan to the heat, whisking to melt any hardened caramel. Whisk in
milk.

4. In a mixing bowl, whisk together egg yolks; whisk in about 8 liq oz (237 ml) of the caramel mixture to temper. Whisk in remaining caramel mixture. Strain and skim off any froth. Pour mixture into
prepared sheet pan and sprinkle evenly with hazelnuts. Bake 20 minutes or until set but still wobbly.
Cool; freeze until firm but not hard, about 1 hour.

*Following page: "The Stratus is as much a textural as a visual or gustatorial experience," says Jim Graham. "There is a dramatic and*
*oddly satisfying sensation associated with pushing a fork down through those ordered layers, shattering and wreaking havoc along the*
*way. I associate this with a childhood memory—the thin chocolate coating of an Eskimo Pie shattering as you bite into the ice cream."*

### CHOCOLATE LEAVES

*1 lb/454 g bittersweet chocolate couverture, melted and tempered*

1. Place 1 plastic sheet on a smooth surface. Spoon about 1 tsp (4 g) of couverture onto the center of the square. Cover with another sheet and press firmly with a piece of plexiglass until the chocolate measures 4" (10 cm) in diameter and is paper-thin.

2. Set aside to cool and repeat process to form a total of 24 chocolate leaves. Allow the leaves to set at room temperature for at least 1 hour.

### CARAMEL GARNISH

*10.6 oz/300 g granulated sugar*

1. Place sugar in a heavy saucepan and cook to a rich, golden brown. Immediately pour onto a silicon baking sheet. Quickly spread the caramel into a thin layer. Allow to cool for a few minutes, until set.

2. Peel the caramel away from the baking sheet and break into small shards. Reserve in an airtight container until ready to use.

### ASSEMBLY

1. Peel plastic away from each side of the chocolate leaves using a brisk motion.

2. Remove custard from freezer. Invert pan onto a sheet pan covered with plastic wrap. Carefully peel away foil and, using a 2" (5 cm) round cutter, stamp out 18 disks of the semifrozen custard.

3. Place a chocolate leaf on dessert plate. Top with a custard disk. Repeat layering 2 times, ending with a custard disk. Cover plate with plastic wrap and refrigerate until custard has thawed.

4. Before serving, top custard disk with chocolate leaf and garnish plate with caramel shards.

*To spread caramel thinly, Jim Graham recommends using a drywall taping knife, available at hardware stores.*

# WHITE CHOCOLATE DELIGHT

. . . . . . . . . . . . . . . . . . . . . . . . . . . . . . . . . . . . . . . . . . . . .

SEBASTIEN CANONNE, RITZ-CARLTON, CHICAGO ILLINOIS

*Refreshing and lemony, spicy linzer cookies are topped with white chocolate mousse and lemon verbena granité;*
*even the steeped plums reinforce the lemon theme.*

### YIELD: 15 SERVINGS

Special Equipment: Fifteen 3" (7.6 cm) oval ring molds

### LINZER DOUGH
*6.5 oz/184 g unsalted butter*
*7 oz/198 g granulated sugar*
*3.5 oz/99 g whole eggs*
*12 oz/340 g cake flour*
*5 oz/142 g almond flour*
*2.5 tsp/10 g baking powder*
*pinch ground cinnamon*
*pinch allspice*
*pinch clove*
*melted white chocolate for coating dough*

1. In a mixer with paddle attachment, cream butter and sugar. Add eggs slowly and mix well together.

2. Sift dry ingredients together and mix into creamed mixture. Chill dough overnight.

3. Preheat oven to 350°F (175°C). Roll dough out to 1/8" (.32 cm) thickness and chill. Dock dough well. Using a 3" oval mold, cut dough and bake until lightly browned, about 8 minutes. When cool, spray both sides with melted white chocolate.

### WHITE CHOCOLATE MOUSSE
*9 oz/255 g white chocolate, chopped*
*2.5 liq oz/74 ml water*
*12 liq oz/355 ml heavy cream*
*zest of 1 lemon, grated*

1. In a saucepan, melt chocolate and water together over low heat. Set aside to cool.

*Facing page: Sebastien Canonne is enamored with the sleek look of art deco, and of clean plates. "I will see a shape or a sculpture in a book and I will wonder, can I get close to that shape with food?" he says.*

2. In a mixer with whisk attachment, whip cream with lemon zest. Fold 1/3 of the whipped cream into cooled chocolate to lighten. Fold in remaining cream. Chill.

3. Line the bottom of the oval molds with linzer dough. Pipe in white chocolate mousse. Level off top and freeze. Remove mold and keep mousse frozen until ready to wrap.

### STEEPED PLUMS

*15 fresh plums*
*2 oz/57 g granulated sugar*
*1 qt/.95 L water*
*8 oz/227 g lemon verbena tea leaves*

1. Cut each plum into 8 wedges. Place in a bowl with sugar.

2. Bring water to a boil, add tea leaves and steep 5 minutes. Strain tea over plums. Let cool completely.

### LEMON VERBENA GRANITÉ

*1 qt/.95 L water*
*8 oz/227 g lemon verbena tea leaves*
*2 oz/57 g granulated sugar*
*1 liq oz/30 ml lemon juice*

1. In a saucepan, boil water and add tea. Steep 5 minutes.

2. Strain and add sugar and lemon juice. Pour into a shallow pan and freeze, stirring with a fork every 1/2 hour during freezing. Scrape the granité into large crystals.

### MARBLED CHOCOLATE RECTANGLE WRAP AND TRIANGLE SHAPE

*1 lb/454 g bittersweet chocolate, coarsley chopped*
*1 lb/454 g white chocolate, coarsley chopped*

1. Cut acetate rectangle strips to fit around oval molds, approximately 8 3/4" x 1 3/4" (22.2 x 4.5 cm). The height should extend approximately 1/2" (1.25 cm) over mold. Cut out triangle shapes 2" x 8" x 8"(5 x 20 x 20 cm).

2. Melt and temper white and dark chocolates. Drizzle white chocolate over rectangle-shaped plastic. Drizzle dark chocolate on top of white. Using a small offset spatula, spread chocolate evenly over entire surface and wrap around frozen mousse. Let set before removing the plastic.

3. Drizzle white chocolate on triangle shape. Drizzle dark chocolate on top of white. Spread evenly over entire surface. Bend plastic slightly. Let set before removing plastic.

### ASSEMBLY

*Red currants*
*Candied citrus zest*
*Mint*

1. In a large shallow bowl, place white chocolate mousse. Arrange plum wedges around it. Pour enough steeping liquid to almost cover plums. Place triangle shape on top of dessert.

2. Place a spoonful of granité on top and garnish with red currents, candied zest and a sprig of mint.

# LEMON TART

RUBEN FOSTER, ARIZONA BILTMORE, PHOENIX, ARIZONA

*Dense, buttery shortbread dough is topped with tart lemon cream and swims in a rosé wine jelly and lingonberries. A light, simple dessert.*

### YIELD: 10 SERVINGS

Special Equipment: 10 plastic cone molds, 4 1/4" deep x 3 1/8" wide (10.8 x 8 cm)

### SHORT DOUGH

*5 oz/142 g confectioners' sugar*
*10.75 oz/305 g unsalted butter*
*1.7 oz/48 g whole eggs*
*1 tsp/4 ml vanilla extract*
*14 oz/397 g all-purpose flour*

1. In a mixer using the paddle attachment, cream together the sugar and butter.

2. Whisk together eggs and vanilla. Gradually add to the creamed ingredients, scraping down the bowl once.

3. Add the flour and mix until just combined.

4. Roll the dough into a ball and refrigerate 1–2 hours.

5. Roll out the dough to 1/8" (32 cm) thickness and chill in the freezer.

6. Using a 5 1/2" x 4" (14 x 10 cm) triangular template, cut the short dough out and bake at 350°F (175°C) for 12–15 minutes until just starting to brown.

### LEMON CREAM

*8.5 oz/241 g whole eggs*
*1.3 oz/37 g egg yolks*
*1 lb/454 g granulated sugar*
*6 liq oz/177 ml fresh lemon juice*
*7 oz /198 g unsalted butter, softened, cut into pieces*
*bittersweet chocolate, melted, for decoration*

*Following page: "Something a little different," comments Ruben Foster. "It started as a sunburst, flat and round with a caramel decoration in the background, but it didn't work—the caramel spray you see is the remnant of that design. I then took a conical mold and cut it in half, and it developed into this."*

1. Whisk together eggs, yolks, sugar, and lemon juice in a large double boiler. Whisk the mixture constantly until thick and doubled in volume. Remove from heat.

2. Whisk the butter into the mixture until completely melted.

3. Pour the mixture immediately into the 4 1/4" x 3 1/8" (10.8 x 8 cm) plastic cone molds (or wine glass with similar dimensions). Freeze completely for 24 hours in a very cold freezer, around 0°F (-18°C) or colder. To unmold, run briefly under running hot water. If necessary, insert a fork into the wide end of the dessert and twist to remove. Return frozen cream to freezer again to refreeze the surface completely. Using a hot knife, cut cone-shaped cream in half lengthwise.

4. Drizzle with melted chocolate and place on short dough triangle until thawed completely.

### ROSÉ WINE SAUCE

*11.25 liq oz/333 ml red wine*
*20.75 liq oz/614 ml white wine*
*8 liq oz/237 ml water*
*4 oz/113 g powdered pectin*
*9.5 oz/269 g granulated sugar*

1. In a large, nonreactive saucepan, combine the wines and bring them to a boil.

2. Combine the water and pectin and add to the wines. Bring the mixture to a boil.

3. Add the sugar, and bring back to a boil for 1 minute. Remove from heat; chill.

### CARAMEL GARNISH

*7 oz/198 g granulated sugar*
*8 liq oz/237 ml water*
*pinch cream of tartar*

1. Lightly grease the surface of a metal cake turntable.

2. In a nonreactive, heavy saucepan over high heat, combine all ingredients. Wash down the sides of the pan with a small pastry brush dipped in cold water. Bring the ingredients to a boil, and boil vigorously until the sugar caramelizes.

3. Transfer saucepan to an ice bath, and cool the caramel until it thickens slightly but is still pourable.

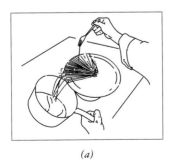
(a)

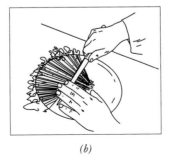
(b)

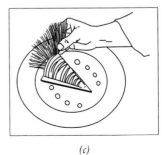
(c)

4. Using a fork, drizzle caramel in lines from the turntable's center to its edge, so that 1/4 of the turntable is covered with lines of caramelized sugar (see illustrations on page 219). With scissors, trim off the excess along the edge of the turntable. Carefully lift the garnish and trim a straight line of sugar from the piece's pointed end to form a flat bottom.

### ASSEMBLY
*Lingonberries*

1. Place the short dough triangle with thawed lemon cream on the center of a plate.

2. Fill the plate with the rosé wine sauce, and garnish with lingonberries.

3. Stand the caramel garnish behind the large end of the lemon cream, and lightly press it into place.

# BITTERSWEET ESPRESSO MOUSSE CONES

MARY CECH, THE CULINARY INSTITUTE OF AMERICA AT GREYSTONE, ST. HELENA, CALIFORNIA

*A blast of chocolate and a hint of espresso, as a crisp chocolate cone is filled with bittersweet espresso mousse.*

### YIELD: 12 SERVINGS

Special Equipment: 12 acetate or parchment cones with a 2" (5 cm) opening

#### BITTERSWEET ESPRESSO MOUSSE

*1.5 pt/710 ml heavy cream*
*1 lb/454 g extra-bitter chocolate, coarsely chopped*
*6 oz/170 g espresso, coarsely ground*

1. In a mixer with whisk attachment, beat cream just until it begins to thicken (it should be the consistency of a thick purée).

2. Melt the chocolate with the espresso over hot water. Keep the chocolate warm for 30 minutes to allow the espresso flavor to infuse. Strain the chocolate through cheesecloth and warm to 110°F (43°C). Immediately whisk the warm chocolate into the cream.

3. Chill the mousse several hours or overnight.

#### CHOCOLATE CONES

*6 oz/170 g bittersweet chocolate, melted and tempered*
*1 lb/454 g white chocolate, melted and tempered*

1. Use a medium artists' brush to dab random streaks of the tempered bittersweet chocolate on the interior of the acetate or parchment cones. Allow the chocolate to set.

2. Drizzle a heaping spoonful of the tempered white chocolate into one of the cones. Turn the cone upside down and allow the chocolate to coat the interior of the cone. Repeat with remaining cones. Lay the cones on their sides and allow to set completely.

#### CHOCOLATE PLATE AND GARNISH

*3 lbs/1.36 kg bittersweet chocolate, melted and tempered*

*Following page: "The visual is really crazy," admits Mary Cech. "The cone rests on a chocolate platter I made—I elect not to use plates sometimes. Of course you're not going to do this in a restaurant. It's not feasible."*

# LE CIRQUE FLORA

ROXSAND SCOCOS, ROXSAND'S, PHOENIX, ARIZONA

*A strawberry-rhubarb cinnamon compote is folded into a tangy fruit yogurt mousse, placed atop a pistachio dac-*
*quoise and wrapped in a crisp chocolate band. Crunchy deep-fried cellophane noodles dusted with cinnamon sugar*
*top the dessert.*

### YIELD: 8 SERVINGS

Special Equipment: Eight 3" ring molds, 2 1/2" high (7.6 x 6.3 cm)

#### STRAWBERRY-RHUBARB COMPOTE

*3 lbs/1.36 kg fresh rhubarb*
*3 lbs/1.36 kg fresh strawberries*
*7 oz/198 g granulated sugar*
*1 liq oz/30 ml vanilla extract*
*.5 oz/14 g ground cinnamon*

In a saucepan, combine all ingredients and cook over medium heat until thick. Refrigerate for 2 hours.

#### FRUIT-YOGURT MOUSSE

*2 tsp/8 g powdered gelatin*
*1 liq oz/30 ml lemon juice*
*.5 liq oz/15 ml kirsch*
*1.3 oz/37 g egg yolks*
*1 oz/28 g granulated sugar*
*8.5 oz/241 g plain nonfat yogurt*
*1 vanilla bean, split and scraped*
*12 oz/340 g strawberry-rhubarb compote (recipe above)*
*4 liq oz/118 ml heavy cream, whipped to soft mounds*

1. Soften gelatin in lemon juice and kirsch. Heat in hot water bath until clear.

2. In a mixer with whisk attachment, beat egg yolks and sugar until they are pale and double in volume.

3. Combine yogurt and vanilla bean in a saucepan and heat to a simmer.

*Facing page: "I was inspired by seeing this incredible European turn-of-the-century-style circus called Circus Flora," says Roxsand Scocos.*
*"I was mesmerized by it, and wanted to create a dessert in its honor."*

# P E R F O R M A N C E   A R T

*"What is the good of making dainties, if they are not served*

*in the proper way?"*

PAUL RICHARDS

*"Rule Number One is, don't harm the customer."*

DAVID PANTONE

Cherries Jubilee, Crêpes Suzette, Baked Alaska. All were staples of fine dining, French-service restaurants. Flames jumping, sauces flowing — they were show business and fine food fused into one. Now they are found mostly on cruise ships; legal entanglements, government regulations and the changing sensibilities of both the public and the chefs brought such waitstaff spectacles in fine dining environments to an end in the 1970s. Then came nouvelle cuisine.

"In the 1980s, people came to restaurants for the chef, and we forgot the show," says Claude Troisgros of C.T. in New York. "But for the past few years, with the end of nouvelle, we are coming back to show business. A customer who comes to your restaurant is not just coming to eat, he is coming for the decor, the show. He wants fun."

"We are part of the entertainment business," agrees David Pantone of the Florida Culinary Institute, "and I love it. It allows the chefs, the cooks and the waitstaff not only to entertain the guests, but to be proud and excited about what they're serving."

A *Performance Art* plated dessert is one which, by design, *displays some action* when set before the customer, or when the customer applies fork or spoon. By 'action' is meant *movement of ingredients, flaming accompaniments or garnishes* which need to be *removed* before reaching the main dessert component.

**CLAUDE TROISGROS**
*Claude Troisgros is chef and owner of C.T. in New York as well as several restaurants in Brazil, including Claude Troisgros, Roanne and Restaurant Terramater. The son of Pierre Troisgros, Claude was born on April 9, 1956, in Roanne, France. "I was born inside a restaurant and raised in the kitchen," he says, referring to his father's celebrated restaurant, Troisgros of Roanne. At age 16, Claude studied at the Hotel School of Thonon-les-Bains, then undertook an apprenticeship with Paul Bocuse. He worked in several restaurants and hotels in Europe before Gaston Lenôtre offered him the position of chef for his restaurant in Rio de Janeiro, Pré Catelan. The contract was for two years; Troisgros stayed in Brazil for 15. "I opened five restaurants and traveled a good deal," he says. In Brazil, "I made French food," he confirms, "but pastry created big problems. The ingredients were different, the results were completely different. We had to start over." One restaurant after another was a success; in 1994, he opened C.T. in New York. He is the author of the book, Da Cabeça à Panela (from the head to the saucepan). Troisgros' plans for the future include a catering operation and possibly a produce label. "I hope my business will continue to grow," he says. "America gives such opportunity for growth."*

## TRINKETS AND GIMMICKRY

Not everyone is pleased at the infusion of show business into the restaurant business of the 1990s; it is a mixed blessing to the lover of fine food, for where there is show biz, excess, vulgarity and pure bad taste are sure to follow. But there are degrees to which show business snatches the spotlight from good food: The Jekyll & Hyde restaurants in New York City feature animatronic and live performers in a ghoulish atmosphere which not only distracts from the food, but for most people stifles appetite entirely. At chain establishments like the Hard Rock Cafe, Planet Hollywood and Harley Davidson, food is a tertiary consideration to the theme decor and the selling of knick-knacks, although decent fare is sometimes available in such spots. There are restaurants where food is the *raison d'être*, but gimmicks drive the machine: Japanese-style restaurants like Benihana, where the chef puts on a show with knife and fire, have been doing business for years. Truth be told, there is a show business patina to even the most dedicated fine dining restaurants: food is the star, but there had better be beautiful people, well-turned-out waitstaff and designer interior decor. Dan Budd, now of the Culinary Institute of America, grows animated when he recalls how his Windy City Sailing Sundae is served in the Park Avenue Cafe Chicago: The sundae, which is formed with cookies and ice cream scoops into a boat with sails, prow and masts "is wheeled from the pastry shop and across the dining room on garadons," says Budd proudly. "It looks like it's sailing." The promise of wonderful food, the excitement of live performance. Show business.

# MOLTEN

Performance in a dessert can be coaxed from flaming liqueurs or poured sugar barriers, but most performance desserts are molten or have cool liquid centers. This can be achieved in a number of ways. The soufflé cake features a cake base made with a high ratio of butter and sugar, which is baked at a high temperature so it crusts on the outside and is molten on the inside. Truffle cakes are high in sugar and eggs, and use cornstarch rather than flour for structure, with a richer, yolk-based ganache at center; this ganache is formed into a disk for better melting when the cake is baked. An ice cream bombe, such as the one served by Lincoln Carson in New York City's Cascabel, features ice cream infused with chocolate syrup which is high in sugar to inhibit freezing; once the bombe is brought to 10–15 degrees above freezing for service, the center melts and is completely liquid. A chocolate disk is inserted in the center to add a chewy, chocolaty factor. Eric Gouteyron devises cakes with centers including alcohol and/or invert sugar such as glucose to inhibit freezing; at the Plaza Hotel he makes an orange and lemon parfait filled with a liquid center of black currant coulis glucosé. The parfait is piped into ring molds, frozen, the coulis center is filled in, allowed to set in the freezer, and the rest of the parfait is piped on top.

The chef who creates Performance Art desserts must be a master of precise ingredients, and temperature is often a leading actor. But there is no mystery to this creation; it is all method. Alain Roby of the Hyatt Regency Chicago keeps a chart of flavors and colors, which he constantly updates. "Flavor is like color," says Roby. "By mixing them you can get a beautiful rainbow, and sometimes you get a disaster." Maintaining the chart is one way to ensure a rainbow.

David Pantone of the Florida Culinary Institute also is striving to de-mystify the alchemy of flavor in the pastry kitchen. He attributes his ability to extract flavor to his experience as a savory chef. "Chefs are always saying, 'Oh, baking is such an exact science, so precise,'" Pantone observes, and he adds, with tongue in cheek: "I think pastry chefs told them that to make sure they keep their jobs, and to squeeze some extra money out of management.

"Sure, some recipes do need to be measured exactly," Pantone continues, "but after that, to me, it's cooking, it's flavor." His instructor at the Culinary Institute of America, Walter Schreyer, de-mystified the cooking process for him. "You take a recipe and break it down to the least common denominators. From that you can learn why it works, how

**DAVID PANTONE**
*David Pantone, Chairperson of the Florida Culinary Institute in West Palm Beach, Florida, was born in Pittsburgh on March 3, 1961. He had six years' kitchen experience in quality restaurants before he applied to the Culinary Institute of America in 1981. Pantone also studied at the Notters' International School of Culinary Arts and Albert Kumin's International Pastry Arts Center. He was an assistant pastry chef at the Waldorf Astoria in New York, then pastry chef at restaurants, bakeries and hotels in Florida, including the Pavilion Hotel, the Mayfair House, Chef Allen's, Lucky's and The Breakers. He also acted as a pastry consultant before becoming an instructor at the Florida Culinary Institute. After becoming director of the pastry program there, in 1994 he became director of the school. His philosophy of education is grounded in both aesthetics and practicality: "I advise all my students to get a solid background in cooking, and also in business administration," he says.*

**ALAIN ROBY**
*Alain Roby, Executive Pastry Chef at the Hyatt Regency Chicago, was born on June 7, 1955, in Mulhouse, France. He received his training in pastry and confectionary at Le Nôtre in Paris, earning his certificate in the customary four years, then spending three more years in the decoration department to learn sugar, chocolate and other centerpiece work. "Phillip Rousselet was the head of the department, and a real genius," says Roby. "It was a very exclusive department, very peaceful and quiet." After Le Nôtre, Roby served in the French navy, worked in a hotel in Japan, then he became the private pastry chef for the Shah of Iran. "When the revolution came," he says, "I had to leave." He worked at the Hilton Park Lane in London and opened the Vista Hotel in New York, before joining the Hyatt Regency Chicago "I love what I'm doing, I love the hotel. The freedom I have in my work, you cannot put a price on that," he says.*

*CHRIS NORTHMORE*
*Chris Northmore, pastry chef of the Cherokee Town and Country Club in Atlanta, Georgia, and an A.C.F. Certified Master Pastry Chef, was born on February 23, 1954, in Detroit. He attended the Culinary Institute of America, and upon graduating spoke to many chefs about what he should do next. The consensus was that if they could re-take their education, many would have wanted to learn more about baking. "So I decided, heck, why not work in a bakeshop for a year?" he says. "I lucked into a good position with a Gunter Heiland in Atlanta at the Omni International Hotel in 1979." When Heiland moved to Philadelphia to open the Fairmount Hotel, he asked Northmore to be his assistant. During that two-year period, Northmore got involved in competitions and continued to take classes, including sugar work with Ewald and Susan Notter and pastry and chocolate with Albert Kumin. In 1981, he became Executive Pastry Chef at the Parker House Hotel in Boston and in 1986 took the position at the Cherokee Town and Country Club. "I'm probably at that point in my career when I should be trying to decide whether I want to own my own business or shoot off in a totally different direction," he says. "I just know that I love bread baking and I love pastry."*

it works, and how it derives its flavors. From those simple basic recipes you can build millions of variations. For example, when I was first studying baking, I found 36 different pâte à choux recipes. I broke them all down and looked into the ratios, and came up with one. And that recipe works just fine."

For Pantone, there is no routine to the creation of desserts, but experience counts for a lot. "If there is a flavor I know I want to use, I will figure out the best way to show off that flavor. Should it be baked? Frozen? Which texture will match it the best? Other times it's visual, something I might see on the street or a flashback from Gilligan's Island, and I will try to match the flavor with it. The skyline of South Beach, where everything is deco, we created desserts based on that."

For Chris Northmore of the Cherokee Town & Country Club in Atlanta, temperature is a crucial element to be exploited in the pastry kitchen. "Temperature brings out certain flavors," he says. "Apple is better warm, while strawberries are better cold. And for me, nothing beats a warm chocolate anything." Northmore strives for balance in his desserts. "The correct balance of flavors, temperatures and textures," he says. "If there's a sweetness, there should be something to balance it out: a tart element." He adds that, when designing a plate, he tries to anticipate how the customer will eat it — to know how it will perform, so to speak.

## HANS VS. MADAME D'OR

The term "Performance Art" is derived from an avant-garde artistic tradition that embraces a wide variety of live performances and dates back to the 1920s; its antecedents include the theatrical branches of the Dadaists, the Futurists and the Surrealists. Only a portion of Peformance Art pieces actually take place in a theater. (In the dead of winter of 1971, artist Vito Acconci invited audiences to visit him in a shed on the Hudson River on a certain night from 1 to 2 a.m.; from the darkened shack, Acconci whispered secrets to anyone who attended.) The goals and meanings of much Performance Art are often elusive. Under the term, many events defy categorization. (Yoko Ono's contribution to a Museum of Modern Art exhibit in 1970 instructed the museum-goer to draw an imaginary map, then go walking on actual New York City streets according to the map.) Performances can involve video, slide projections, actors, dance, poetry or music or any combination in a narrative or non-narrative format. (California artist Chris Burden, in a work entitled *Shooting Piece,* instructed a friend to shoot him with a pistol from 15 feet away, grazing the artist's arm; the friend mistakenly blew a portion of Burden's shoulder away.) Performance art is always experimental. Each work is intended as an event, a unique moment in time, not to be repeated. Transitory — like dessert.

The interrelationship of food and performance has been seen throughout history, often running the gamut from vulgarity to elegance. The Romans of the ancient world prided themselves on presenting lavish and (to modern sensibilities) decadent banquets. Chronicles tell of one host who served a "food chain" dish — inside a calf was a pig, inside the pig was a lamb, inside the lamb a chicken, then a rabbit, then a dormouse; mechanical devices were sometimes employed to lower the food from high ceilings; dishes were occasionally devised so that they sprayed the guests with aromatic saffron or rosewater, or birds might fly from an item when it was cut open. This lively presentation of food continued through the centuries. In 1430, a banquet was held in a French court in honor of a Portuguese duchess: inside a huge pie that was presented was a sheep painted blue and a human giant named Hans. When the pie was cut open, Hans jumped out and wrestled with Madame d'Or, a blond dwarf who was nationally famous for playing the Fool at many an occasion. At the more elegant end of the spectrum, Antonin Carême, the innovative 19th-century French chef, presented a pie from which doves would fly when cut open. From the London of 1846 comes this description of a Twelfth Cake on display in the shop of Messrs. Batger & Co. of Bishopsgate Street: "...decorated with sponge-cake birds which dip their beaks in basins of translucent sugar candy while blancmange dolphins spouted streams of almost irresistible barley-sugar." The cake was topped with a pineapple, from which sprang jets of "apparently falling water."

## PURE MAGIC

When Eric Gouteyron, one of the world's finest pastry chefs and an acknowledged master with chocolate, defines beauty in a plated dessert, movement is very much a part: "Beauty is a combination of originality, creation, flavor, movement and fragility," he says. "When a dessert is brought to a customer, I like to see amazement and their smile deepening."

The artistry of these plates is not skimped because of the necessity of performance: David Pantone's Cascade of Coulis is set, appropriately enough, in a cavernous environment created by the huge sugar backdrop that looms over the dessert. The dessert components, pure sleek geometrics, contrast with the rough-hewn cavern. The cocoa pear shadow over Chris Northmore's Pear Bavarian is a thoughtful, surreal touch, as if the dessert is throwing a shadow. Once the raspberry coulis appears, it has a perfect stage of snowbound white on which to flow. Alain Roby's Merlin's Crystal Fantasy is pure magic, with blown sugar used as God intended: to create an enchanted, Christmas snowball effect, enclosing the dessert and raising it on a crystalline pedestal. Sebastien Canonne's Green Apple Surprise is likewise reminiscent of Christmas; it is like a welcome package, with the colors of that season vividly represented in sugar. Interesting also is the free-form whorl of sugar that Canonne adds to lend sweep and looseness to forms that are strict. Alain Roby's Wings of Sugar boasts pearl luminescence, graceful lines and verticality, with the dark fruit for contrast and focus.

Action in these plates includes involving the customer in some way: they must crack open Roby's Merlin's Crystal Fantasy and Sebastien Canonne's Green Apple Surprise to find their

**GALE GAND**
*Gale Gand, pastry chef/co-owner (with husband Rick Tramonto) of Brasserie T in Chicago, was born on November 21, 1956, in Evanston, Illinois. While living the college-age artist's life, she applied for a job as a waitress. "Then one day a cook didn't show up. They threw the apron at me." Terrified at first, Gand very quickly ("two seconds," she says) grew to love cooking. "I loved the color, the life of the produce, the flavors, the textures. I was dizzy. I'd had plans to be an artist, and then this bolt of lightning hit me." Gand eventually started her own catering company, and worked at the Strathallen Hotel in Rochester, New York, where she met Rick Tramonto. She studied pastry at La Varenne in Paris, then moved to New York and worked in several restaurants, including the Gotham Bar & Grill. Moving to Chicago, she worked in, and opened, several restaurants including Café 21, Bice and Bella Luna. She worked at a hotel outside London for a time before returning to Chicago and taking a position at Charlie Trotter's. In 1993, Gand and Tramonto joined Henry Adaniya to open the wildly succesful Trio restaurant. In 1995, Gand and Tramonto opened Brasserie T. Gale Gand is working on a book, tentatively titled* Brasserie U.S.A., *and is hoping to open a fine dining establishment and a bakery in the near future.*

# THE PALM BEACH

. . . . . . . . . . . . . . . . . . . . . . . . . . . . . . . . . . . . . . . . . . . . . . . . . . . . . . . .

ERIC GOUTEYRON, THE PLAZA, NEW YORK, NEW YORK

*Distinct flavors abound, as a demisphere of orange sorbet filled with cassis coulis and ginger parfait is crowned with a circle of genoise, drizzled with chocolate and glazed. Fresh fruit and raspberry coulis round out the experience.*

### YIELD: 8 SERVINGS

Special Equipment: Eight 8 oz/227 g demi-sphere molds

#### ORANGE SORBET
*11 oz/312 g turbinado sugar*
*3 oz/85 g glucose*
*1 oz/28 g dextrose*
*.25 oz/7 g stabilizer (such as trimoline)*
*4.5 liq oz/133 ml water, warmed*
*1 pt/.95 L orange juice, freshly squeezed*

1. In a saucepan, combine sugar, glucose, dextrose, stabilizer and water. Bring to a simmer and add orange juice. Strain through a fine chinois; chill.

2. Freeze in an ice cream machine.

#### CASSIS COULIS
*8 liq oz/237 ml black currant purée*
*4 liq oz/118 ml honey*
*6 oz/170 g granulated sugar*
*2.5 oz/71 g glucose*
*3 liq oz/89 ml kirsch*

Mix all ingredients and freeze until hard but still pliable.

#### GINGER PARFAIT
*5.5 oz/156 g granulated sugar*
*2 liq oz/59 ml water*

*Facing page: A touch of show business is not outside the sphere of Eric Gouteyron, considered by many to be one of the finest pastry chefs working with chocolate. "The art of pastry is a business," he concedes, "but first it is a passion."*

# GREEN APPLE SURPRISE

. . . . . . . . . . . . . . . . . . . . . . . . . . . . . . . . . . . . . . . . . . . . . . . .

SEBASTIEN CANONNE, RITZ-CARLTON, CHICAGO, ILLINOIS

*It is no surprise that green apple and chocolate blend beautifully. The pairing is given a twist as a blown sugar apple filled with green apple sorbet is placed inside a white and dark chocolate box. Calvodos-flavored financiers and dried apple chips garnish the dessert.*

## YIELD: 8 SERVINGS

Special Equipment: Financier molds
Eight 2" (5 cm) ring molds
Woodgrain impression tool

### CALVADOS FINANCIER

*2.5 lb/1.13 kg unsalted butter, cut in cubes*
*14.4 oz/408 g almond flour*
*43.2 oz/1.22 kg confectioners' sugar*
*14.4 oz/408 g all-purpose flour*
*36 oz/1.02 kg egg whites*
*3 Tbs/36 g apple compote*
*3.5 liq oz/103 ml Calvados*

1. Preheat oven to 375°F (190°C). Butter financier molds. In a saucepan, melt butter and cook until nut brown. Cool slightly and strain through cheesecloth.

2. In a large bowl, combine almond flour, sugar and all-purpose flour.

3. In a mixer with whisk attachment, whisk egg whites until foamy. Add apple compote and flour mixture and mix just until combined. On low speed, mix in butter. Cool 5 minutes.

4. Stir in Calvados. Fill molds 3/4 of the way with batter. Bake 10 minutes or until golden. Remove from molds and cool.

### DRIED APPLE CHIPS

*2 green apples*
*2 red apples*

1. Preheat oven to 200°F (95°C). Core apples. Using slicer, cut into rings 1/16" (.16 cm) thick.

2. Lay rings on silicon baking sheet and bake 1 hour or until dry. Store in airtight container.

*Facing page: "I sometimes make this dessert in a more architectural fashion," says Sebastien Canonne. "For this, we tried to do something that no one had thought of, with no molten chocolate running at its center."*

1. In mixer with whisk attachment, beat whites until foamy. Turn off mixer while preparing sugar syrup.

2. In a saucepan over low heat, combine sugar and water. Cook, stirring frequently, until sugar dissolves. Increase heat to medium-high and boil without stirring until mixture reaches 240°F (117°C).

3. Remove syrup from heat, and gradually add in a steady stream to the egg whites while continuing to beat. Beat until the meringue is cool, about 8 minutes.

### ASSEMBLY
*2 liq oz/59 ml Armagnac*
*10 limes, cut in half*

1. Fill a pastry bag fitted with a medium plain tip (Ateco #4) with meringue. Pipe mounds of meringue over ice cream bases, covering each completely. Place each bombe on dessert plate. Squeeze juice of 1 lime around each bombe.

2. In a saucepan over low heat, warm Armagnac. Immediately before serving, sprinkle bombe with warm Armagnac and flambé. Serve immediately.

# ROASTED FRUITS IN PARCHMENT

GAIL GAND, BRASSERIE T, CHICAGO, ILLINOIS

*Plums, peaches and pears are tossed in honey, brown sugar, red wine and cinnamon, then roasted in parchment paper and topped with glazed almonds and caramel spirals.*

### YIELD: 4 SERVINGS

#### GLAZED ALMONDS

*5.3 oz/150 g sliced almonds*
*2 oz/57 g granulated sugar*
*.5 oz/14 g egg whites*

1. Preheat oven to 300°F (149°C). Lightly grease a sheet pan.

2. In a bowl, toss together almonds and sugar. Stir in egg whites until well mixed; spread onto sheet pan and bake, turning frequently, 15–20 minutes or until golden brown. Break up slightly.

#### RED WINE-GLAZED FRUIT

*2 plums*
*2 peaches*
*2 pears*
*1.47 oz/42 g honey*
*.95 oz/27 g brown sugar*
*1 liq oz/30 ml red wine*
*.5 oz/14 g ground cinnamon*

1. Preheat oven to 400°F (205°C). Cut fruit in quarters and remove pits or seeds.

2. In a bowl stir together remaining ingredients and toss with fruit.

3. Divide glazed fruit among 4 sheets of parchment paper, gathering up corners and securing with string to form packets. Roast in preheated oven (or wood oven, if desired) until tender, 20–30 minutes.

#### ASSEMBLY

*Pulled sugar spirals*
*Mint leaves*

1. Untie string on each packet and place on dessert plate.

2. Garnish with glazed almonds, pulled sugar sprials and mint leaves.

*Facing page: "When we decided to build a brasserie, we wanted a wood-burning oven," says Gale Gand. "So I tried to design food that would benefit from being cooked in this magnificent oven. The pears and peaches were the choice of that particular season."*

# WINGS OF SUGAR

. . . . . . . . . . . . . . . . . . . . . . . . . . . . . . . . . . . . . . . . . . . . . . . . . . . . .

ALAIN ROBY, HYATT REGENCY, CHICAGO, ILLINOIS

*A ginger-flavored crème caramel is garnished with fresh berry compote and julienned crystallized ginger.*

### YIELD: 12 SERVINGS

Special Equipment: Twelve 4 oz/113 g ramekins

#### CARAMEL
*10.5 oz/298 g granulated sugar*
*2 liq oz/59 ml water*

1. In a saucepan, combine sugar and water and cook to caramel stage. Immediately divide caramel among twelve 4 oz ramekins, swirling the caramel to evenly coat the bottom of each ramekin.

2. Set ramekins aside at room temperature.

#### GINGER CRÈME CARAMEL
*1 qt/.95 L milk*
*2 Tbs/24 g coarsely shredded ginger*
*1 vanilla bean, split*
*10.5 oz/298 g whole eggs*
*2.6 oz/74 g egg yolks*
*8 oz/227 g granulated sugar*

1. Preheat oven to 325°F (165°C).

2. In a saucepan, bring milk to a boil. Remove from heat, add ginger and vanilla bean and allow to infuse 10 minutes; strain.

3. In a large bowl, whisk together eggs, yolks and sugar. Gradually add the hot milk mixture to the egg mixture, whisking. Divide the mixture among the caramel-lined ramekins.

4. Bake the custards in a water bath until set, about 35 minutes. Cool and chill.

*Facing page: "When I was in Japan I created this dessert," says Alain Roby. "The problem is, people don't believe I can mass-produce this dessert, but I have produced 300 of them for a single dinner. Each swan takes me about 15 minutes."*

## ASSEMBLY

*Pulled sugar swans*
*Fresh berry compote*
*Julienned crystallized ginger*
*Dry ice*

1. Unmold crème caramels and place each on pulled sugar swan display piece. Garnish with fresh berry compote and crystallized ginger.

2. Before serving dessert, lay some dry ice around the base of the swan for a smoky effect.

*Dry ice is actually crystallized carbon dioxide. Touching dry ice with bare hands can result in burns. Always handle it with heavy tongs or heavy garden-type gloves.*

# PEAR BAVARIAN

. . . . . . . . . . . . . . . . . . . . . . . . . . . . . . . . . . . . . . .

CHRIS NORTHMORE, CHEROKEE TOWN & COUNTRY CLUB, ATLANTA, GEORGIA

*A timbale of pear Bavarian infused with pear purée, pear concentrate and Poire Williams is sprinkled with almond praline and chocolate ornaments. Poached pears and pear sorbet also appear.*

### YIELD: 25 SERVINGS

Special Equiptment: Twenty-five 2" (5 cm) ring molds, 2" (5 cm) in height

#### RASPBERRY SAUCE

*4 oz/113 g granulated sugar*
*1 oz/28 g Triquel instant thickener\**
*1.5 lb/680 g strained raspberry purée*
*1 liq oz/30 ml raspberry liqueur*

In a bowl, combine sugar and Triquel. Whisk the mixture into raspberry purée until thickened. Whisk in raspberry liqueur. Transfer the sauce to a squeeze bottle.

#### PEAR BAVARIAN

*6 oz/170 g granulated sugar, divided*
*4.5 oz/128 g egg yolks*
*2 Tbs plus .25 tsp/20 g powdered gelatin*
*1 pt/473 ml milk, divided*
*1 pt/473 ml heavy cream*
*1 pt/454 g Bartlett pear purée (from ripe pears)*
*8 oz/227 g pear concentrate*
*2 liq oz/59 ml Poire Williams liqueur*
*3 oz/85 g pasteurized egg whites*
*citric acid, to taste*

1. In a bowl, whisk together 4 oz (113 g) of the sugar and egg yolks.

2. Soften the gelatin in 4 oz (133 g) of the milk.

*\* Dreidoppel brand, available from Continental Foods, (800) 345–1543*

*Following page: "This is a modern variation of Pear Belle-Helene," says Chris Northmore. "It has similar flavors but a more dramatic presentation. Dramatic but simple — that's what I try to do with all my desserts if I can."*

PEAR BAVARIAN

3. Whip the cream to soft peaks and reserve.

4. Bring the remaining milk to a boil. Temper the yolks with some of the hot milk and add this mixture to the milk. Cook as an anglaise until thickened. Pour the hot anglaise over the bloomed gelatin to melt it. Stir the anglaise over ice until cool but not to the point of setting.

5. Add the pear purée, concentrate and liqueur.

6. In a mixer with whisk attachment, whip the whites and remaining 2 oz (57g) sugar to soft peaks and fold into the anglaise. Fold in the whipped cream. Add citric acid to taste.

7. Pipe the mixture into the 2" ring molds until 3/4 full.

8. Pipe the sauce directly into the center of each Bavarian. Fill with sauce until the cream comes up to the top of the mold. Seal off the hole with a bit of the Bavarian. Chill immediately.

*Pear Bavarian.*

**PEAR SORBET**

*1.5 lb/680 g Bartlett pear purée*
*1 pt/473 ml simple syrup (28° baume)*
*12 liq oz/355 ml water*
*Poire Williams liqueur, to taste*

Combine pear purée with syrup and water. Freeze in an ice cream machine. Add the Poire Williams during the last minute of freezing.

**ASSEMBLY**

*Leaf-shaped tuile cookies*
*Modelling chocolate*
*Cocoa powder*
*Almond praline, finely ground*
*Poached Pear sorbet slices*

1. Make a leaf-shaped tuile cookie and a stem from modeling chocolate to detail the pear shape stenciled on the plate.

2. Using a large pear stencil, dust plates with cocoa prior to service. Glue stem and leaf to the plate with melted chocolate.

3. Sprinkle the top of the Bavarian with some almond praline.

4. Leaving it in the mold, lift the Bavarian with a spatula and place it on the plate. Once in place, lift the ring mold off. (The ring should slip off easily. If you handle the Bavarian without the ring, the sauce inside may rupture the cream and spill out.)

5. Garnish each plate with poached pear slices and a quenelle of pear sorbet.

# E C L E C T I C I S M

*"When you do not know what you are doing and what you are doing is*

*the best — that is inspiration."*

ROBERT BRESSON

*"It's everyone's worst nightmare when I come in and say, 'This is what I*

*dreamed last night.'"*

JANET RIKALA

Apastry chef talks about creative inspiration: "A lot of it comes to me when I'm alone, during long drives, listening to music. I start drawing plate designs on a pad on the passenger seat. So I guess I'm not very safe to drive near, but I find it relaxing, and all these things will come to me in floods. I draw and write and list ingredients, and eventually I pair ingredients. Many desserts are created in this spurt, driving to loud rock and roll music—oh, and I sing, which is another reason I have to be alone."

Sources of visual inspiration for pastry chefs are as varied as the desserts in this chapter— *Eclectic Desserts,* which have *recognizable features from two or more other schools of plated desserts* as delineated in this book.

Pastry chefs talk about the things that spur their creativity: "Travel," says Gerard Partoens of the Peabody Hotel in Orlando, Florida. "Travel impels one to look at things with a sense of newness. It gets you away from the routine and forces you to take notice of your surroundings."

"Nightclubs," says Martin Howard of the Hudson River Club in New York City. "The clothing, the lighting. It helps to be constantly visually stimulated, and to be out there among the crazy people."

"The competition experience made me realize that I could develop my eye," says Martha Crawford of Johnson & Wales University. "My cleanness, sharpness. It has me thinking of new ideas."

**GERARD PARTOENS**
*Gerard Partoens, pastry chef at the Peabody Hotel in Orlando, was born on April 25, 1961, in Antwerp, Belgium. For six years he attended the Piva Hotel School, which provided a conventional curriculum along with pastry, baking, confectionery and glacier. "My mother was a garde manger. Her work was detailed but simple and elegant," says Partoens. "I always loved sweets, and always loved to make them." Partoens apprenticed at several patisseries before becoming head patissier at the exclusive Bruynseels Patisserie in St. Niklaas. He then came to America and won executive pastry chef positions at a series of hotels and resorts, including the Ritz-Carlton Mauna Lani, where he worked with Phillip Padovani, the Westin La Paloma in Tucson, the Scottsdale Princess and the Golden Mushroom in Southfield, Michigan. He joined the Peabody Orlando in 1995. "I love the profession," he says. "I don't know if I love the business." Ultimately Partoens would like to open a specialized, upscale glacier shop, bakery and deli. "I'd like to give everyone the opportunity to treat themselves a little more often."*

"One of the biggest influences to me is fashion," says Eric Bedoucha. "The windows in New York are the greatest in the world. So elegant and clean."

"I find inspiration in window designs," agrees Kurt Walrath of Rainbow! in New York City. "Some of the most creative people in New York do window designs."

Mary Cech of the Culinary Institute of America at Greystone, St. Helena, California, says she is inspired by art stores, jewelry stores, china, ceramic, furniture, hardware and plastic stores. "As a matter of fact, I have to keep out of stores or I get too inspired," she says.

Ann Amernick of Ann Amernick Cakes in Washington, D.C., says that her collection of antique children's books, art books, and Victorian scrapbooks inspire her. "I visualize things that are old, and I try to see shapes," she says. "I love oval."

"A lot of it is memory, things that evoke a good response," says Janet Rikala of Postrio in San Francisco. "Also, travel, museums and looking at books. Even the weather here, if it's a beautiful day, might influence what we prepare."

"Everyday experiences are factors of influence," agrees Eric Gouteyron of the Plaza Hotel in New York City. "But in order to adapt in the art of pastry, it will have to be handled with love and soul and an open mind."

# DARWIN, EINSTEIN, PICASSO, ET AL.

Creativity is more than inspiration, of course. Method must follow the madness. The contemporary writer Howard Gardner has written two books on the subject of creativity: *Art, Mind & Brain* and *Creating Minds.* In them, he tries to dispel the notion of the creative act as mystical, irrational and romantic, proceeding in stormy fits and starts. Certainly, there is magic in creativity, but there is also method, experience and labor.

In *Art, Mind & Brain,* Gardner follows the accounts of historian Howard Gruber, who studied Charles Darwin during Darwin's most creative and productive time of life, when he was developing his theory of evolution. What Gruber discovered was that, although many of Darwin's ideas tumbled forth chaotically, they were rigorously studied and ordered. According to his journals, Darwin gathered lists of thoughts, images, questions, dreams, sketches, comments and arguments. He constantly revised and reorganized. Insights that would eventually prove crucial might have been scribbled carelessly months before, discarded, only to be rediscovered later and fit into the puzzle.

Gruber generalized that the minds of creative people are constantly organizing the facts at their disposal and the theories they develop to create a synthesis, the path to which is often found in a dominant metaphor. In Darwin's case, a branching tree was the metaphor which best represented the evolutionary process he was seeking to define, but before the tree dominated he wrestled with metaphors of the evolutionary process as a river bank and as organs of a body. The creative person, according to Gruber and Gardner, also has a guiding purpose, an overt one, not a system of unconscious motivations; this purpose compels the creative person to develop the skills to achieve the purpose.

In his second book, *Creating Minds,* Gardner explores the creative lives and methods of people as diverse as Einstein, Picasso, Martha Graham, and Gandhi. Some generalities based on his findings: in producing revolutionary thought or work, an artist is system building — examining past concepts and phenomena relating to the problem and developing new models, rethinking. Each of the persons Gardner examines has different "symbol" or metaphor systems: Freud was strong in terms of language and was a sharp observer of people, while Einstein had few personal skills or interest in people and modest linguistic skills, but his thought was rich in visual-spatial images; many of the creative people Gardner studies have strong ties to child-

**MARTHA CRAWFORD**
*Martha Crawford, an instructor in the pastry arts program at Johnson & Wales University in Providence, Rhode Island, was born on June 20, 1962, in Philadelphia. She went to the Culinary Institute of America and, upon her graduation, took a job on the line at Country Epicure, working nights decorating cakes. Meanwhile, she looked for work elsewhere, and in 1986 she took a job at a new business, Desserts International, which had been opened a mere four months earlier by Gunter Heiland. "He was desperate for help, so he hired me," says Crawford. "I worked with him for eight years." Crawford eventually became Heiland's assistant. "I learned everything from him," she says. "He made me what I am today." In 1993, she joined the faculty of Johnson & Wales, teaching baking formulas, cake decoration, and plated desserts. "I feel I've found my niche in teaching," she says. "I feel that I have a lot to offer my students in terms of my experiences with Gunter."*

**PATRICIA MURAKAMI**
*Patricia Murakami, pastry chef at Chinois East/West in Sacramento, California, was born on November 28, 1951, in New Brunswick, New Jersey. She honed her skills in the pastry kitchens of the French restaurant at the Domaine Chandon winery, then took the position at Chinois East/West. "The restaurant was a work of art, the decor, the whole experience," says Murakami, "and they were doing such a great job at Fusion cooking. But there was no attention being paid to desserts. It was a crime, because the rest of the operation was so sophisticated, so perfect." Murakami continues to work the pastry kitchen of the original Chinois, even as the restaurant expands to several new locations. She is also acting as a consultant to food companies and creating special food events for select clients. "Some day I would like to have my own shop," says Murakami, "and I have definite ideas on what I want it to be—a European-style tea salon where you can purchase desserts to eat in and take out, with some savory foods."*

*RICHARD RUSKELL*
*Richard Ruskell, pas-*
*try chef at The*
*Phoenician in*
*Scottsdale, Arizona,*
*was born on November*
*7, 1956, in Nebraska*
*and was raised in*
*southern Minnesota,*
*and worked as a*
*breakfast cook*
*throughout college.*
*With ambitions as an*
*actor, he moved to New*
*York but had only modest success, so he enrolled at the French Culinary*
*Institute. When the six-month program was over, he was still not sure*
*what his specialization would be. "An instructor shook my hand and he*
*said, 'You have very cold hands, that would be good for pastry,'" Ruskell*
*remembers. "Then he added, 'Just remember that the pastry chef is always*
*the first to arrive and the last to leave, single quote'" Ruskell worked in a*
*series of hotels, including Hotel Maxxim's (now the Peninsula) and the*
*Stanhope, and undertook more training at Le Royal Grey in France. He*
*credits Jean Michel Diot and Jacques Chibois as major influences. "It was*
*exciting to see how they respected food over in France," he says. "I screwed*
*something up and Diot screamed at me in French, with someone translat-*
*ing behind me. It had to do with desserts coming from the heart. And it*
*does. It's a feeling thing. I think all good food comes from the heart."*

hood, in the sense of asking the fundamental, unexpected questions that children often raise, in the sense of joking, wordplay and daydreaming; they master the symbol system in their respective disciplines relatively early, but spend their lives stretching or changing it; they are all craftpersons, in the sense that they work regularly and with patience, their most important work often taking years and years to complete.

Cognitive scientists are still delving into the relationship between mundane activities and creative output, between memory and creativity, between invention and repetition...but such analysis in no way diminishes the beauty of works of creative art. A joke closely examined ceases to be funny, a poem deconstructed loses some of its magic...but a dessert examined head to toe will still taste as sweet.

## VISION AT 3 A.M.

Eclecticism is an honored school in the visual arts; it is the practice of borrowing and combining the stylistic features from other art movements or from the works of other artists. In theory, by taking what is best from other masterworks, the eclecticist can create work that surpasses the original.

The chefs in this chapter did not borrow from other chefs to create these plates, of course; creative inspiration is a blessing, but ingredients and equipment still call the tune in the pastry kitchen and inevitably limit the chef's options. And, of course, the schools defined in this book were recently minted by the authors and are being imposed on the chefs and their desserts.

Thus, who can say where the visions come from, the images that dance on the eyelids of chefs when they are conjuring tomorrow's plates? For many of the chefs in this book, creativity begins with visualization. And, in most instances, flavor is an essential part of the vision.

"I use a lot of visualization in my work," says Bruno Feldeisen of the Four Seasons Hotel in New York City. "If I am planning a pear dessert, I try to think of a pear on a plate. That helps me think of what will go with it. I let my unconscious work. Don't push it. Just let it come out. I almost smell it when I think of it."

"I taste it first in my imagination, then I visualize it," says Patricia Murakami of Chinois East/West in Sacramento. "It comes from my mind pretty quickly," says Judy Doherty of the Hyatt Regency Scottsdale. "I do get a vision of it but it will come to me at odd times, driving to the store or watching TV. I also look through southwestern art books and at Indian designs. I tend to get inspired that way." "I see forms in my head and try to find food that matches it," says Pat Coston, formerly of Moose's in San Francisco.

"I can see it visually, it comes to me right away," says Alain Roby of the Hyatt Regency Chicago. "Many of the decisions come to me during my drive to work. If the theme of an upcoming event is tropical, I will see colors; sand, sea, sun, tropical birds, flowers maybe. It must be something different. It cannot just be cake and sauce." "When I really need to come up with something, it always comes from my head. It's spontaneous," says Mary

Cech. "Flavor components come first, then the visual. I'm inspired at the conscious level but when conceiving it does come from the unconscious."

Janet Rikala uses her unconscious — sometimes to the chagrin of her staff. "One time, I dreamed of a sophisticated milk shake," she says. "So I came in and had my whole staff start making cookies in the shape of a milk shake glass and chocolate-coating them. It was difficult, tedious work. Then we found that at the lightest touch, the milk shake would spill out of the cookie. Well, it was a good idea at 3 a.m."

The plates found here running wild in the halls of the Eclectic school fall into no category, though there are obvious threads which tie them, by flavor or presentation, to one school or another. There is a strong vertical element in Richard Ruskell's Phoenician Crunch Cake, which might place it in the Architectural category, but the way the cookie peels away from the cake suggests a modernist touch, a statement, an ironic commentary. There are Neo-classic overtones to Jeff Barnes' Roasted Hazelnut-White Chocolate Mousse: the ring form is classic, the vivid colors of the sauce and fruit at its base are classic, but the sugar spiral rising very, very high off the plate is Architectural. Ruben Foster's Chocolate Sampler has one of the primary qualifications of an Architectural dessert — beautiful forms

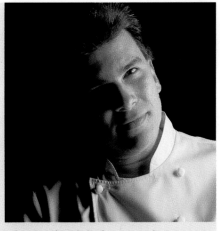

MARSHALL ROSENTHAL
*Marshall Rosenthal, Executive Pastry Chef of the Renaissance Harborplace Hotel in Baltimore, was born on September 10, 1959, in Baltimore. When he was 22 years old, Rosenthal took a job in a small soup-and-salad restaurant that was also equipped with a complete French-style boulangerie and pâtisserie. In his spare time, Rosenthal would observe and volunteer to help. Rosenthal took a series of jobs in bakeries in the Baltimore area before finding work in the pastry kitchens of the Hyatt Baltimore. He was then appointed pastry chef at the Hyatt in Greenville, South Carolina, before helping to open the Hyatt Grand Cypress as Assistant Pastry Chef. Leaving the Hyatt organization, he took the position of pastry chef at the Royal Sonesta in Boston before returning to Baltimore, and the Harborplace Hotel. A major avocation of Rosenthal's is the chocolate sculptures he creates for competitions and special events. "I enjoy what I do," he says. "Eventually I would like to teach. If you don't teach people what you know, then learning what you learned had no purpose at all."*

in a carefully composed arrangement — but some of the forms are pure geometry and others are modern or primitive. There are many towers in the Architectural chapter, but in Martha Crawford's Dueling Towers plate included here, one of the towers is deliberately upended, making this an exercise in form with no dominant vertical component; the vivid fruits and spray of sugar are Neo-classic touches. François Payard's Pistachio Cake wants to be Neo-classic — it has vivid fruit colors and simple, classic forms — but there is that pesky tuile in a sail form rising vertically, and that egg-like mound of mousse, a Minimalist touch; it's an exercise in harmonious colors and dissonant forms. Marshall Rosenthal's Tiramisù Grande contains Modernist forms (the letter 'A' cocoa tuile, the unfurling, rising tuile and the coil of sugar in co-dependence) as well as Architectural verticality and a classic recipe. The Architectural nature of Richard Leach's Glazed Coconut Custard Tart with Sorbet and Caramel Sauce lies solely in the tuile arches; the soul of this is a classic ring mold dessert.

These plates feature dazzling colors, unexpected forms and pleasing compositions: François Payard's serene pistachio green; the bright fruit colors of Jeff Barnes' Roasted Hazelnut-White Chocolate Mousse; Martha Crawford's contrasting colored towers with the brilliant fruit at their feet; the raspberry piggy tail protruding from the otherwise earth-toned tiramisù plate; the ultra-chocolate brown and blacks of the Chocolate Sampler; the pleasing brown and beige of the Phoenician Crunch Cake; the soaring arch of Richard Leach's Glazed Coconut Custard Tart with Sorbet and Caramel Sauce; the sheer verticality of the Phoenician Crunch Cake with, at its base, a joyous studded puddle of chocolate, praline and sauce; the whimsical sailboat form astride the stately Pistachio Cake; the luxuriant sugar spears of the Roasted Hazelnut-White Chocolate Mousse.

## WHAT'S IN THE WALK-IN?

To create such plates, no two chefs employ the same method. For example, John Hui: "The visual comes first. Then I think of the flow of it on the plate and the combination of flavors. Then I might diagram it, with all the different components." Fairly standard procedure so far, but then he adds: "My first visual is do-able — what I see, I can do. Usually it comes out exactly as I envision it." Far more chefs are like Ruben Foster: "I sketch very roughly," he says, "and it never ends up being what I drew."

Method can be nebulous: "As for the placement of the food on the plate, it's a gut feeling," says Richard Ruskell of the Phoenician in Scottsdale. "I can say that you want things off center, or that odd numbers are more interesting than even, but that isn't always true. Symmetry can be interesting too."

The practical approach works for others: "I'll see what's in the walk-in and go from there," says Jeff Barnes of the Ritz-Carlton, Palm Beach. "What's fresh and what needs to be used up. It's a business. That's where you can have fun, and I think that's where I've been most creative." "The ideas come from anywhere, but mostly — what time of year is it?" agrees Ruben Foster. "What type of fruit do I have? I think of the price range of the dessert I'm planning. Okay, I want chocolate, fruit sorbet, a poached fruit, something baked, so I have warm and cold. It has to be physical. You can't do food on paper. You have to work with what you have, and make it work for you."

"When I'm designing desserts, I have difficulty putting things on paper," says Norman Love of the Ritz-Carlton Hotel Company, Naples, Florida. "I work best in two different stages. I may be driving in my car or watching TV, and ideas will come to me. Then when I get to work, I start cutting pieces of chocolate and assembling molds."

"My philosophy is to follow the 1-2-3 step," says Gerard Partoens of the Peabody Hotel in Orlando. "Base, garnish, sauce, but add constructive and inventive design to every element. I try to contrast a classic component, such as almond cake, against the sweetness of chocolate and fruit — that is usually the start of my desserts. I use classic techniques and give them a modern twist."

"When I create a dessert, I work that recipe out on paper, usually late at night, alone in my office," says Hubert Keller. "I take the main ingredient and ask, what else will work with this? Then I think of my own favorites, and I wonder whether the public will like it. You have to ask, how will they respond? Then comes the creative step, the challenging part. We have to be a little bit different. Do we bake it? What kind of crust? A sauce? I like to play with the contrast, something cold, something hot, and play with textures and temperatures. I make a sketch. The next day we go into the kitchen and see how it works."

"I don't sketch, I do it all in my head, but I definitely see it visually," says Roxsand Scocos of RoxSand in Phoenix. "I approach any new formulation of a concept in a semi-organized way. Let's say peaches are coming into season. So I'll isolate the flavor of a peach and what it is I like about it. The first thing that comes to mind is the smell. I take apart the sensual components that make that item exciting and worth while. For me, the peach is fragrance, so I wouldn't want to distract from that. I would want to highlight it. The second concern is textural. Texture and smell are really important; they galvanize the taste. Some things don't taste like anything, but they have a lot of texture. A fruit mousse — you don't really taste the fruit. If I use a mousse I want it to taste like what it is. It's a matter of building a dessert that doesn't distract. From that point it's almost architecture. Form follows function — what is this thing's innate beauty?"

Imagination for visual presentation and the preparation of food—there are no limits, just as there seems to be no limit to the variety of foods the planet will provide, as evidenced by the Fusion chapter to follow. But imagination and creativity, as we've seen, are not the province of dark-cloaked, moody youths, brooding on the moors and coming up with desserts of uncanny flavor and boggling presentation. There is much to be said for method and maturity. "When I was 17, 18, I didn't have the vivid, quick imagination I have now," says Gerard Partoens. "When you're young you spend so much time worrying, what am I going to do? Younger people have awkwardness. They go too wild. Doing well is partly habit — if you have a variety of foods around and the proper background and training..."

The child's eye is important, then; but so is maturity. One sparks, the other guides. One is restless and fidgety and given to outbursts; the other is steady, calm, hard-working. "Having a playful attitude inspires me to create whimsical, fantastical desserts," concludes Partoens.

# SUMMER BERRIES WITH WHITE CHOCOLATE MOUSSE

GERARD PARTOENS, PEABODY HOTEL, ORLANDO, FLORIDA

*Circles of almond cake soaked in orange liqueur are topped with white chocolate-honey mousse and swim in a pool of fruit sauces studded with fresh fruit.*

## YIELD: 12 SERVINGS

### ALMOND CAKE

*6.3 oz/179 g egg whites*
*3.5 oz/99 g granulated sugar*
*6.25 oz/177 g almond flour*
*1.6 oz/45 g all-purpose flour*
*4 oz/113 g confectioners' sugar*

1. Preheat oven to 360°F (180°C). Line a half sheet pan with parchment paper.

2. In a mixer with whisk attachment, beat egg whites with sugar to stiff peaks.

3. Sift together almond flour, all-purpose flour and confectioners' sugar. Fold flour mixture into whipped egg whites. Spread batter into prepared pan and bake for 20 minutes or until set.

### WHITE CHOCOLATE MOUSSE

*18.6 liq oz/550 ml heavy cream, divided*
*2 Tbs/24 g honey*
*8 oz/227 g white chocolate couverture, finely chopped*

1. In a saucepan, bring 5.3 liq oz (157 ml) heavy cream to boil. Stir in honey. Pour hot cream over white chocolate. Whisk until chocolate is melted. Cover and chill at least 4 hours.

2. Whisk together white chocolate ganache and remaining 13.3 liq oz (393 ml) heavy cream until stiff peaks form.

### ASSEMBLY

*Orange liqueur*

*Page 260: "There is a reason that the Masters painted fruit in so many of their works," says Gerard Partoens. "It is a simple, natural way to portray beauty. I always use fruit to give the plate a luscious, succulent appeal."*

1. Cut twelve 3 1/2" (8.9 cm) circles of almond cake. Place on baking sheet and soak with orange liqueur.

2. Fill a pastry bag fitted with a medium plain tip with white chocolate mousse. Pipe mousse onto rounds to a height of 1 1/4" (3.2 cm). Set aside while making white chocolate fans.

### WHITE CHOCOLATE FANS

*2 liq oz/59 ml vegetable oil*
*2 lbs, 3 oz/992 g white chocolate couverture, melted and tempered*

1. Whisk oil into tempered chocolate. Pour fine line of chocolate onto marble slab. Spread evenly in long strip. Just before chocolate sets, form fans with palette knife.

2. Immediately place the fans around the top edge of the prepared mousse rounds, leaving a hole in the center for berries.

### PLATING

*Assorted fruit sauces, such as raspberry, mango and kiwi*
*Assorted berries*
*Cocoa powder*

1. Pipe concentric rings of fruit sauces on dessert plate. Secure plate with clay to turntable and spin forcibly to achieve an abstract plate design.

2. Place dessert in center of plate and decorate center of mousse ring with assorted berries and a dusting of cocoa powder.

# DUELING TOWERS

............................................................

M A R T H A  C R A W F O R D,  J O H N S O N  &  W A L E S  U N I V E R S I T Y,  P R O V I D E N C E,  R H O D E  I S L A N D

*Towers of chocolate molded from dark chocolate and white chocolate enclose rum-scented bittersweet mousse and orange-scented white chocolate mousse. Raspberry sauce, fresh fruit and caramelized sugar sticks complete the dessert.*

### Y I E L D :  2 0  S E R V I N G S

Special Equipment: Forty 1 3/4" x 4" high (4.45 x 10 cm) tube molds.

#### D A R K  T O W E R S

*4 oz/113 g white chocolate, tempered*
*8 oz/227 g semisweet chocolate, tempered*

1. Cut 20 pieces of acetate to fit inside a 1 3/4" diameter x 4" high tube mold.

2. Lay the plastic pieces on a piece of parchment paper. Place a small amount of white tempered chocolate into a parchment cone and pipe diagonal lines across the plastic. The lines should be approximately 1/8" (.32 cm) apart. Pipe criss-crossing lines 1/8" (.32 cm) apart to create a lattice effect. Allow the chocolate to set completely.

3. Once the white chocolate has hardened, spread a thin layer of dark chocolate on top of the white lines. Let chocolate set just a few minutes. Pick up each plastic strip and place inside of each tube with the plastic side against the mold. Let set until completely hardened.

#### W H I T E  T O W E R S

*4 oz/113 g semisweet chocolate, tempered*
*8 oz/227 g white chocolate, tempered*

1. Cut 20 pieces of acetate to fit inside a 1 3/4" diameter x 4" high tube mold.

2. Lay the plastic pieces on a piece of parchment paper and place a small amount of dark tempered chocolate into a parchment cone and pipe lines across the plastic. The lines should be approximately 1/8" (.32 cm) apart. Then pipe lines in the other direction 1/8" (.32 cm) apart. This will create a lattice effect. Let the chocolate cool and become hard.

*Facing page: "I was just playing around with two towers and came up with this," says Martha Crawford. "I wanted something modern—I don't make things to represent anything else."*

3. Once the dark chocolate has hardened, spread a thin layer of white chocolate on top of the dark lines. Let chocolate set just a few minutes. Pick up each plastic strip and place inside of each tube with the plastic side against the mold. Let set until completely hardened.

### WHITE CHOCOLATE MOUSSE

*13 liq oz/384 ml heavy cream*
*4.5 oz/128 g egg yolks*
*2.5 oz/71 g granulated sugar*
*.25 oz/7 g powdered gelatin*
*5 liq oz/148 ml milk, divided*
*4.5 oz/128 g white chocolate, finely chopped*
*vanilla extract, to taste*
*Triple Sec, to taste*

1. Whip cream to soft peaks and set aside.

2. In a bowl over simmering water, whisk together yolks and sugar until light and fluffy and the mixture reaches 140°F (60°C).

3. Soften gelatin in 2 liq oz (59 ml) of the milk. Heat in a water bath until dissolved. Place the white chocolate in a bowl.

4. Place remaining milk in a saucepan and bring to a boil. Pour over the white chocolate. Let sit for 1 minute then stir until smooth. Add the melted gelatin and stir until combined.

5. Fold the yolk mixture into the chocolate mixture and let cool until it starts to become slightly thickened. Add the flavorings.

6. Carefully fold in the whipped cream. Scrape mousse into pastry bag fitted with plain tip and pipe into prepared dark chocolate-lined tube molds, filling them completely. Level top of tubes with spatula and chill until mousse is set, at least 4 hours.

7. Carefully remove mousse tubes from molds and peel away acetate. Chill until serving.

### DARK CHOCOLATE MOUSSE

*9 liq oz/266 ml heavy cream*
*6 oz/170 g semisweet chocolate, finely chopped*
*3.25 oz/92 g egg yolks*
*4.5 oz/128 g granulated sugar, divided*
*2.5 oz/71 g egg whites*
*2 liq oz/59 ml dark rum*
*rum extract, to taste*
*vanilla extract, to taste*

1. Whip the heavy cream to soft peaks and set aside.

2. Place chopped chocolate in a bowl and melt over a double boiler.

3. Place egg yolks and 2.25 oz (64 g) sugar in a bowl and place over a double boiler. Whisking constantly, bring yolk mixture to 140°F (60°C).

4. Beat the egg whites and remaining sugar to stiff peaks.

5. Stir flavorings into yolk mixture and then fold yolk mixture into the chocolate mixture.

6. Fold whipped cream into chocolate mixture and then fold in beaten egg whites. Scrape the mousse into a pastry bag fitted with a plain tip and pipe it into the prepared white chocolate-lined tube molds, filling them completely. Level tops of molds with spatula and chill until mousse is set, at least 4 hours.

7. Carefully remove mousse tubes from molds and peel away acetate. Chill until serving.

### SPUN SUGAR
*8 oz/227 g granulated sugar, divided*

1. Place 1/2 of the sugar into a stainless steel pot. Constantly stir the sugar until it becomes a light brown caramel.

2. Slowly add the remaining amount of sugar until all the sugar is a light golden brown color.

3. Remove the pot from the heat and shock the bottom of it in cold water to cool the sugar and make it begin to thicken.

4. Once thickened, place a fork into the sugar and wave it back and forth over 2 dowels placed over the edge of a table, creating strands of sugar. Repeat until the sugar has completely hardened.

### ASSEMBLY
*Bow stencil (cut to fit dessert plate)*
*Cocoa powder for dusting bow stencil*
*Raspberry sauce*
*Raspberries*
*Blueberries*
*Kiwis, peeled and sliced*

1. Place 5" x 5 1/2" (12.7 x 14 cm) bow stencil (see pattern) on dessert plate and dust with cocoa powder.

2. Place white chocolate mousse tower on center of plate, laying it down.

3. Place dark chocolate mousse tower on plate next to the white tower, standing it up. Garnish plate with raspberry sauce and fruit.

4. Place raspberry sauce in a squeeze bottle and pipe around the base of the chocolate tower in a circle. Garnish plate with fruit and spun sugar.

# PISTACHIO CAKE

. . . . . . . . . . . . . . . . . . . . . . . . . . . . . . . . . . . . . . . . . . . . . .

FRANÇOIS PAYARD, RESTAURANT DANIEL, NEW YORK, NEW YORK

*Pistachio accented with chocolate and a hint of tartness: A pistachio biscuit layered with pistachio Bavaroise is lightly flavored with kirsch and praline and topped with a quenelle of milk chocolate chantilly cream.*

### YIELD: 12 SERVINGS

Special Equipment: Twelve 3" (7.6 cm) ring molds
Wood grain impression tool

#### MILK CHOCOLATE PRALINE LAYER

*4.4 oz/124 g hazelnut praline*
*4.4 oz/124 g hazelnut butter*
*2.2 oz/63 g milk chocolate, melted and cooled to 35–40°F (2–4°C)*
*4.4 oz/124 g crushed feuilleté or oven-toasted rice cereal*
*.88 oz/25 g unsalted butter, melted and cooled to room temperature*

1. In a mixing bowl, stir together all ingredients until combined. Spread onto parchment-lined sheet pan to a thickness of 1/4" (.63 cm). Chill until set.

2. Cut chocolate praline into 2" (5 cm) rounds and set aside.

#### VANILLA TUILE

*3.8 oz/108 g egg whites*
*3.5 oz/99 g confectioners' sugar*
*3.5 oz/99 g all-purpose flour*
*1 vanilla bean, split and scraped*
*3.5 oz/99 g unsalted butter, melted and boiled slowly for 1 minute*

1. In a bowl of a electric mixer, whisk together egg whites and sugar over simmering water until sugar is dissolved. Place bowl in mixer stand fitted with whisk attachment and beat on medium speed; gradually add the flour and vanilla bean seeds and beat until smooth. Beat in the warm butter and mix until smooth. Cover bowl and chill batter several hours or overnight.

2. Preheat oven to 350°F (175°C). Spread a 1/8" (.32 cm) thick layer of batter across a silicon baking mat. Bake the tuile half way, about 5 minutes, just until the batter is set but still white. With a rolling wheel cutter, cut the tuile sheet into 3 1/2" x 1 1/2" (8.9 x 3.8 cm) triangles. Just below the tip of each

*Facing page: "Many desserts look beautiful but their taste is often disappointing," says François Payard. "My desserts can look simple, but once you involve the stomach, you forget about looks."*

triangle stamp out a small hole (that a cigarette can fit through) with a plain pastry tip. Return the mat to the oven and bake until the tuiles are golden, about 5 minutes. Remove the tuiles from the oven and immediately bend them over a bain-marie or jar. Cool completely.

### BISCUIT

*9.9 oz/280 g almond flour*
*11.3 oz/320 g confectioners' sugar, sifted*
*12.7 oz/360 g egg whites*
*1 liq oz/30 ml lemon juice*
*4.2 oz/119 g granulated sugar, divided*
*1.75 oz/50 g pistachio paste*
*1.5 oz/43 g chopped pistachio nuts*

1. Preheat oven to 400°F (205°C). Line a sheet pan with parchment paper. In a bowl, combine almond flour and confectioners' sugar; set aside.

2. In a mixer with whisk attachment, beat egg whites with lemon juce and 1/3 of the granulated sugar on medium speed, gradually beating in the remaining sugar. Beat on high speed until the whites form stiff peaks. Stir a small amount of the whites into the pistachio paste; fold the pistachio mixture into the remaining whites along with the flour mixture. Scrape batter into prepared sheet pan and sprinkle with chopped nuts.

3. Bake until golden, about 10 minutes. Cool; cut out twelve 3" (7.6 cm) rounds and twelve 2" (5 cm) rounds from the biscuit.

### PISTACHIO BAVAROISE

*6.7 oz/190 g pistachio paste*
*25.4 liq oz/750 ml milk*
*9.5 oz/269 g egg yolks*
*4.1 oz/115 g granulated sugar*
*8 gelatin sheets, soaked in cold water*
*.84 liq oz/25 ml kirsch*

1. Place pistachio paste in a saucepan and gradually whisk in milk. Bring mixture to a boil.

2. Meanwhile, in a mixer with whisk attachment, beat yolks and sugar to ribbon stage. While mixing at low speed, pour some of the hot milk mixture into the yolk mixture to temper it. Pour the entire mixture into the saucepan and cook, whisking, until thickened (178°F [81°C]). Add the drained gelatin and stir until smooth.

3. Line a hotel pan with plastic wrap. Strain the Bavaroise mixture through a chinois into the prepared pan. Cover with plastic wrap and refrigerate until cold.

### MILK CHOCOLATE CHANTILLY

*12.2 liq oz/360 ml heavy cream*
*8.5 oz/241 g milk chocolate, finely chopped*

1. In a saucepan, bring cream to boil. Add the chocolate and whisk until smooth.

2. Cover and chill several hours or overnight.

## CHOCOLATE PISTACHIO WOOD GRAIN DECOR
*9 oz/255 g bittersweet chocolate, melted and tempered*

Spread chocolate out on silicon baking mat. Before it sets, drag a wood grain tool over it (See illustrations *a* and *b* below). Allow to set completely; set aside.

### ASSEMBLY
*28.7 liq oz/850 ml heavy cream*
*Vanilla crème anglaise*
*Shelled pistachio nuts*
*Chocolate cigarettes*
*Mint sprigs*

1. Place ring molds on parchment-lined sheet pan. Place a 3" (7.6 cm) biscuit round, nut side up, in the bottom of each mold.

2. Remove pistachio Bavaroise from refrigerator and whisk in kirsch. Whisk the mixture over a very low flame just until smooth (do not warm it).

3. Beat the 24 liq oz/850 ml of heavy cream to stiff peaks. Gently fold the whipped cream into the Bavaroise mixture. Place the mousse into a pastry bag fitted with a plain tip.

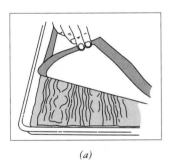 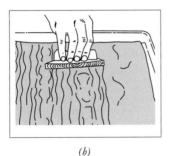  

*(a)*        *(b)*        *(c)*        *(d)*

4. Pipe a small amount of mousse on top of the biscuit in ring molds. Place a praline round on top of the mousse. Pipe on another layer of mousse. Place the 2" (5 cm) biscuit round, nut side down, on top, and cover with another layer of mousse, filling the mold. Level off each mold with a spatula. Freeze the molds for several hours.

5. Spread some of the remaining pistachio mousse onto the chocolate woodgrain decor in a thin layer (see illustration *c* above). Freeze until set.

6. Cut the chocolate-pistachio decor into 3" (7.6 cm) rounds (see illustration *d* above).

7. Two hours before serving, unmold the cakes. Place a woodgrain decor round on top of each cake and place in refrigerator.

8. Slowly whip the milk chocolate chantilly until thick; do not overwhip or it will become grainy. With hot spoons, form quenelles from the chantilly and refrigerate.

9. Place the pistachio cake on dessert plate. Set a tuile standing up alongside the cake. Place a chantilly quenelle in front of the tuile to anchor it. Insert a chocolate cigarette into the hole in the tuile. Spoon some vanilla crème anglaise onto the plate randomly and garnish with pistachio nuts and mint.

# PHOENICIAN CRUNCH CAKE

. . . . . . . . . . . . . . . . . . . . . . . . . . . . . . . . . . . . . . . . . . . . . . . . .

RICHARD RUSKELL, THE PHOENICIAN, PHOENIX, ARIZONA

*A toffee cake layered with bittersweet ganache and honey caramel and topped with ganache is served with vanilla crunch ice cream. The dessert is served with chocolate and caramel sauces. "I was in a caramel phase at the time," admits Richard Ruskell.*

### YIELD: 24 SERVINGS

#### TOFFEE CAKE

*12 oz/340 g unsalted butter*
*10.5 oz/298 g granulated sugar*
*1.5 lb/680 all-purpose flour*
*25.5 liq oz/754 ml buttermilk*
*.75 oz/21 g baking soda*
*5.25 oz/149 g whole eggs*
*1 Tbs/12 ml vanilla extract*
*12 oz/340 g Heath Bar, crushed*
*12 oz/340 g sugar-toasted pecans, crushed*

1. Preheat oven to 350° F (175°C). Butter 3 half sheet pans and dust with flour.

2. In a mixer with paddle attachment, cream together butter, sugar and flour until smooth.

3. In a mixing bowl, whisk together the buttermilk, baking soda, eggs and vanilla. Add to the flour mixture.

4. Divide evenly among the 3 pans. Sprinkle each pan with Heath Bar pieces and pecans. Bake for 20 minutes or until golden and firm. Cool.

#### GANACHE

*32.5 liq oz/961 ml heavy cream*
*2 lb 12 oz/1.25 k bittersweet chocolate, chopped*

Bring cream to a boil. Pour over chocolate and mix until smooth. Cool.

*Facing page: "My chef asked me if I would make something from his childhood—a Heath Bar cake," recalls Richard Ruskell. "I told him I didn't want to make something that other people were making, but I started playing around with the idea until I came up with something I could call my own. Not everything needs height, but if you can get it, hey, go for it."*

### CARAMEL LAYER

*14 oz/397 g granulated sugar*
*7 liq oz/207 ml honey*
*1.75 oz/50 g trimoline*
*28 liq oz/828 ml heavy cream, warmed*
*2 oz/57 g unsalted butter, cubed*

1. In a saucepan, heat sugar, honey and trimoline to 360°F (180°C).

2. Add the heavy cream and butter, stir until the butter melts and immediately pour over one of the layers of the toffee cake.

### ASSEMBLY

*4 oz/113 g Heath Bar, chopped*
*4 oz/113 g sugar-toasted pecans, chopped*

1. Spread half of the ganache on the first cake layer and top with the layer that is covered with caramel. Sprinkle this layer with Heath Bar and pecans.

2. Top with the third cake layer and freeze.

3. Warm the remaining ganache and spread over the entire cake. Let cool and slice.

### CHOCOLATE SAUCE

*1.75 liq oz/52 ml water*
*1.5 oz/43 g unsalted butter*
*2.25 oz/64 g granulated sugar*
*1.5 liq oz/44 ml corn syrup*
*1.5 oz/43 g extra-bitter chocolate, chopped*
*.5 oz/14 g cocoa powder*
*1 Tbs/15 ml vanilla extract*

In a saucepan, bring water, butter, sugar and corn syrup to boil. Add chocolate and cocoa powder and boil for 2 minutes more. Mix until smooth. Strain, add vanilla and cool.

### CARAMEL SAUCE

*1 lb 5 oz/595g granulated sugar*
*2 liq oz/59 ml lemon juice*
*1 lb/454 g crème fraîche, warmed*

Heat sugar and lemon juice to 370°F (188°C). Remove from heat and slowly add crème fraîche. Return to boil, stirring constantly and cool.

### CRUNCH MIX

*4 oz/113 g Grape Nuts cereal*
*5 oz/142 g bittersweet chocolate, melted*
*8 oz/227 g Heath Bars, crushed*

1. Coat the cereal with chocolate, add crushed Heath Bar and spread onto sheet pan; cool.

2. Break into small pieces.

### PHOENICIAN CRUNCH ICE CREAM
*16.24 liq oz/480 ml heavy cream*
*17 liq oz/502 ml milk*
*2 vanilla beans, split and scraped*
*6.5 oz/186 g egg yolks*
*3 oz/89 g granulated sugar*
*1 lb/454 g crunch mix (recipe above)*

1. In a saucepan, combine the heavy cream, milk and vanilla seeds and bring to a boil.

2. Whisk the yolks with the sugar until smooth. Temper yolks with milk mixture. Return mixture to the saucepan and cook until thickened. Strain and cool in an ice bath. Freeze in ice cream machine.

3. After processing, fold crunch mix into ice cream and freeze.

### WHITE TUILE
*8 oz/227 g confectioners' sugar*
*4.5 oz/128 g unsalted butter, melted*
*5.5 oz/156 g all-purpose flour*
*6.3 oz/179 g egg whites*

1. Preheat oven to 300°F (149°C).

2. In a mixer with the paddle attachment, combine sugar, butter and flour. Add egg whites gradually at high speed and mix until smooth.

3. On a nonstick baking sheet, spread batter thinly into desired shape. Bake for 6–8 minutes or until firm to the touch.

4. Remove from oven, bend tuile to desired form, and allow to cool completely.

5. Store in an airtight container.

### FINAL ASSEMBLY
Place the cake on a dessert plate, standing on end, with 1 scoop of ice cream. Decorate with tuiles and chocolate and caramel sauces.

# TIRAMISÙ GRANDE

. . . . . . . . . . . . . . . . . . . . . . . . . . . . . . . . . . . . . . . . . . . . . . . . .

MARSHALL ROSENTHAL, RENAISSANCE HARBORPLACE HOTEL, BALTIMORE, MARYLAND

*Chocolate and vanilla sponge layers are soaked in espresso syrup. The chocolate layer is topped with bittersweet ganache and the vanilla layer with rum-scented mascarpone cheese. Crème anglaise, raspberry sauce, chocolate spirals and marbled sweet biscuit triangles complete this dessert.*

### YIELD: 12 SERVINGS

#### CHOCOLATE SPONGE LAYER
*1.75 oz/50 g sifted cake flour*
*2 Tbs/24 g dark cocoa powder*
*5.25 oz/149 g whole eggs*
*4 oz/113 g granulated sugar*
*.75 Tbs/10 g unsalted butter, melted*
*1 tsp/4 ml bourbon vanilla extract*

1. Preheat oven to 350°F (175°C). Line a half sheet pan with parchment.

2. Sift together cake flour and cocoa powder; set aside.

3. In a mixer with whip attachment, beat eggs and sugar on medium-high speed until light and fluffy.

4. Gently fold flour mixture into egg mixture. Fold in the melted butter and vanilla.

5. Spread batter into prepared pan and bake 10 minutes or until set. Cool.

#### LADYFINGER SPONGE LAYER
*1.95 oz/55 g egg yolks*
*3 oz/85 g granulated sugar, divided*
*3.15 oz/89 g egg whites*
*3.25 oz/92 g sifted cake flour*

1. Preheat oven to 375°F (190°C). Line a half sheet pan with parchment.

2. In a mixer with whip attachment, beat yolks with 1 oz (28 g) of the sugar at medium-high speed until light and fluffy. Transfer to a large bowl.

*Facing page: "Pastry is perfection," says Marshall Rosenthal. "It is very important that your lines be perfect and your cuts straight. If it's not perfect, it's not going to work."*

3. In a mixer with clean bowl and whisk attachment, beat egg whites at medium speed, gradually adding the remaining 2 oz (57 g) sugar. Beat until stiff.

4. Gently fold egg whites into yolk mixture.

5. Lightly fold in cake flour. Spread batter into prepared pan and bake 10–12 minutes until golden brown. Cool on rack.

### CHOCOLATE FILLING

*10 oz/283 g semisweet chocolate, finely chopped*
*8 liq oz/237 ml heavy cream*

1. Melt chocolate over bain-marie.

2. In a saucepan, bring cream to a gentle boil and slowly whisk into melted chocolate. Set mixture aside.

### ESPRESSO SOAKING SYRUP

*8 oz/227 g granulated sugar*
*8 liq oz/237 ml water*
*1.25 Tbs/16 g instant espresso powder*

1. In a saucepan, combine sugar and water and bring to boil.

2. Remove from heat and whisk in espresso powder until completely dissolved.

### MARBLED SWEET BISCUIT TRIANGLES

*8 oz/227 g unsalted butter*
*4 oz/113 g granulated sugar*
*1.75 oz/50 g whole eggs*
*.5 oz/15 ml vanilla extract*
*6 oz/170 g bread flour*
*6 oz/170 g pastry flour*
*.25 oz/7 g dark cocoa powder*

1. In a mixer with paddle attachment, cream butter and sugar until smooth. Beat in egg and vanilla.

2. In a bowl, combine bread and pastry flours. Gradually add flours to butter mixture and mix just until incorporated. Form dough into disk, wrap in plastic and chill 30 mintues.

3. Place dough on a lightly floured work surface and sift cocoa powder directly onto dough. Lightly fold the dough to incorporate the cocoa, but do not overknead. There should be streaks of cocoa in the dough.

4. Roll dough out to 1/8" (.32 cm) thickness. Using a stencil as a guide, cut out 12 triangles measuring 8" (19.6 cm) on two sides and 1 3/4" (4.45 cm) at base. Transfer triangles to sheet pan.

5. Bake at 350°F (175°C) 15 minutes or until golden. Cool.

### MASCARPONE FILLING

*.5 oz/14 g powdered gelatin*
*4 liq oz/118 ml dark rum*
*15.75 oz/447 g whole eggs*
*1 lb/454 g granulated sugar, divided*
*.5 liq oz/15 ml light corn syrup*
*6 liq oz/177 ml water*
*34 oz/964 g mascarpone cheese*

1. In a small bowl, sprinkle gelatin over rum; set aside.

2. In a mixer with whisk attachment, beat eggs with 2 oz (57 g) of the sugar at medium speed until light and fluffy. Reduce speed slightly and continue to mix while preparing syrup.

3. In a small saucepan, combine remaining 14 oz (397 g) of sugar with corn syrup and water and cook to a very light amber color. Remove from heat immediately and add in a fine stream to egg mixture while continuing to beat. Beat until cool.

4. Place bowl of gelatin in water bath over heat and stir until dissolved.

5. In a medium bowl, stir mascarpone cheese to soften. Slowly add cooled egg mixture to cheese, stirring until no lumps remain.

6. Temper gelatin with about 8 liq oz (237 ml) of the cheese mixture. Fold the gelatin mixture into the cheese mixture.

### ASSEMBLY

*Cocoa powder*
*Crème anglaise*
*Raspberry coulis*
*Chocolate spirals*
*Pulled sugar spirals*

1. Cut the chocolate sponge layer and ladyfinger layer to fit into a half hotel pan. Carefully peel off the fine "skin" layer of the sponge cake.

2. Place the chocolate sponge layer in the bottom of a half hotel pan and soak with 1/2 of the espresso syrup. Scrape the chocolate filling over the cake and spread evenly. Top with the ladyfinger layer, pressing down firmly. Soak the ladyfinger layer with the remaining espresso syrup.

3. Top with the mascarpone filling. Chill, uncovered, 8 hours. Dust with cocoa before serving. Cut tiramisù into squares and garnish plate with crème anglaise, raspberry coulis, marbled sweet biscuit triangles, chocolate spirals and pulled sugar spirals.

1. In a saucepan, bring cream to a boil. Place chocolate in mixer with paddle attachment and pour cream over. Mix on low speed until chocolate is completely melted. Pour into half hotel pan, cool and chill.

2. Cut ganache into 1" (2.5 cm) cubes. Dredge each cube in cocoa powder.

### CHOCOLATE POTS DE CRÈME
*1 qt/.95 L heavy cream*
*12 oz/340 g bittersweet chocolate, chopped*
*8.75 oz/248 g whole eggs*
*8 oz/227 g granulated sugar*

1. Preheat oven to 350°F (175°C). In a saucepan, bring cream to boil. Remove from heat; add chocolate to hot cream and stir until chocolate is melted.

2. In a bowl, whisk eggs and sugar together. Add some of the chocolate mixture to the egg mixture to temper; add the remaining chocolate mixture. Pour into a hotel pan and bake in a water bath 30–35 minutes. Cool and chill. Cut into 1 5/8" (4.1 cm) disks and return to refrigerator.

### CHOCOLATE SORBET
*12 oz/340 g bittersweet chocolate, chopped*
*4 oz/113 g cocoa powder, sifted*
*1 qt/.95 L water*
*1 lb/454 g granulated sugar*

1. In a bowl, combine chocolate and cocoa powder.

2. In a saucepan, cook water and sugar until sugar is dissolved and syrup is boiling. Remove from heat and cool for 1 minute. Pour hot syrup over chocolate and stir until completely melted.

3. Strain the mixture through a fine chinois and chill. Freeze in an ice cream machine.

### CHOCOLATE MOUSSE
*14.8 oz/420 g egg yolks*
*4.6 oz/130 g granulated sugar*
*4 liq oz/118 ml heavy cream*
*14 oz/397 g bittersweet chocolate, melted*
*20 liq oz/591 ml heavy cream, whipped to soft peaks*

1. In a mixer with whisk attachment, beat yolks with sugar until light. Add heavy cream and mix just until combined. Remove the bowl from mixer stand and add the warm melted chocolate all at once, stirring until combined.

2. Fold 1/3 of the whipped cream into the chocolate-yolk mixture; fold in the remaining whipped cream.

### CHOCOLATE SAUCE
*13.3 liq oz/393 ml water*
*10.5 oz/298 g granulated sugar*

*2 Tbs/24 g cornstarch*
*3 oz/85 g bittersweet chocolate, chopped*
*1.7 oz/48 g cocoa powder*

1. In a saucepan, bring 11.3 liq oz (339 ml) water and sugar to a boil.

2. In a small bowl, dissolve cornstarch in remaining water. Stir cornstarch mixture into sugar syrup; simmer 3 minutes.

3. Add chocolate and cocoa to syrup and stir until melted. Bring sauce to boil and boil for 2 minutes. Strain and cool in an ice bath.

### VANILLA PRALINE SAUCE

*16 liq oz/473 ml milk*
*16 liq oz/473 ml heavy cream*
*14 oz/397 g granulated sugar, divided*
*1 vanilla bean, split and scraped*
*6.3 oz/179 g egg yolks*
*2 oz/57 g praline paste*

1. In a saucepan, bring milk, heavy cream, 7 oz/198 g of the sugar and vanilla bean to boil.

2. In a bowl, whisk together yolks and the remaining 7 oz/198 g of sugar until blended. Gradually whisk in 1/2 of the hot milk mixture. Return the entire mixture to the saucepan and cook, stirring constantly, until mixture coats the back of a spoon. Whisk in praline paste. Chill the sauce over an ice bath.

### CHOCOLATE SPRITZ COOKIES

*12 oz/340 g unsalted butter*
*7 oz/198 g confectioners' sugar*
*3.5 oz/99 g whole eggs*
*1 lb/454 g cake flour*
*4 oz/113 g cocoa powder*

1. Preheat oven to 350°F (175°C). Line a baking sheet with parchment paper. In a mixer with paddle attachment, cream together butter and sugar until smooth. Gradually beat in eggs.

2. Sift together flour and cocoa powder and add to butter mixture at low speed. Fill a pastry bag with the batter and, using a plain tip (Ateco #3), pipe out cookies in decorative design. Bake 12–15 minutes. Cool completely.

### CHOCOLATE MARZIPAN

*9.9 oz/280 g confectioners' sugar*
*1.9 oz/54 g cocoa powder*
*13.9 oz/395 g almond paste*
*2.9 oz/87 ml corn syrup*

1. Sift together confectioners' sugar and cocoa powder. In a mixer with paddle attachment, combine marzipan with dry ingredients and corn syrup until combined.

2. Turn the marzipan onto a work surface and knead it until it is smooth. Roll out chocolate marzipan to 1/8" (.32 cm).thickness. With a 4 1/4" (10.8 cm) fluted round cutter, cut out rounds and set aside.

## ASSEMBLY

*Forty-eight 1 1/2" (3.8 cm) chocolate disks*
*Melted bittersweet chocolate*
*Deep-fried linguini, dusted with cocoa powder*
*Chocolate triangles*

1. Place a chocolate marzipan round in the center of dessert plate. Pour chocolate sauce into a squeeze bottle and pipe a wavy ring of sauce around the disk. Pipe dots of vanilla praline sauce around plate.

2. Place a chocolate disk on top of the marzipan round, near the edge. Pipe a small amount of chocolate mousse onto the chocolate disk; repeat layering twice, and top with another chocolate disk.

3. Place a chocolate pot de crème round next to the layered mousse, toward the back of the marzipan disk. Place a ganache cube on top of the pot de crème.

4. Using melted chocolate, "glue" a chocolate spritz cookie to the marzipan disk, positioning it behind the mousse layers. Glue the pasta sticks and triangle garnish to the marzipan disk, positioning them behind the spritz cookie.

5. Dip one end of the biscotti into melted chocolate and place it behind the pot de crème.

6. Place a scoop of sorbet at the front of the disk and serve immediately.

# GLAZED COCONUT CUSTARD TART WITH SORBET AND CARAMEL SAUCE

. . . . . . . . . . . . . . . . . . . . . . . . . . . . . . . . . . . . . . . .

R I C H A R D   L E A C H ,   L A   C ô T E   B A S Q U E ,   N E W   Y O R K ,   N E W   Y O R K

*Creamy glazed coconut custard is complemented by its macaroon crust and the pool of caramelized coconut crème anglaise. Honey tuiles and coconut sorbet add crunch and coolness.*

## Y I E L D :   8   S E R V I N G S

Special Equipment: Eight 4" (10 cm) ring molds
Eight 4" (10 cm) ramekins

### MACAROON CRUST

*7 oz/198 g unsweetened coconut*
*8.6 liq oz/254 ml light corn syrup*
*3.5 oz/99 g granulated sugar*
*6 oz/170 g egg whites*
*2.1 oz/60 g all-purpose flour*

1. Preheat oven to 300°F (149°C). Combine all ingredients in a small bowl. Whisk until smooth.

2. Arrange ring molds on parchment-lined sheet pan. Press mixture into bottom of ring molds.

3. Bake for 10-15 minutes or until a light golden brown.

### COCONUT CUSTARD

*16.2 liq oz/479 ml heavy cream*
*17 liq oz/502 ml milk*
*6 oz/170 g unsweetened shredded coconut, divided*
*5.85 oz/166 g egg yolks*
*5 oz/142 g granulated sugar*

1. Preheat oven to 275°F (135°C). In a saucepan combine cream, milk and 2 oz (57 g) of the coconut and bring to a boil. Remove from the heat and let steep for 30 minutes. Let cool.

2. In a medium bowl, whisk the yolks and sugar until pale. Slowly whisk in the coconut-milk-cream mixture.

3. Strain through a fine chinois. Add the remaining 4 oz (113 g) of shredded coconut to the custard mixture.

*Following page: "Everything contributes to coconut here," says Richard Leach. "The cookie was added as a practical solution to the problem I had with the sorbet—it was melting."*

4. Pour the custard base into eight lightly greased 4" ramekins to a depth of 1". Place ramekins in a water bath and cover with aluminum foil. Bake until custard is firm, approximately 45 minutes. Cool and chill at least 3 hours.

5. Run a paring knife around the sides of the ramekin to release the custard. Unmold a custard onto a prebaked macaroon crust.

## COCONUT SAUCE

*3.5 oz/99 g granulated sugar*
*2 drops lemon juice*
*8.3 liq oz/245 ml water*
*16.2 liq oz/479 ml heavy cream*
*2 oz/57 g unsweetened coconut, shredded*

1. Combine sugar, lemon juice and water in a saucepan. Bring mixture to a boil and cook until it turns a light amber caramel color.

2. Remove from heat and whisk in cream. Add coconut and set steep for 20 minutes.

3. Strain sauce through fine chinois. Let cool until room temperature.

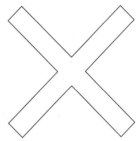

## HONEY TUILE

*4 oz/113 g unsalted butter*
*5.9 oz/167 g honey*
*8 oz/227 g confectioners' sugar*
*8.5 oz/241 g all-purpose flour*
*6 oz/170 g egg whites*

1. Preheat oven to 300°F (149°C). In a mixer with paddle attachment, beat the butter and honey until smooth. Add the confectioners' sugar and flour and mix until smooth. Slowly add the egg whites to the mixture. Mix until smooth.

2. Make an 8" (20 cm) long and 1" (2.54 cm) wide X-shaped stencil (see pattern) from a thin piece of plastic. Place the stencil on a nonstick pan. Spread tuile batter thinly over stencil. Remove stencil and bake until tuile is light golden brown, about 15 minutes.

3. Remove tuile from oven and, while still warm, carefully press over a domed object (such as an upside-down bowl) to create an arch shape. Let cool and repeat to form 8 tuiles.

## COCONUT SORBET

*7 oz/198 g granulated sugar*
*4 liq oz/118 ml water*
*1 pt/.95 L coconut milk (fresh or frozen)*

1. In a saucepan, bring sugar and water to boil. Cool and chill syrup.

2. Combine the coconut milk and simple syrup. Process mixture in an ice cream machine and freeze until ready to serve.

## ASSEMBLY

1. Lightly sprinkle granulated sugar on top of each custard. Glaze lightly with a blow torch until golden.

2. Place a ladle of the coconut sauce in a large bowl. Place the coconut tart on top.

3. Place a X-shaped tuile over the tart and top with a scoop of coconut sorbet.

# ROASTED HAZELNUT–WHITE CHOCOLATE MOUSSE

JEFF BARNES, RITZ-CARLTON, PALM BEACH, FLORIDA

*An almond joconde is crowned with hazelnut-white chocolate mousse lightly flavored with Kirschwasser. Kahlua crème anglaise is a smooth accent while the mixed berries add a tart touch.*

## YIELD: 15 SERVINGS

Special Equipment: Fifteen 2 1/2" (6.3 cm) tube molds
Wood grain impression tool

### PÂTE DECOR

*4 oz/113 g unsalted butter*
*4 oz/113 g granulated sugar*
*4 oz/113 g egg whites*
*4 oz/113 g all-purpose flour*
*1 oz/28 g cocoa powder*

1. In a mixer with the paddle attachment, cream butter and sugar until smooth.

2. Slowly add the egg whites and flour alternately. Sift in the cocoa powder. Blend just until incorporated.

3. Spread onto a silicon baking mat; drag the wood grain tool over the pâte decor. Freeze until solid and place on a sheet pan.

### JOCONDE

*17.5 oz/496 g whole eggs*
*3.5 oz/99 g all-purpose flour*
*10 oz/283 g almond flour*
*12 oz/340 g egg whites*
*11 oz/312 g granulated sugar*
*2.5 oz/71 g unsalted butter, melted*

1. Preheat oven to 400°F ( 205°C). In a mixer with whisk attachment, beat the eggs on high speed until doubled in volume.

2. With the machine on low, add the flours to the egg mixture.

*Facing page: "For a plate to be beautiful you should be able to see that it's all fresh ingredients," says Jeff Barnes. "A quality product comes first. If there's no freshness, no quality, presentation won't help you much."*

3. In a mixer with whisk attachment, beat egg whites to soft peaks. Add sugar and whip to stiff peaks. Fold whites into flour mixture. Fold butter into the mixture.

4. Spread the batter into a even, thin layer on top of the frozen pâte decor.

5. Bake for 8–10 minutes.

### HAZELNUT-WHITE CHOCOLATE MOUSSE

*4.5 oz/128 g granulated sugar*
*5.5 oz/156 g egg yolks*
*1 lb/454 g white chocolate, melted*
*.5 oz/14 g powdered gelatin*
*4 liq oz/118 ml water*
*4 liq oz/118 ml kirsch*
*32 liq oz/946 ml heavy cream, whipped to soft peaks*
*6 oz/170 g hazelnuts, roasted and finely chopped*

1. In a small saucepan, cook sugar to 250°F (121°C).

2. In a mixer with whisk attachment, whip egg yolks on high speed. While whipping slowly, pour sugar syrup into the yolks. Add melted white chocolate.

3. Place the gelatin, water and kirsch in a bowl and dissolve over a water bath. Add to the yolk mixture.

4. Fold the whipped cream and hazelnuts into the yolk mixture.

### CRÈME ANGLAISE

*1 pt/473 ml half-and-half*
*4 oz/113 g granulated sugar*
*1 vanilla bean, split and scraped*
*4 oz/113 g egg yolks*
*Kahlua, to taste*

1. In a saucepan, combine half-and-half, sugar and vanilla bean and bring to a boil.

2. Remove the vanilla bean and temper in yolks; cook to custard stage. Strain and cool in an ice bath. Stir in Kahlua.

### ASSEMBLY

*Cocoa powder*
*Apricot glaze, warmed*
*Fresh berries*
*Mint*
*Chocolate decorations*

1. Cut out fifteen 1 1/4" (3.1 cm) strips from the joconde. Cut out fifteen circles from the remaining joconde. Line fifteen 2 1/2" (6.3 cm) tube molds with acetate. Place 1 circle of joconde in the bottom of each mold. Wrap 1 strip of joconde around the interior of the mold, on top of the cake circle.

2. Pipe the hazelnut mousse mixture into the cake-lined molds and freeze until solid.

3. Remove desserts from the freezer and unmold. Dust the tops with cocoa powder and then glaze with the warm apricot glaze. Remove the acetate.

4. Spoon vanilla and Kahlua crème anglaise onto plate. Place mousse in center of plate. Garnish with fresh berries, mint, and chocolate cigarettes.

# F U S I O N I S M

*"The smell and taste of things remain poised a long time, like souls, ready*

*to remind us..."*

MARCEL PROUST

*"It can jump off the plate at you but it doesn't have to chase you out of the*

*restaurant."*

MARSHALL ROSENTHAL

The restaurants may be crowded, the decor precious, the experiments boldly successful or wildly off-key — Fusion cooking has all the hallmarks of a trend, but it is not. Just ask Hugh Carpenter, the author of *Fusion Food Cookbook*. "To say it's a trend is idiocy," he says. "It's been going on for centuries. Look at the history of the tomato or the potato. There wasn't even tempura in Japan until the Portuguese arrived. Caribbean cooking was tuber-level primitive before Columbus."

Carpenter defines Fusion cooking as cooking which combines one or more elements from different cooking traditions, either techniques or ingredients. It is also called cross-cultural cooking, or cooking without barriers. Thus, a *Fusion dessert* is one that *includes at least one ingredient or seasoning which is not found in the French/European or American dessert tradition*. Fusion ingredients usually come from Asia, Central America or South America. This windy definition ignores the fact that Fusion cooking is all around us. "David Bouley of Bouley's in New York adds lemongrass to a dish, invisibly," Carpenter points out. "He'd never call it Fusion." For the purpose of this book, a true Fusion Dessert incorporates such ingredients not as an accent, but as a central flavor or ingredient.

Fusion is, appropriately enough, global. "It's happening all over Europe and in Singapore," Carpenter points out. "And it's not just a New York and Los Angeles phenomenon. All over America, food is changing. Americans' palates are changing. We want food that has more flavor."

Hans Peter Graf of Red Sage in Washington, D.C., agrees. "Americans say they want to go light, but for the most part they don't," he says. "Americans want strong, heavy flavors. Here, spices must be stronger."

*HANS PETER GRAF*
*Hans Peter Graf, pastry chef of Red Sage in Washington, D.C., and a food consultant, was born on September 30, 1966, in Switzerland. "I've always been in the food business," he says. "My father was a baker, and he was the biggest influence on me. He would never accept a cutback in quality on anything. Ever. I hate compromise. I hate anything that compromises the quality of food." At age 16, he began his apprenticeship in pastry at a bakery, then worked as a pastry cook in hotels in Switzerland and at the Hyatt Regency Hotel in Grand Cayman. He opened bake shops in South America, Canada and Europe and worked as a chef at hotels in Switzerland and Thailand, also finding the time to earn degrees in food management and international resource management at the University of Bangkok and the University of Maryland. In 1995, he took the position of pastry chef for Mark Miller at Red Sage. Graf, who is in the process of establishing an ice cream company in Vietnam, has ambitions to start a food distribution company. "This country is so big, and has so many people to serve," he says. "It's fascinating, introducing real Asian foods to the American people."*

So American palates are changing. But there must be other reasons for this contemporary Fusion infusion. Carpenter points to the communication revolution ("A chef can fax a recipe or shipment request in seconds") as well as the improved quality and speed of overseas food transportation. Plus, Asian fascination with the flavors of the West, including desserts, is ongoing. Asians in particular have been dessert-deprived: "The dessert traditions of India, Thailand and China are sorry," says Carpenter. "Without the use of dairy, liqueurs, coffee or chocolate, you can't have a deep, complex tradition."

Claude Troisgros, chef and owner of C.T. in New York City and several restaurants in Brazil, believes that Fusion has filled the void left by the slow fade of nouvelle. "Fusion cuisine in America today is the nouvelle of the 90s," he says. "Nouvelle, which my father [Pierre Troisgros] helped develop, started with impeccable chefs evolving and turned into something else. In about 1985, nouvelle stopped. Why? Chefs from nowhere, with no tradition, were doing beef with chocolate, salmon with strawberry." At the same time, Troisgros is grateful for the innovative chefs, even the ones who go overboard. As he says, "You need crazy chefs to experiment."

## DID SOMEONE CALL FOR A CRAZY CHEF?

"There are no rules when it comes to pairing these flavors," says Patricia Murakami of Chinois East/West in Sacramento. "Just try anything, it's more fun that way. People do combine ingredients that make no sense at all," she concedes. "I try to combine ingredients that are soul mates—tropical flavors, for example, which were born and raised in the same part of the world."

Other chefs share this sense of adventure, as long as the adventure doesn't plunge the customer into unwanted peril. "I love experimentation," says D. Jemal Edwards of Nobu in New York City. "You should keep experimenting or quit. But that doesn't mean you have to praise the outcome of every experiment. An experiment is to be respected, but not necessarily the end product. If it doesn't work it should never make it to the menu."

What Andrew MacLauchlan of the Coyote Cafes is shooting for in his plates is "extreme intensity" of flavor, and Murakami agrees. "In pastry, I prefer not to have too many flavors," she says. "I like to concentrate on a few things, and I want an intense flavor. When I want something chocolate, I want it to be really chocolaty."

## THIS BUD'S FOR PAIN

As human beings, we have roughly 10,000 taste buds in our mouths, located in peg-like projections called papillae, which are grouped according to receptivity to salt, sour, sweet and bitter. Inside each bud are some fifty taste cells relaying information to neurons, which report to the brain. We primarily taste sweet things at the tip of the tongue, sour substances at the sides, salty all over the surface (but mainly toward the front), and bitter at the back. But the "map" analogy is faulty: every taste is the result of a combination of the four primary tastes. Ice cream, for example, tastes very sweet when swiped with the tip of the tongue, less sweet when it slides over the back of the tongue.

When we smell a dish or when we bring a forkful of food to our mouths, the procedure begins: Vaporized chemicals from the food enter our nasal passages through the nose and past the back of the mouth. It requires many fewer food molecules for us to smell a food, and smelling food causes us to salivate, aiding the actual tasting of it.

We can only taste a food when it begins to dissolve; it is through saliva that the taste buds are stimulated. Stimulation of the taste buds is joined by stimulation of other receptors in the mouth, which gauge temperature and

**ANDREW MacLAUCHLAN**
Andrew MacLauchlan, Executive Pastry Chef of Coyote Cafes in Santa Fe, Las Vegas and Austin, was born in Vermont on March 24, 1963. He worked in Vermont and Maine then moved to Colorado and found a position as pastry chef of a resort hotel. He was 22. "This is where I grew up," he says, "and where I started doing pastry seriously." After two years, MacLauchlan moved to Boulder and worked in a French restaurant. "You could not talk in the kitchen," he says. "You'd go to work and there'd be nothing but heads down and the sound of clicking knives." Two years later, in 1991, MacLauchlan moved to Chicago and was hired as pastry chef at Charlie Trotter's eponymous restaurant. "That experience was another turning point," he says. "It was a defining experience. Charlie was extremely demanding of me, wanting desserts that had extreme intensity of flavor." In 1995, MacLauchlan joined Mark Miller at Coyote Cafe. MacLauchlan is the author of New Classic Desserts and Mark Miller's Famous Flavored Breads, and is currently working on another dessert book.

**DAVID NOWACK**
David Nowack, Executive Pastry Chef of Arizona 206, New York City, was born on June 23, 1965, in Buffalo, New York. He wanted to be a chef, he earned a degree in food service administration, then attended the Culinary Institute of America and served as an extern at the Trellis Restaurant in Virginia under Marcel Desaulniers. "That's when I knew what I wanted to do," says Nowack. Returning to the CIA, Nowack studied pastry and baking and, upon graduation, found a position as pastry chef at the Whitehall and Tremont Hotels in Chicago. "It was probably the wrong choice to take a pastry chef position right out of school," he says. "I didn't feel I knew enough." Nowack decided to join the kitchens of the Hotel Inter-Continental, which was to open in a few months, as a pastry cook so that he could work under an executive pastry chef. "But, as it turned out, there was no executive pastry chef," says Nowack. "So five of us opened the hotel." Nowack then worked as pastry chef of Ritz-Carlton hotels in Philadelphia, Aspen and Mauna Lani, then the Hilton at Short Hills and the Sea Grill in New York. Nowack hopes to teach someday.

pressure. The longer we allow food to linger in our mouths, the more of our senses are applied to appreciating it. The technical definition of "flavor" includes temperature, texture, aroma, color and pain, by which food scientists mean spiciness or heat. We also derive pleasure from the sound food makes it our heads — crunch. Pain and crunch in our heads are not always "flavorful" though: if a food has crunch when it shouldn't, or disagreeable spicing when combined with other food, our taste buds will not be fooled.

The old saying, "There's no accounting for taste," is not entirely accurate. There are several factors which account for peoples' differing tastes in food, as well as each individual's change in taste over time, or over moods. For example, taste buds themselves only last about a week to ten days; the body replaces them. As we get older, however, they are not replaced as quickly, so it takes more intense flavor to create the same sensation in the mouth. (Lesson for today: be kind to cranky older customers.) Additionally, some foods contain substances that help "deceive" the tongue — the glutamate in MSG blocks our mouth's ability to taste the true salt content of soy sauce. The flavor of food affects our food selection (called the hedonistic response); that much is obvious. But our state of hunger and nutrition level can affect our appreciation of salt and sour. (Our desire for sweet seems to remain stable. Notify the boss.) Then there is the tricky issue of acids and sugars: acids produce a sour taste and sugars a sweet taste, of course, but different acids produce different tastes and they are affected by other chemicals, including those found in saliva. Plus, acids and sugars interact in complex ways; sweetness and acidity are related at the chemical level. And the chemical composition of our saliva is affected by heredity, diet, perhaps even mood, and so this combination of the different chemical makeup of saliva plus the interactions of acids and sugars, plus the different arrangements and emphases of taste buds in each customer and dinner guest adds up to different tastes in different moods at varying times of our lives — no two of us taste the same *tarte tatin* exactly the same way.

Humans like to stimulate their senses, which is why we heli-ski and go to IMAX theaters and try new foods. We like sharp jolts to our taste buds.

"I like Thai food because there are so many different flavors that are applying in your mouth at the same time," says Patricia Murakami. "There is hot and sweet...you really can't detect one ingredient from another. They're all mingled."

"Most succesful dishes have a range of flavor levels, not all of which are perceived at first," says Hugh Carpenter. "Secondary flavors can ultimately make a dish succesful. You'll have peaks of flavor from one bite to the next. It adds an element of surprise as well. Americans are no longer interested in living in a flavor-deprived area."

## JASMINE AND GINGER

The chefs who work with Fusion ingredients demonstrate how artful intensity can be in a dessert. In D. Jemal Edwards' Coconut Passion Fruit Napoléon, coconut meringues are filled with the slightly acidic, extremely fragrant passion fruit mousse. A warm fruit compote serves as the garnish. Ginger is the accent in Stanton Ho's Fresh Peach Melba Canton and Hans Peter Graf's Grilled Chinese Pear with Galangal-Chocolate Truffles and Mekong Litchies. Ho presents ginger-vanilla ice cream in a raspberry coulis under glazed, broiled peaches, while Graf uses a ginger simple syrup to poach his pears. Graf's accompaniment is a soothing sensorial assault: chocolate truffles are flavored with galangal (a commonly used spice in Indonesia and Thailand with a taste reminiscent of saffron) and litchies (a sweet, musky-flavored fruit that originated in China and is now found in the Far East and West Indies) simmered in a Mekong whiskey caramel-passion fruit sauce. The plate is garnished with lemongrass and candied kumquats (a citrus fruit originating in central China).

Perfume-scented jasmine rice is featured in two dishes presented here: In Patricia Murakami's Tropical Fruit Sushi, it is cooked in coconut milk and heavy cream, giving this rice pudding a distinctive taste and smoothness. The rice rolls are filled with kiwis, mango and strawberries which have been marinated in a rum-flavored simple syrup. In David Nowack's Lemongrass Rice Pudding with Dried Fruit Medley, the jasmine rice and the mild scent of lemongrass are combined in a rice pudding served with a smooth coconut sauce. Deep-fried cellophane noodles tossed in cinnamon sugar add a sweet crunch to the smooth, silky pudding.

In Andrew MacLauchlan's Cajeta Caramel Panna Cotta, evaporated goat's milk is the essence of the cajeta caramel (a traditional Mexican caramel with a very distinct, pronounced tinge) which flavors the panna cotta. The chili-lime syrup of habanero, arbo and New Mexico red chili peppers add a spiciness and burn to the pears. Crunchy pinon brittle and oven-dried pear chips add crunch and a sweetness to the dessert.

This is a flavor-driven school, so we shouldn't necessarily expect visual themes to run from plate to plate. And yet white dominates — in Murakami's Tropical Fruit Sushi, in the spun sugar ball of Stan Ho's Fresh Peach Melba Canton, in Roxsand Scocos' Lillikoi Mousse, and David Nowack's Lemongrass Rice Pudding with Dried Fruit Medley as well as D. Jemal Edwards' Coconut Passion Fruit Napoléon. The vibrant, deep, lustrous color of Hans Peter Graf's Grilled Chinese Pear with Galangal-Chocolate Truffles and Mekong Litchies is also to be admired; much of this color is provided by the plate, but it is a beautiful fusing of plate and food — the orange-golden candied kumquats, the deep tones of the truffles, the pale litchies and above all the pear — earth tones orchestrated by terracotta.

Norman Love's Chocolate Oolong Mousse with Caramelized Orange Sauce is like a meditation on the sphere: on that one plate are disks, circles, half-circles, crescents, a dome — and in witty contrast, an insistent tile pattern.

Chefs love their food, and when you get these pastry chefs talking about the ingredients they've found in their travels, research and visits to other kitchens, there's no stopping them.

Andrew MacLauchlan sings the praises of tamarind. "Extremely tangy," he comments. "I use it to augment other fruits such as plums or ginger. It really takes you over." Other favorites: "Hoja santa is a broad leaf that has a kind of licorice type of flavor. It goes well with other fruits, makes a great ice cream and sorbet, and you can crystallize it and make candy with it.

"Canela is an extremely fragrant cinnamon," MacLauchlan continues. "It gives you a whole new perspective on cinnamon. Juniper berries are indigenous to the southwest. I dry them in the oven and make them into a juniper gin cake served with caramelized apples and quince sauce and triple cider ice cream."

Patricia Murakami extols the virtues of jasmine rice, Chinese five-spice, orange tea sauce and bean paste (for its "funky texture"). Jacquy Pfieffer frequently uses ginger, litchie nuts and red bean paste. ("It's very strange," he admits. "It has the texture of lotus seed paste. We sometimes put it in danishes.") Claude Troisgros, who has opened five restaurants in Brazil, tends to use passion fruit, mango, guava and jabuticaba ("I made my own liqueur from this; we called it Jabukir"). He has also made a liqueur from the pods of cashews and a sauce from cachaça ("Lime, cachaca, pineapple, sugar and butter makes an interesting pastry cream.")

"I came back from Singapore with pandan," reports Norman Love, who travels extensively in his role as Corporate Pastry Chef for the Ritz-Carlton Company in Naples, Florida. "It looks like a palm frond, and has a coconut and toasted almond type essence. It brings an earthy, distinct flavor, especially in combination with coconut." Love also sampled a palm syrup used in Asia, made from actual palm trees ("Wonderful, wonderful sweet flavor," he enthuses. "Very distinct. You could use it as a substitute for sugar, sort of like sugar in the raw") and a powdered coconut, manufactured in Malaysia. Love is fond of green tea infusions as well. "I don't use it in excess but I do make green tea ice cream and truffles. I make one cake with it too: a green tea and saki teabread with golden raisins."

Andrew MacLauchlan, whose territory is now the southwest and who takes seriously his mission of incorporating ingredients of the region, lists a few: pistachios and quince from southern Mexico, Gravenstein apples and black mission figs. "I haven't gone crazy with the chiles," he says. "I like hot food but when it comes to dessert, I go with tropical fruits. Anything tropical goes well with this restaurant concept."

D. Jemal Edwards is pastry chef at Nobu, the elegant Japanese restaurant in New York, so his mission is clear. "There's a citrus indigenous to Japan called yuzu," he says. "It reminds me of a Meyer lemon. The only problem is, the yuzu juice we get here is shipped and preserved with salt. I can sometimes get a freeze-dried yuzu skin, which I use more, but I'm game to try anything once, and I tried making an ice cream with the juice. Incredibly salty. The ice cream was terrible." Edwards confesses to using "a ton of ginger. It works incredibly well with pastry, and is one of the best combinations with chocolate I've used. Chocolate can be hard to pair because it overwhelms most things. Ginger has a delicate taste on the palate." He also uses it in a brûlée, in a ganache for petits fours, and as an accent in whipped cream — but always fresh, never powdered. (In Edwards' opinion, the best way to use ginger is to steep it or grate it, process it and squeeze out all the juice. "You can use it like any other spice, and not use very much of it.") Edwards also uses shiso syrup. "It's sometimes called Japanese mint," he says. "It's got a very very strong flavor, very light and clean. I paired it with chocolate and it works really well." He has also found a use for saki — "in the same capacity you would use any other liqueur. In a sabayon, for example. It has the same consistency as wine.

"Sesame works really well with pastry," Edwards continues, "especially with cream products or creamy-type desserts. I use something called neri goma, which is literally puréed sesame. It's basically a tahini which I can get in black or white. I can steep that in cream and whip it, then fold in white chocolate for a mousse, or fold in black sesame seeds and pipe it into an almond cake." Edwards, like Norman Love, finds uses for green tea, "which we get in a powdered form," he says. "That seems to be the best way to use it. We've made buttercreams and genoise—you can use it the same way you use cocoa. I like it with fresh fruits. If you overuse it it turns bitter, but there's still a touch of bitterness in it, no matter how little you use."

Hans Peter Graf lists as some of his favorites star anise, cumin ("I've had great success with it in bread."), cactus syrup (which he uses as a simple syrup to sweeten light desserts), passion fruit ("My customers seem to like it"), sticky rice with fruit on the side, soy ("I've had good success with soy ginger ice cream; Asian soy is awfully strong for palates here, but

Western soy is good"), horned melon, kiwanos ("It's a cross between a banana and a kiwi. I like it but it never caught on here."), goat's milk ("I'm selling a lot of goat milk caramel reduction with chocolate and cream on top"), Asian pear, tart Thai whiskey, and burnt honey. Burnt honey? Graf confesses that he never would have considered burnt honey as a pastry ingredient, "Except that I tasted it in San Francisco and I liked it," he says. "Now I make a burnt honey ice cream. It destroys the flavor of the honey but at the same time it creates a new flavor."

To keep one's mind pried wide open, willing to try new ingredients and combinations — that is one facet of the complex, contradictory definition of a succesful chef. To see failure not as a defeat, but as an opportunity to learn. Patricia Murakami recalls a culinary contest years ago: "I thought they were looking for something more interesting," she says. "So I did cayenne peppermint ice cream layered with crushed chocolate cookies. It was pink with brown layers. It was cold in the mouth, then when you swallowed there was fire. We called it Fire and Ice. It only sold to adventuresome people, and it did poorly at the contest. I think vanilla pudding won. I was completely off track."

To work as the member of a team. To remember that this is above all a business. David Nowack says that he trusts his waitstaff to be honest with the customers when trying to sell his offerings. The waiters want a happy customer, and Nowack doesn't want a hard sell, so he is willing to shorten portions, to put some items on the side. His Chocolate Jalapeño Sorbet, for example. Or his Black Pepper Red Wine Sorbet. Chocolate Cognac Sorbet. His 23 Karat Gold Ice Cream. "I made a honey garlic ice cream," he confesses. "Some people liked it, others didn't. A journalist said I'd created fireworks in the mouth. I liked that."

To have a passion for food. A love that demands honesty. "Some chefs start with an idea of the form of a dessert they are planning," says Andrew MacLauchlan. "I choose to start with an ingredient. I try to best and most simply present the flavors of, say, a peach. I'm not presenting geometry or architecture, I'm presenting food. Cooking is about presenting the flavors that are already there. There's nothing you can do to make a white peach better. It's already perfect."

# CAJETA CARAMEL PANNA COTTA

. . . . . . . . . . . . . . . . . . . . . . . . . . . . . . . . . . . . . . . . . . .

ANDREW MACLAUCHLAN, COYOTE CAFE, SANTA FE, NEW MEXICO, LAS VEGAS, NEVADA,
AND AUSTIN, TEXAS

*The classic combination of pear and caramel is given fusion tinge with this slightly sweet panna cotta served with pears poached in a chili-lime syrup of haba, arbo, and New Mexico red peppers. Pinon brittle and oven-dried pear chips add crunch and sweetness.*

### YIELD: 6 SERVINGS

Special Equipment: Six 3 1/2" (8.9 cm) one-piece tart tins

#### CAJETA CARAMEL
*34 liq oz/1 L goat's milk*
*12.75 liq oz/377 ml milk*
*.69 oz/20 g cornstarch*
*.088 oz/2.5 g baking soda*
*10.5 oz/298 g granulated sugar*

1. In a large stainless steel pot, bring goat's milk and milk to a boil. Reduce heat to a simmer.

2. In a small bowl, combine the cornstarch and baking soda. Whisk in some of the hot milk until dissolved and add the mixture to the pot.

3. In a stainless steel saucepan, melt the sugar until it becomes a deep amber color.

4. Slowly ladle some of the hot milk into the caramel until it no longer bubbles up. Add this mixture to the remaining goat's milk mixture. Cook the mixture until reduced by 1/2, approximately 1 hour.

#### CHILI-LIME POACHED PEARS
*35 liq oz/1.03 L fresh lime juice*
*14 oz/397 g granulated sugar*
*2 habañero or Scotch bonnet peppers, cut in half*
*4 New Mexican dried red chilies, chopped*
*4 arbo chilies, chopped*
*4 slightly underripe pears, peeled, cored and halved*

*Page 298: "I've gone from classic French training to a more free sense," says Andrew MacLauchlan. "Now I follow the French model of regionality and seasonality and some forms and techniques of French cuisine, but as an American, I do American food. My influences are from all around the world."*

1. In a medium stainless steel pot, bring the lime juice, sugar and peppers to a simmer. Add the pears and cook until easily pierced with a knife.

2. Cut the pears into 1" x 2" (2.54 x 5 cm) wedges.

### PEAR CHIPS

*1 Comice pear*
*confectioners' sugar as needed*

1. Preheat oven to 220°F (105°C). Using a mandoline, slice the pear lengthwise in slices 1/32" (.08 cm) thick.

2. Arrange the pears on a silicon baking mat and bake for 20–25 minutes or until crisp.

3. Peel the slices from the baking mat while still warm and transfer to a baking sheet. Sprinkle the pears with confectioners' sugar and caramelize with a blow torch. Turn the slices over and repeat on the other side.

### PHYLLO DISKS

*4 phyllo dough sheets*
*2 oz/57 g unsalted butter, melted*
*2 oz/57 g confectioners' sugar*

1. Preheat oven to 350°F (175°C). Brush 1 sheet of phyllo with melted butter and sprinkle with confectioners' sugar. Repeat with remaining phyllo sheets; stack the sheets on top of one another.

2. Cut 5" (12.7 cm) circles from the phyllo and place on a parchment-lined sheet pan. Bake for 8–10 minutes or until evenly browned.

### PIÑON BRITTLE

*2.08 liq oz/62 ml water*
*1.75 oz/50 g granulated sugar*
*3 oz/85 g piñons (raw)*

1. Preheat oven to 350°F (175°C). Line a sheet pan with lightly oiled parchment paper. Place the water and sugar in a stainless steel saucepan and bring to a boil for 2–3 minutes. Let cool.

2. Add the nuts to the simple syrup and spread onto the prepared sheet pan. Roast the nuts for 10–12 minutes, stirring occasionally.

### CAJETA PANNA COTTA

*6.08 liq oz/180 ml heavy cream*
*20 liq oz/591 ml cajeta caramel (recipe above)*
*10.6 liq oz/313 ml milk*
*3.1 oz/88 g granulated sugar*
*1 vanilla bean, split and scraped*
*3.5 gelatin sheets, softened*

1. In a stainless steel pot, bring the cream, caramel, milk, sugar and vanilla bean to a simmer. Remove from heat.

2. Whisk the softened gelatin into the hot cajeta mixture. Strain into an ice bath and fill six 3 1/2" one-piece tart tins. Refrigerate until set (about 45 minutes).

### ASSEMBLY

1. Arrange the poached pear wedges on each plate. Drizzle some of the remaining cajeta caramel over them and sprinkle with the piñon brittle.

2. Dip each panna cotta-filled tart tin into hot water for several seconds.

3. Place a phyllo disk on top of the panna cotta and quickly invert it. Carefully remove the tart tin and settle each panna cotta-topped phyllo disk onto the pears. Stick 2 slices of crispy pear chips in panna cotta and serve immediately.

# LILLIKOI MOUSSE

ROXSAND SCOCOS, ROXSAND RESTAURANT & BAR, SCOTTSDALE, ARIZONA

*The subtle tang of passion fruit is showcased in a mousse wrapped in white chocolate and a ginger macaroon.*

### YIELD: 11 SERVINGS

Special Equipment: Eleven 3" ring molds, 2 1/2" high (7.6 x 6.3 cm)

### LILLIKOI MOUSSE

*19 oz/539 g bottled passion fruit purée*
*34.5 liq oz/1.02 L heavy cream, divided*
*11 oz/312 g granulated sugar, divided*
*3.5 oz/99 g egg yolks*
*.5 oz/14 g powdered gelatin, bloomed and clarified*

1. In a saucepan, bring purée and 16.5 liq oz (488 ml) of the heavy cream to a boil.

2. In a stainless steel bowl, combine 5.5 oz (156 g) of the sugar and egg yolks; temper the purée mixture into the yolks.

3. Add the gelatin to the mixture.

4. Cook the mixture until it coats the back of a spoon. Strain and cool to room temperature.

5. Whip the remaining 18 liq oz (532) ml heavy cream with the remaining 5.5 oz (156 g) sugar together to soft peaks. Fold the whipped cream into the cooled passion fruit mixture.

6. On a sheet pan lined with parchment paper, fill eleven 3" ring molds with mousse; refrigerate at least 2 hours until set.

### WHITE CHOCOLATE BORDER

*1.5 lb/680 g white chocolate couverture, melted and tempered*

1. Unmold the mousse rings and return to the refrigerator.

2. Cut out eleven 3" x 10" (7.6 x 25.4 cm) strips of parchment paper. Cover the strips with melted white chocolate, and allow the chocolate to set up slightly.

3. Wrap the chocolate-covered strips of parchment around the mousse and return them to the refrigerator. Once white chocolate has set up completely, remove the parchment from around the mousse.

*Following page: "I wanted to create something that reflected my life in Hawaii," says Roxsand Scocos. "It's a classic preparation, nothing revolutionary—a nice blending of tropical flavors in a classic form."*

### WHITE CHOCOLATE FANS
*2 lbs 3 oz/992 g white chocolate couverture, melted and tempered*
*2 liq oz/59 ml vegetable oil*

Whisk oil into tempered chocolate. Pour fine line of chocolate onto marble slab. Spread evenly in long strip. Just before chocolate sets, form fans with a palette knife.

### ASSEMBLY
*Confectioners' sugar, for dusting*

Immediately place the fans around the top edge of the prepared mousse rounds in a flower pattern. Dust the fans with confectioners' sugar and serve.

# GRILLED CHINESE PEAR WITH GALANGAL-CHOCOLATE TRUFFLES AND MEKONG LITCHIES

. . . . . . . . . . . . . . . . . . . . . . . . . . . . . . . . . . . . . . . . . . . . . . . . . . . . . .

H A N S   P E T E R   G R A F ,   R E D   S A G E ,   W A S H I N G T O N ,   D . C .

*A complex interaction of flavors, as whole pears poached in ginger simple syrup are accompanied by chocolate truffles flavored with galangal and litchies simmered in a Mekong whiskey caramel-passion fruit sauce.*

### Y I E L D :   1 0   S E R V I N G S

#### GALANGAL-CHOCOLATE TRUFFLES
*3.9 oz/110 g egg yolks*
*3 oz/85 g granulated sugar*
*4 oz/113 g semisweet chocolate, melted*
*2 oz/57 g unsweetened chocolate, melted*
*2 oz/57 g galangal, finely chopped*
*16 liq oz/473 ml heavy cream, whipped to soft peaks*
*cocoa powder, for dusting*

1. In a bowl with whisk, beat together yolks and sugar until creamy. Whisk in semisweet and unsweetened chocolates and galangal. Fold in whipped cream. Chill 4 hours.

2. Scoop out 1" (2.45 cm) balls of truffle mixture and freeze until firm, about 30 minutes. Roll in cocoa powder and refrigerate until serving.

#### POACHED PEARS
*1.5 qts/1.4 L water*
*21 oz/600 g granulated sugar*
*7oz/198 g ginger, chopped*
*10 Chinese pears, peeled and cored*

1. In a large saucepan, combine water, sugar, and ginger. Bring to boil and add pears. Cook pears in simmering syrup until tender.

2. Cool pears in syrup.

*Facing page: "I like to feature a strong flavor surrounded by tidbits of other flavors," says Hans Peter Graf. "Your palate should receive a line of flavors. Visual is a good selling point, but visual content cannot be crucial. We do a lot of covers at Red Sage. I can't be playing with a plate for five minutes."*

# COCONUT PASSION FRUIT NAPOLÉON

· · · · · · · · · · · · · · · · · · · · · · · · · · · · · · · · · · · · ·

JEMAL EDWARDS, NOBU, NEW YORK, NEW YORK

*Light, crispy toasted-coconut meringues are filled with slightly acidic, extremely fragrant passion fruit blended
into a mousse. A warm fruit compote of mango, papaya, pineapple, kiwi, and plum serves as the garnish.*

## YIELD: 12 SERVINGS

### COCONUT WAFERS
*8 oz/227 g egg whites*
*12 oz/340 g granulated sugar*
*5 oz/142 g lightly toasted flaked coconut*

1. Preheat oven to 250°F (120°C). Line a sheet pan with a silicon baking sheet.

2. In a mixer with whisk attachment, beat whites, gradually adding sugar until stiff peaks form. Fold
in coconut. Spread meringue into 3" circles, 1/8" thick (7.6 x .32 cm) and bake 40–45 minutes, until
dry. Cool and store in airtight container.

### PASSION FRUIT MOUSSE
*12.75 liq oz/377 ml passion fruit juice*
*7.8 oz/221 g granulated sugar*
*12 oz/340 g unsalted butter*
*7.8 oz/221 g egg yolks, lightly beaten*
*3 gelatin sheets, softened in cold water, drained*
*16 liq oz/473 ml heavy cream, whipped to stiff peaks*

1. In a mixing bowl combine passion fruit juice, sugar, and butter. Place bowl over a pot of simmering water and stir until butter is melted and mixture is warm.

2. Temper in the egg yolks and continue to cook over water 15–20 minutes until slightly thickened.
Strain through fine sieve and stir in drained gelatin. Chill the curd for at least 4 hours.

3. In a mixer with whisk attachment, beat passion fruit curd until smooth. Fold in whipped cream.
Refrigerate until ready to serve.

*Facing page: "We have a lot of very interesting plateware imported from Japan at Nobu," says Jemal Edwards. "But I stay away from
the plates the chefs use. Even though they're thoroughly washed, the perception from the customer is, wow, there was fish on this thing."*

**ASSEMBLY**

*Tropical fruit compote*
*White chocolate cigarettes*

1. Fill a pastry bag fitted with a medium star tip with the passion fruit mousse. Pipe a small amount of the mousse onto the center of a dessert plate. Place a coconut meringue on top and press down to secure. Pipe a layer of mousse on the meringue and top with another meringue; repeat layering once. Top meringue with a rosette of mousse.

2. Spoon some tropical fruit compote around the dessert and garnish with white chocolate cigarettes.

# LEMONGRASS RICE PUDDING WITH DRIED FRUIT MEDLEY

DAVID NOWAK, ARIZONA 206, NEW YORK, NEW YORK

*Perfumed jasmine rice and the mild lemon scent of lemongrass are combined for a rice pudding served with a smooth coconut sauce. Deep-fried cellophane noodles tossed in cinnamon sugar add sweet crunch.*

## YIELD: 6 SERVINGS

Special Equipment: Six 6 oz/170 g ramekins

### RICE PUDDING

*9 oz/255 g jasmine rice*
*1 qt/.95 L milk*
*7 oz/198 g granulated sugar*
*1 vanilla bean, split and scraped*
*1 lemongrass stalk, cut in thirds*
*3 sheets gelatin*
*1.95 oz/55 g egg yolks*
*1.5 liq oz/44 ml Grand Marnier*
*8 liq oz/237 ml heavy cream, whipped to soft mounds*

1. Rinse the rice well; drain.

2. In a large saucepan, combine the rice, milk, sugar, vanilla bean, and lemongrass. Over medium-high heat, bring the mixture to a gentle boil; lower heat and simmer, stirring occasionally, for 30 minutes or until rice is tender.

3. Meanwhile, soak gelatin sheets in cold water. When rice is cooked, whisk drained gelatin leaves into hot milk mixture; cool 10 minutes. Whisk in yolks and Grand Marnier. Cool the pudding completely in an ice bath.

4. Gently fold in whipped cream. Divide the pudding among 6 lightly greased 6-oz ramekins. Chill 6 hours, or until set.

*Following page: "I learned about theme from Stacy Radin at the CIA," says David Nowack. "She taught me that when you look at a plate it should portray the flavor in your mind. If it's a cake, you can't see what's on the inside, so the garnish should somehow convey the flavor."*

## COCONUT SAUCE

*2 tsp/8 g cornstarch*
*2 Tbs/30 ml cold water*
*14 liq oz/414 ml coconut milk*
*1.75 oz/50 g granulated sugar*

1. In glass measuring cup, dissolve cornstarch in water.

2. In a saucepan, cook coconut milk and sugar over medium-high heat, stirring occasionally, until boiling. Whisk in cornstarch mixture and allow to boil for 1 minute. Cool the sauce completely.

## DRIED FRUIT MEDLEY

*8 oz/227 g dried apricots, diced*
*8 oz/227 g dried strawberries, diced*
*8 oz/227 g dried cranberries, diced*
*8 oz/227 g dried currants, diced*
*8.3 liq oz/245 ml water*
*1 liq oz/30 ml Grand Marinier*

Place fruits, water and Grand Marnier in a saucepan. Bring to a boil; strain, discarding liquid.

## ASSEMBLY

*Mint*

Unmold rice pudding onto serving plate. Arrange some of the dried fruit next to the pudding. Garnish with pools of coconut sauce and mint.

# CHOCOLATE OOLONG MOUSSE WITH CARAMELIZED ORANGE SAUCE

. . . . . . . . . . . . . . . . . . . . . . . . . . . . . . . . . . . . . . . . . . . . . . .

NORMAN LOVE, RITZ-CARLTON HOTEL COMPANY, NAPLES, FLORIDA

*The classic pairing of chocolate and orange is given a pleasing hint of bitterness with the infusion of oolong tea.*
*Candied oranges and a shiny glaze add texture to this smooth dessert.*

## YIELD: 10 SERVINGS

Special Equipment: Ten 4 oz/113 g demi-sphere molds,
Checkerboard silk screen stencil

### CARAMELIZED ORANGE SAUCE

*7.9 oz/225 g granulated sugar*
*3.9 liq oz/115 ml water*
*5.9 liq oz/175 ml orange juice, warmed*
*1.05 oz/30 g unsalted butter*

In a saucepan, cook sugar and water to medium caramel color. Slowly add the warmed orange juice and whisk in butter.

### ORANGE CONFIT

*26 oz/737g whole oranges*
*3.5 oz/99 g unsalted butter*
*4 cloves*
*12.3 oz/350 g turbindado sugar, divided*

1. Place the oranges in a large pot and cover with water; bring the water to a boil and boil for 1 hour to wash away bitterness. Dry the oranges and cut into eighths.

2. In a sauté pan, melt butter with cloves. Add the orange pieces and sauté until juice has evaporated and oranges caramelize. Cover the orange pieces with water and 3.5 oz/99 g of the sugar and let simmer until almost dry. Repeat process with remaining sugar and more water. Spread oranges onto parchment paper and allow to cool. Chop coarsely.

*Facing page: Norman Love travels extensively in Asia. "The more I travel the more I bring back and implement in my pastry," he says. "I spend hours in tea shops, finding things I can use to infuse flavor."*

### CHOCOLATE OOLONG MOUSSE

*2.1 oz/60 g egg yolks*
*1.75 oz/50g eggs*
*1.75 oz/50 g granulated sugar*
*.5 liq oz/15 ml water*
*.35 oz/10 g oolong tea leaves*
*7 liq oz/207 ml heavy cream, whipped to soft peaks*
*5 oz/142 g bittersweet chocolate, melted*

1. In a mixer with whisk attachment, whip yolks and eggs on medium-high speed until pale.

2. In a saucepan, bring sugar and water to a boil. Add the tea leaves and allow to steep for 5 minutes. Pass the infusion through a sieve, return to the saucepan and continue cooking until the syrup reaches 253°F (123°C). Immediately add the tea syrup to the whipping egg mixture and continue to beat at medium speed until cool.

3. Fold 1/2 of the whipped cream into the melted chocolate; fold this mixture into the egg mixture. Fold in the remaining whipped cream. Fill ten 4 oz (113 g) demi-sphere molds with the mousse and chill until set.

### CHOCOLATE GLAZE

*1.4 oz/40 g bittersweet couverture, finely chopped*
*4.4 oz/124 g pâte à glacer*
*2.5 liq oz/74 ml milk*
*1.4 liq oz/40 ml heavy cream*
*.88 oz/25 g granulated sugar*
*.88 oz/25 g glucose*

1. Place couverture and pâte à glacer in medium bowl.

2. In a saucepan, bring milk, cream, sugar, and glucose to a boil. Pour hot mixture over chocolate and whisk until smooth.

### CHOCOLATE STENCILING

*30 oz/850 g white chocolate, tempered*
*60 oz/1.7 kg dark chocolate, tempered*

1. Place a checkerboard silkscreen stencil on work surface. Evenly spread some of the dark chocolate over the squares. Allow to set 2–3 minutes. Remove the stencil and freeze until completely set. Spread some of the white chocolate over the dark chocolate and let set completely.

2. Spread some of the dark chocolate over the back of a sheet pan lined with acetate. Allow to set.

3. Using a 6" (15.2 cm) metal cutter, cut out 10 circles from the set dark chocolate. Cut 1/4 of each circle off.

4. Cut out fifteen 6" (15.2 cm) circles from the set checkerboard chocolate. Set aside 10 of the checkerboard circles. Cut the remaining 5 checkerboard circles in half to form 10 half-circles.

5. Using a metal cutter, cut the remaining 10 checkerboard circles into thirds (making 30 1/3 moon-shaped pieces of chocolate). Cut out twenty 1" (2.54 cm) circles from the dark chocolate. Cut out ten 3" (7.4 cm) circles from the dark chocolate. Cut out ten 1" (2.54 cm) circles of the checkerboard chocolate.

## ASSEMBLY

1. Place a dark chocolate 3/4-circle on a plate. Spread a little melted dark chocolate near the edges. Place a 1" (2.54 cm) dark chocolate circle on each end on the melted chocolate. Place some melted chocolate on the top edge of the 1" (2.54 cm) circles and place a 3" (7.6 cm) dark chocolate circle on top.

2. Place the oolong mousse on top of the 3" circle. Place a 1" (2.54 cm) checkerboard circle on top of the mousse. Place the half circle of the checkerboard chocolate in front of the dark chocolate 3/4" (1.9 cm) circle. Glue 3 of the 1/3 moon-shaped checkerboard chocolates with melted chocolate, graduating slightly, and glue to the back of the dark chocolate circles.

# BIBLIOGRAPHY

Ackerman, Diane. *A Natural History of the Senses*. New York: Random House, 1990.

Arnheim, Rudolf. *Visual Thinking*. Berkeley: University of California Press, 1969.

Beardsley, Monroe C. *Aesthetics*. New York: Harcourt, Brace and Co., 1958.

Carpenter, Hugh. *Fusion Food Cookbook*. New York: Artisan Press, 1994.

Carraher, Ronald G. and Jacqueline B. Thurston. *Optical Illusions and the Visual Arts*. New York: Reinhold Publishing, 1996.

Charsley, Simon R. *Wedding Cakes and Cultural History*. London: Routledge, 1992.

Ching, Francis D.K. *A Visual Dictionary of Architecture*. New York: Van Nostrand Reinhold, 1995.

Gardner, Howard. *Art, Mind & Brain*. New York: Basic Book Publishers, 1982.

Gardner, Howard. *Creating Minds*. New York: Basic Books, 1993.

Henisch, Bridget Ann. *Cakes and Characters*. London: Prospect Books, 1984.

Maguelonne, Toussaint-Samat. *A History of Food*. Cambridge: Blackwell Reference, 1992.

Mayer, Ralph. *A Dictionary of Art Terms and Techniques*. New York: Thomas Y. Crowell Company, 1969.

Panofsky, Erwin. *Meaning in the Visual Arts*. Chicago: University Chicago Press, 1955.

Rader, Melvin. *A Modern Book of Esthetics*. New York: Holt, Rinehart and Winston, 1935.

Smith, Jillyn. *Senses & Sensibilities*. New York: John Wiley & Sons, 1989.

Tannahill, Reay. *Food in History*. New York: Stein and Day, 1973.

Yenawine, Philip. *How to Look at Modern Art*. New York: Harry N. Abrams, 1991.

# INDEX

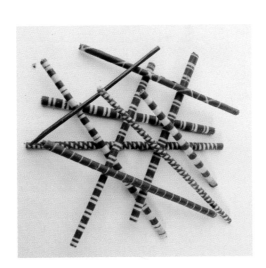

**L**

Ladyfingers, 237-238
Ladyfinger sheets, 107
Ladyfinger sponge, 282-284
*La répertoire de la cuisine*, 10
Laurier, Philippe, 79, 103, 155, 156, 195, 197,
          198, 203
Leach, Richard, 112, 116, 117, 118, 119, 132,
          265, 291
Leaves, tuile, 192
Le Cirque Flora dessert, 196, 224-227
Lemon cream, 217-219
Lemongrass Rice Pudding, 303, 325-327
Lemon strips, candied, 110
Lemon Tart, 196, 197, 217-220
Lemon verbena granité, 216
Lillikoi Mousse, 303, 309-311
Lime cream, 158
Linzer crust, 25
Linzer dough, 214
Litchies, caramel, 314
Love, Norman, 116, 117, 118, 119, 122, 266, 303,
          304, 328
Luchetti, Emily, 6, 45, 47, 49, 65, 68

**M**

Macadamia nut cake, 19
Macaroon crust, 291
MacLauchlan, Andrew, 6, 301, 303, 304, 305, 306
Manet, Edouard, 152-153
Mango mousse, 206
Mango saffron coulis, 206
Marshmallow, roasted, 56
Marzipan, 76-77
   chocolate, 289
Mascarpone filling, 285
Masi, Noble, 5
Matisse dessert, 153, 176-180
Melon Cream, 48, 71-73
Meringue, 249-251
   chocolate, 142-144
   cloud, 165
   Italian, 105

Meringue Basket dessert, 154, 157-158
Meringue straws, 210
Merlin's Crystal Fantasy, 233, 243-245
Metz, Ferdinand, 4
Minimalist desserts, 12, 13, 45-73
Minimalist movement, 46-48
Mocha buttercream, 43
Mocha Panna Cotta, 48, 65-67
Modernist desserts, 195-228
   abstraction in, 197
Mold, face, 185
Monet, Claude, 154
Monet Painting dessert, 79, 100-102
Morello sauce, 124
Mousse
   banana, 57, 181
   bittersweet chocolate, 116, 132-135
   bourbon, 81
   caramel, 161
   chestnut, 17
   chocolate, 39-40, 93, 115, 134, 146, 159-161,
          191, 288
   chocolate coconut, 120
   chocolate oolong, 303, 328-331
   chocolate-orange, 243
   chocolate passion fruit, 125-127
   dark chocolate, 272-273
   fruit-yogurt, 224-226
   gianduja, 181-183, 187
   green apple, 40
   Hawaiian vintage chocolate and Kahlua, 21
   hazelnut-white chocolate, 294-297
   Lillikoi, 309-311
   mango, 206
   milk chocolate, 60, 142
   passion fruit, 322
   passion fruit and strawberry, 165
   praline, 139
   silken milk chocolate, 130
   white chocolate, 214-216, 268, 272
Mousse cake, pumpkin and milk chocolate, 60-62
Mousse cones, bittersweet espresso, 196, 221-223
Mousse pyramid
   coffee, 136-138
   pistachio, 116, 122-124